6205

Eating apples : knowing women's lives / Caterina
Edwards and Kay Stewart, editors. -- Edmonton :
NeWest Press, c1994.
310 p. ; 22 cm.

07725744   ISBN:0920897797 (pbk.)

1. Canadian essays (English) - Women authors. 2.
Women. I. Edwards, Caterina, 1948- II. Stewart, Kay
L. (Kay Lanette), 1942-

Eating Apples

Knowing Women's Lives

~

Caterina Edwards and Kay Stewart
Editors

NeWest Press
Edmonton

Canadian Cataloguing in Publication Data

Main entry under title:

Eating apples

ISBN 0-920897-79-7

1. Canadian essays (English) — Women authors.* 2. Women.
I. Edwards, Caterina, 1948- II. Stewart, Kay L. (Kay Lanette), 1942-

PS8235.W6E17 1994   C814'.5408'0352042   C94-910593-7
PR9194.5.W6E17 1994

Editors for the Press: Janice Dickin McGinnis and Aritha van Herk
Editorial Coordinator: Eva Radford
Cover and interior design: Brenda Burgess
Financial assistance: NeWest Press gratefully acknowledges the financial assistance of The Canada Council; The Alberta Foundation for the Arts, a beneficiary of the Lottery Fund of the Government of Alberta; and The NeWest Institute for Western Canadian Studies.

Printed and bound in Canada by Best Book Manufacturers Inc.

NeWest Publishers Limited
Suite 310, 10359 – 82 Avenue
Edmonton, Alberta T6E 1Z9

To the women who sustain us.

~

Contents

~

We would like to thank Flora Pavich, Linda Schultz, and Marguerite Meyer for help with the typing; Astrid Blodgett for both her typing and her comments; Sheryl Nixon for copy-editing; Eva Radford, Janice Dickin McGuiness and Aritha van Herk at NeWest Press for their expertise; and, in particular, Elizabeth Entrup, who gave much of her time, enthusiasm, and intelligence to this book.

Introduction

*T*HIS COLLECTION OF AUTOBIO-
graphical essays by women began very simply. We began with no
preconceptions, no particular ideological stance, and with no
predetermined theme beyond that of *Knowing Women*. We sent
out a call for submissions through various writers' newsletters and
through the writers' "party-line." We asked women we knew if
they had anything appropriate that they would like to submit.
And the essays poured in — an embarrassment of riches.

Kay: One of the things that impressed me about the submissions
was their range — in subject, style, and authorship. Younger
women grappling with questions of identity, older women *still*
grappling with questions of identity (like me!) or comfortably sure
of themselves, at least for the moment; women from small towns
and big cities, from coast to coast; the much-travelled and the
firmly rooted, Canadians born and made; heterosexual and lesbian women; novice writers, seasoned pros, others somewhere in
between. Women writing about growing up and growing old,
making a living and making a life, confronting the present and the
past. The essays we chose are, indeed, eating apples: juicy and satisfying, sweet and sour.

Caterina: The seed for these eating apples is an import. At the
home of a friend, I came across a book of autobiographical essays

by American women writers. I was immediately interested. I asked my friend if I could borrow her book. "No," she said, "you can't. Ever since I bought that book five different women have walked out of my house with it. No one seems to be able to resist it." So I was left with the seed of an idea. I wanted to work with someone; I had always wanted to try a collaboration but had never had the chance. Kay and I had talked about our writing for years, both in our writing group and in brisk walks together around the neighbourhood. The walks became the soil for the idea.

Kay: We decided we would like to put together a book that we, personally, would want to read. I found nearly all the submissions interesting; the ones we chose seemed to be most successful in marrying form and content. They also shared a generosity of spirit that made them, for me, a pleasure to read.

Caterina: Our first criterion was that they be well-written. But then, looking over the essays, we realized certain thematic patterns were emerging. I suppose, inevitably, our personal interests and concerns influenced our critical decisions. Yet we did *try* to work inductively, rather than deductively. And I don't want to make our judgements sound too arbitrary or quirky. We both have years of background in essay writing. Actually, I was surprised by how often we agreed on a first reading, before discussion — that that was an essay we wanted, that this one wasn't. The essays were also read and commented upon by Elizabeth, our editorial assistant. And we got responses to some of the essays from Sheryl, a journalist friend who proofread, and from Astrid, one of our typists and an accomplished poet.

Kay: When NeWest decided to publish the collection, we were told that the book was much too long. So we went over all our choices again, this time with the editors from the press, Janice and Aritha. And we discovered that just as we tossed around ideas and judgements on our walks, they had discussed the book over badminton.

Caterina: I now know what collaboration on a project means. And it does seem like a female way of doing things — mixing work and pleasure (or at least exercise), scheduling meetings around hair appointments and children's activities, coming up with a new title over dinner at Aritha's.

Kay: There were other books with titles similar to *Knowing Women*, but we wanted to keep the emphasis on women's desire to know and be known. *Eating Apples*, with its reference to Eve, fit perfectly with the way we had grouped selections to illuminate the many sources of women's knowledge, all rooted in the self. We begin with "Working Knowledge": what we learn about the social world through experience, the repeated activities of our daily lives. Other learning is more indirect — intuited, dredged up from the recesses of memory, painfully pieced together, as the selections in "Forbidden Knowledge" indicate. The essays in "Relative Knowledge" share a sense of double vision, of shifts in perspective that are sometimes troubling, sometimes transforming. "Body of Knowledge" emphasizes that the body is where all knowledge begins — and ends. The selections in "Book of Knowledge" stress the knowing that is available to us through language, and acknowledge gaps in the nets words make. And finally there is a spiritual sense of connection that makes itself felt through image and symbol in "Tree of Knowledge."

Caterina: The desire for integration was a theme that occurred again and again. I found surprising how many writers expressed the difficulties of juggling different roles: daughter, lover, mother, friend, caregiver, writer.

Kay: Surprising? Think of all the juggling we were doing during this project.

Caterina: A multiplicity of selves. I found it instructive that all the women who wrote about the struggle between the competing and contradictory selves decided that the writing self was the most essential self. Because, of course, the writing self is the constructed self. Is it because it is the self we make that it seems so important?

Kay: I have some reservations about the idea of the constructed self. It sounds so "finished," so done. For me, integration, particularly the integration of knowledge, is an ongoing process, not an end I have miraculously achieved — or ever will. There are parts of me still silenced, parts under the conscious or unconscious domination of received ideas, and parts desperately clinging to some hard-won personal truth.

Caterina: But don't you find that those truths often emerge in the act of writing about oneself? For me, autobiography is a method of self-awareness, as well as self-disclosure. We make sense of ourselves when we tell our story. Paradoxically, this self-filled process connects us to others. As Thomas Mann said of autobiography, "[It is] the ego's becoming conscious proudly and darkly yet joyously of its recurrence and typicality." Recurrence, typicality: that's one of the most appealing aspects of reading women's autobiographical writings, for me, that sense of commonality. In making the private public, the writer is less alone. She is speaking to a community and as part of a community. And when we read the written texts, we glimpse ourselves in others and others in ourselves, which — in turn — reinforces *our* sense of being part of the community.

Kay: I loved the fact that this project created its own community.

Caterina: It did, didn't it? It started with the two of us on our walks and grew to include Elizabeth, Sheryl, and Astrid, and then Flora and Lynda and Marguerite, who also typed some of the manuscript, and then Janice and Aritha. The writers who dropped us notes from time to time joined in and all those along the way who have let us share our enthusiasm. And now we welcome our readers into this community.

Working Knowledge

W<small>E GAIN A "WORKING KNOWL-</small>edge" of something, such as a language, through experience. Through repeated trials we learn the principles by which it operates, the beauties it is capable of, and the traps it sets for the unwary. But our knowledge remains imperfect, and we continue to learn. This emphasis on learning through experience runs through the selections gathered here.

These pieces portray not only the world of paid work, but more important, the workings of the world in which women live their lives. J. B. Lundman's "Skating Is More than Walking" shows the beginnings of this learning, as the rituals of the skating rink carry a young girl from the first hesitant steps of childhood to the exciting — and dangerous — games of adolescence. The possibilities — and limitations — of women's lives become more evident when a young woman enters the larger world of work. In "Great Pacific Fish Cannery" Julia van Gorder looks back upon her wartime employment with wry humour and compassion for the working-class women unable to escape its drudgery. That little has changed for women in low-paid manual jobs is clear from "Chicken and Fingers," Mary Maxwell's account of the long-term damage to women's health caused by exploitative working conditions.

Another kind of drudgery, one familiar to many women, is the starting point for Carolyn Pogue's "Motherhood, Eh?" But the tone deepens as the story moves from the tribulations of a young mother to the wisdom of a woman who has experienced motherhood in its amazing and humbling complexities. Lacking a supportive social environment, Pogue turns to Erma Bombeck. When Vera de Jong becomes a "Carpenter's Apprentice," there is nowhere to turn. Her essay clearly brings out both the rewards of physical labour and the emotional costs of entering a male-dominated trade. The results of a different kind of apprenticeship are evident in the comic fantasy "In the Bleak Midwinter," where Dianne Linden reckons the emotional cost of loving.

Experience is a demanding teacher. These writers have learned their lessons well.

Skating Is More than Walking

J. B. Lundman

WHERE I COME FROM, SKATING is a skill you learn early. Before I was in school my brother wadded newspaper into the toes of his old hockey skates and laced me into them. "It's easy as walking," he pronounced, and led me across the road to the local rink.

There was a school yard across from our house, and every October, snow or not, a pile of boards was dumped at the far end of the field. After Halloween, four walls, a sloped roof, and a skate-battered floor were assembled from the jumble of lumber. This was "the shack," and it signalled the start of winter.

When we kids on the block saw smoke rise from the tin chimney, we knew Frank was there stoking the fat-bellied stove. Soon clouds of steam billowing from the frozen field would announce the first flooding of the neighbourhood rink.

Frank did the flooding. He appeared as regularly as the frost every October, and melted from sight with the puddled rink in March. He was dark and squat with a consistent length of stubble on a face too long and large for his stature.

"Best guard against frostbite ever invented," he told the bold ones who asked why he didn't shave.

He answered all our questions and tightened boots. He coached hockey and rubbed frozen feet with snow. He kept old flannel rags to rub off our skates and he kept the big boys from bullying the little ones and fighting with the girls.

On soft nights of smothering snowfall, the only sound in a secret world was Frank's wide shovel scraping against the ice as he trudged the width of the rink. Stolid and patient, he pushed the ridges of fresh falling snow, clearing our path and depositing the piles that grew through the season to shape the banks of white surrounding the edges of the ice.

We learned to land here. The snowdrift took us in. Whether we were chased or stopped to rest, the safe cold embrace of snow stirred depths we had only dreamed about. From this infinitely light and soft retreat our child's world was lost in awe-filled contemplation of a universe we could not yet imagine.

"Just imagine you're walking," my brother coaxed as we staggered onto the ice. He held me from behind, pinning my arms against my ears and forcing my mittened hands to flap free and useless above the pompom on my toque. My head hung forward and down so that I peered at my waddling feet sliding without purchase or direction on the ice.

My brother nudged each of my feet with one of his — poke-kick on the left, push-shove on the right. With each minuscule advance my ankles collapsed closer to the frozen surface until the skate blades were upended and gliding ineffectually over the ice. The situation seemed hopeless from where I was looking, and my brother must have felt the same because hockey claimed him exclusively after that brief diversion.

I learned to skate anyway, but that first lesson taught me that skating was more than walking. Trudging onto solid ground in a series of foot moves was duck soup compared to getting the feel for balancing a bundled body on two thin edges of steel while four limbs were in motion.

No, skating was not the same as walking. It was pushing a foot forward and out, pressing another back and away. It was thrusting your torso into the wind while rocking it competently from side to side. It was swinging your arms in arced loops at the same time as everything else was swaying. It was moving in the direction intended and eventually keeping time to music that crackled into the frosted air above the slick and frozen ground. And finally, it was trusting this effort to move you through these elements with enough grace to attract admiration.

Boys stick-handled as soon as they could skate. Everybody cheered and admired them for their agility on ice. They prepared for the game ahead, competing flat out to get at the puck.

We girls practised figures at the corners of the rink. Shooting the duck was hardest because you had to squat in bulky clothing with one leg raised parallel to the ice. This trick required speed to keep you balanced.

A few girls in our neighbourhood had skating skirts and tights because they wore white fancy skates and took lessons. But they were considered show-offs by us when they wiggled and spun and shot the duck in the middle of the rink.

At the same time that we scorned their display of confidence, we fervidly dreamt of owning fancy skates ourselves. Even black ones would get you into centre ice while the mob circled the outer edge of the rink at "free ice" time when hockey stopped. Our ambitions were modest; black skates would do. Besides, white fancy skates were too public a declaration of commitment to a game that confounded the small group I clung to.

We sensed we were destined to compete, but instinct warned us away from the contest. We withdrew to the safety of the edges. We watched the action at centre ice. We parodied the figures and moves of the older girls as they swooped and twirled down the length of the rink, setting their flounced and pleated skirts aflutter in tantalizing motion. We spun and whooped in triumphant derision. We bent and zagged a jagged line learning to skate backwards. We got fast and accurate at hurling our bodies into the snowdrifts around the ice to elude pursuers. We shot the duck despite lumpy layers of clothing and hand-me-down skates.

And our efforts were rewarded. For a brief magic period before our boisterous spirits were hushed, we could join the gang of skaters hurtling over the ice in games of Red Rover and Crack-the-Whip. Shapes of large and small, thick and thin, fast and slow children scrambled across the frozen expanse after hockey practice and figure skating.

On still, frigid nights, mostly Fridays, we clustered under the globe of yellow light cast by one overhanging pole, and under a dome of navy blue sky with its wild sparkle of new falling snow, we were cradled for a time on our playground of ice by the clouds of snowdrift rising at the margins of our world like hands holding us in a benediction.

Shrieks of terror and delight cracked the frosted air as a small figure was flicked from the end of the line when the "whip" pulled up short to snap the linked skaters around in a burst of heartstopping speed. Or scuttling like insects, the children tore down the length of the rink avoiding the lone crier of "Red Rover, Red Rover, I call my troops over . . . ," and those tagged helped tag in the next surge of players across the ice, until one quick and dodging figure was all that was left evading the wave of skaters moving in the middle of the ice waiting for the final call of Red Rover.

All through the deepening night the banks of snow enclosed us, waiting to receive our bodies flung at breakneck speed out beyond the dark edges of the ice. Cushioned by the snow, we sank into the eternal moment trembling with exhaustion and wonder, contemplating the black and vast sky, and moving our limbs luxuriously against the perilous cold.

The enormity of our contentment was made more delicious by the quivers of promise opening around us. We anticipated an expansion, an enlargement to our lives, and the dark sky and the white snow expressed the limitlessness of the possible. We would choose. For now, we must wait. But we would choose where in the trackless universe we would go.

I chose, in the natural course of social expansion, to skate elsewhere. My choice was hastened by humiliating episodes unbecoming to the dignity of a nine-year-old. A skating rink across the road from our house was far too handy a spot for my parents to lead parties of their friends, where, on crowded Friday nights, they disported themselves on the ice in a grotesque imitation of a game I was beginning to see as essential to the spirit of social progress.

Mother was particularly offensive and talented in her abuse of conventions. What she couldn't achieve, she made fun of, and she was no skater.

One memorable Friday night, she appeared under the cozy dome of light dressed in my father's kilt. Oversized blue bloomers hung below the Black Watch pleats. A sporran swung at her hips, and a tam-o'-shanter sat splendidly atilt on a brush of hair purposely matted and messed for the occasion, I noted hatefully. She clung to a man's — not my father's — arm, and wobbled her way amid the throng of skaters who whooped and hooted their appreciation. She waved queenlike as they passed her by, and from time to time, flipped her false teeth down to bare naked gums in a gracious smile.

This last antic was too much. While my struggle to overlook her desecration of the myths of war (I was still enthralled by my father's renditions of his experience in the trenches) was partially successful, her desecration of the myths of beauty was a betrayal of her sex that revolted me.

I fled a mile away across the proverbial railway tracks to skate at a more generously endowed community centre. There hockey was promoted with a zeal close to obsession. Friday nights a dozen games were played under the brutal arced lights. A succession of teams chopped and checked and crashed against each other and the boards, where parents and coaches pressed to cheer and yell their approval and encouragement.

This was where the boys were, and a few of us followed them there. Bold and uncertain, our tiny clutch of girls shivered at the sidelines trying to catch some enthusiasm for the game. We were grim and silent and longed for the hockey to be over so the music for free skating could start. We darted distractedly from the clubhouse to the edge of the ice in a constant struggle for warmth while we were immobilized watching the games.

Inside, if you had a dime, there were Cracker Jacks and hot cocoa and chocolate bars. More important than the warmth of food, was the chance of significant encounters with a current crush. A look or touch could electrify the evening. Amid the rush of steaming bodies and hectic noise, these random contacts could fire elaborate fantasies of future bliss, or bring quiet moments of solitary consolation. Close analyses of intent, character, and consequence were often parsed and scanned with a view to advising the girl whose fancy had been thus provoked.

But fancies were as fleeting as the winking lights off snow. Dangerous as frost to exposed skin, the game's trick was in playing the lure, testing the waters, interpreting the signs, while evading the unnamed peril. Learning the delicate balance of come-hither allure and get-lost spirit was a business that absorbed us all. Responding with enough insouciance to attract more attention was a triumph. A hint of temper condemned a girl as a witch/bitch.

If Jeannie didn't respond charmingly when her toque was snatched, then some other girl was teased next time. If Linda pranced and squalled appropriately when her mitt or scarf was grabbed, Ward, our local hockey star, might step forward to orchestrate the subsequent horseplay. Panther-smooth and smirking, he held the trophy aloft while Linda jumped and clawed to retrieve it. Tossing the hat or mitt from Trevor to Crossley, from Lloyd and back to Ward, increased the din of whistles and jeers. All the girls joined the pitch-and-grab, pinch-and-shove, shout-and-toss, slap-and-hold fray that followed.

The exhilaration of these preliminaries fired all our blood for the musical parade round the rink. The "Skater's Waltz" and "Blue Danube" crackled under the white lights, and orderly couples swayed in unison to the music, their arms entwined and legs twinned in rhythmic mimicry.

We girls clasped one another to display our art as best we could, threading our way amid the swaying throng. An occasional bump or snatch from one of the boys as they dashed between the couples was a thrilling reminder of games to come when the older crowd left the skating rink.

The games were more dangerous now. We were faster, bolder, more skilled at skating and dodging. We girls dared more, pushing into unexplored territory, pressing the boys to follow. Now when we played Red Rover, we could fling our bodies high over the boards at the edge of the rink and out into the safety of the hidden banks of snow beyond the glare of artificial lights.

Every spring we retreated to books and skipping rope, and every November when frost set the ice, the still magic of a winter night drew us again to the local rink where moving in the elemental cold, we renewed our contact with a universe of light beyond the yellow globe.

But the excitement of hockey and the rough-shouldered players lured us like fish to the darkened edges of the floodlit ice. We waited with less hope for the boys to finish their games. Though now there was some solace in sometimes being partnered around the big rink for a waltz, we dreamed of the old games.

And they were not the same. Something had been lost in the play of Red Rover and Crack-the-Whip, but we couldn't say what. You could no longer count on being alone when you landed in a bank of snow. Before there was time to gaze into the navy blue swirl of sky, Lloyd or Trevor or Crossley might pounce on top of you to snatch at clothes, stuff snow down your back, or force a kiss.

One time after fighting to free myself from a particularly woolly snowbank where I had enjoyed a few moments alone, I heard a shout across the rink.

"*Fuck her, Crossley.*"

The cry swept across the ice and, funnelled by the frozen mounds of snow, lifted into the frosted night, thrusting beyond the arced and savage lights to tear against the pliant velvet sky.

I couldn't tell if it was Jeannie or Linda with Crossley in the snowbank across the ice from me, but Ward's voice was unmistakable. It rose in a triumphant bleat, suffusing air and ice and snow, shrinking the globed night, and blotting out the scattered bits of light.

In the crouching silence that was left, I turned to the clubhouse thinking of hot cocoa.

~

In her own words: J. B. Lundman grew up on the prairies and has lived on the east and west coasts of the United States. She worked as a nurse while attending Hunter College and started teaching in New York City after receiving her degree. She returned to Canada and taught high school in Winnipeg for many years before retiring to Vancouver Island. She still misses the sun and snow of the prairies although she now has time to write.

Great Pacific Fish Cannery

Julia van Gorder

May 21, 1945

Boeing is such a drag. Wonderful pay, but I see Bev only at lunch breaks.

Bev, says my partner Ella, after she zips herself into her white Boeing coverall and ties a white kerchief around her small head, looks like a rivet. Bev is the same size as Ella, but she impresses her female form on whatever she wears. Ella is contained by the uniform. I'm a head taller than either of them. What does the uniform do to me?

We are working in a huge shed on Georgia Street, by Stanley Park. Making parts for B-39 bombers which are assembled in Seattle.

The first night, Ella told me to plug my rivet gun in an overhead socket. Gravity worked. The plug fell out. I pointed this out to Ella. Her lip curled. "Ya tape it."

"Tape?"

"There." She looked at a roll of masking tape on a counter.

I taped the plug to the socket. "Scissors?" I asked.

Ella kept me holding the heavy rivet gun in one hand and the taped plug in the other for five seconds while she stared at me. "Ya tear it." She turned her back.

So much for the usefulness of a B.A. in the real world.

July 23, 1945

It has taken Ella weeks to forgive my initial incompetence, and weeks for me to learn that she doesn't respond to small chat like "Hello" or "How was your time off?" There was work to be done. She does it. At meal times, there is food to be eaten. She eats it. It's strange. She always eats with Bev and me as if we were buddies, but she says nothing.

Last week Hank, our shop steward, told me if I was late once more, my pay would be docked. Oh dear. Night shift is such an adjustment. I have no sense that we are working for victory, or anything idealistic. We're here for the money. I stand bucking rivets hour after hour, thinking of nothing but the lunch break. Is that what has happened to Ella?

August 10, 1945

Oh God, what a way for the war to end — our side incinerating hundreds of thousands of helpless human beings! So what do we celebrate? A victory for humanity?

Boeing gave Bev and me our pink slips.

During the lunch break we sit outside on the wooden wharf, dangling our legs over the dark of Coal Harbour. I am fretting. Money is water in my hands. I need another month's work to see me through next year at U.B.C. Bev is bubbling towards her marriage with Doug, who has a job in forestry lined up for the fall.

Ella sits beside us, focussing on peanut butter and jam squashed between slices of white bread. What is she thinking? Does she have a future like Bev, or is she living day by day like me? She wasn't fired. She's worked on B-29s since the U.S. came into the war. I heard Hank tell her she could stay on until all the existing parts had been assembled and shipped to Seattle. But that is only two weeks' work.

Ella throws her scrunched lunch bag into Coal Harbour, stands, leans against a piling, and looks down on us.

"So someone has churned the butter of your lives."

I can feel Bev suppressing merriment, but I like Ella's image. She's right. My life all through the war has been a tub of butter, with no close losses overseas, no real hardships. Given the job opportunities the war brought, it has been a time of increased prosperity.

"Ya'll have to go into a fish cannery," Ella decides. "They're hiring at Great Pacific, past West Van."

"Let's go," I say to Bev.

"Not my idea of a picnic."

"What do they pay?" I ask Ella.

"Fifty-two cents an hour, more if you're on piecework."

"Let's go," I said. "Are you going, Ella?"

"I dunno."

August 12, 1945 Great Pacific Cannery
Our first night. Bev and I arrive at 10 P.M., just after dark, having waited for the last bus. The only person up — Anna, in running shoes without socks — is setting long trestle tables for breakfast in the cookhouse. She grumbles, as she leads us by flashlight up wooden stairs and down a hall to our room, that people work hard here and go to bed at a decent time. She nods sideways at the washroom across the hall, switches on our light, and leaves.

A single light bulb hanging in the centre of the room. The air alive with buzzing flies, hyped up, I'm sure, by the smell of rotting fish, which permeates the building. I tug at the window. It won't open. The floors and walls unpainted boards. Two metal cots covered with striped mattresses. Dust balls like families of mice huddle under the cots.

We go to the washroom. It has its own supply of flies. We take a broom back to our room and sweep off the mattresses before unrolling our sleeping bags.

"You and your big ideas," Bev says. She is crying. She undresses and gets into her sleeping bag.

I am too stunned to comfort her. She's the comic on our team. I count on her spirits to carry us through situations like this.

"It wasn't my idea. It was Ella's."

"So where is Ella?"

"Maybe this is her revenge for my being a bum riveter."

"Next war you learn to rivet fast. Okay?"

"Okay."

"And I'm not promising to stay here. Understand? As soon as Doug hits town, I'm quitting."

"I hear you." And I'm depressed. I can't imagine life without Bev. But that's not reciprocal. I must accept that. And I have to stay. I must have another month's work. Bev is not going on to do graduate work like most of us. She'll take to the woods when Doug gets his job.

"Sleep tight," I say by habit, turning out the light.

"And none of your little ironies. This is not an ironic situation."

"No, it's awful, but I still hope you can sleep."

"You too. Goodnight."

I can't sleep for wondering if this isn't an ironic situation. Do we deserve it? Is there something we, I, didn't learn at Boeing that I need to learn here? When I read Dante's *Divine Comedy* last year, I felt that I was living in Purgatory — repeating experiences until I had learned from them. But this, this feels like the Inferno. My face crumples and I cry. But crying attracts flies to my face. I slide down into my sleeping bag and try to fasten the cover over my head.

August 13, 1945

The first morning the cookhouse is full of people eating at the trestle tables. A handsome woman of about fifty comes to us. She has an orange-red gladiolus spike pinned to her white smock. Her lipstick and nail polish match the gladiolus. High rubber boots, white kerchief, fine skin.

"So you got here after all," she says. "Well, sit down and get some breakfast. We start work in . . ." She glances at a dainty silver watch. ". . . fifteen minutes."

We sit. No one speaks to us, but food is passed — orange juice, porridge, pancakes, toast, bacon, coffee. Someone hands me an oval platter of fried eggs. The eggs sit in front of me, staring like fish eyes. I can't eat. I am breathing the smell of rotting fish. I read somewhere that the nose turns off its recognition of a foul smell in ten minutes. Not so.

When the bell rings, the handsome forewoman, "Maw" to the work crew, puts a hand on each of our shoulders. "Come and get a clean smock and gloves. I'm glad you've got the sense to wear boots and a kerchief." Her hand on my shoulder has become a comfort. She barks out orders, expecting obedience and hard work. But she coats the harshness with touch, a reminder of a different world.

The main canning space, a huge barn that opens to English Bay when the fish boats come in, is not the white sterile factory I had imagined sitting in, packing orange-red sockeye into tins. We stand on concrete leaning against scrubbed wooden tables, waist high.

Maw is not afraid of getting dirty. She shows us how to gib pilchards, cutting off their heads and dragging their head and guts in one movement across the table and into a bin. Pilchards are the dirtiest fish dead. Half of these seemed bad. I can't gut them in one movement. Maw shows me how to get my finger into the cavity to make sure they are clean. In no time my thin cotton gloves are soaked.

During the smoke break one of the pieceworkers says, "I stop to blow my nose when I'm on time, but when I'm on piecework, I just wipe it on my sleeve."

This place has mass production down pat. The Chinamen bring us fish and take away the tubs of guts. When they come around to sharpen our knives, they hand us another so we won't stop work. Ten hours a day at fifty-two cents an hour! The Chinese — why are they called Chinamen here and Chinese at the university? — are pleasant but distant. Is it a language barrier? No. The others are the same. Here to make money, like me. The older women seem to have stuck it longest. There are a few Native women, shy, not driven like the rest of us. Two grads from Dalhousie, three kids going into first year at U.B.C. The men, a rough-looking lot.

August 20, 1945
Yesterday I was sick to my stomach. We were back to gibbing pilchards, after a couple of days of stringing herring in the smoke

house (a wand forced through the gills and mouth, with the eyes staring their pain at you). Maw decides I am allergic to pilchards, and sends me to clean the women's washroom. A man Bev calls Romeo follows me into the washroom. He has already begun to haunt us in the cannery. His shirt opens to the navel, his hairy belly loops over his pants. He leans against a wall, his bare arms akimbo, as I clean toilets. I don't like having him behind me, so I switch to wash basins.

"You sleeping with that squirt you came with?"

"That's none of your goddam business!"

"Just thought I would give you some of the real thing."

He unzips his fly just as Maw comes in. When she is in the cannery, Maw has a corktip cigarette drooping from her lips. Her fine nose is stained orange by the smoke, and the hairs of her right nostril are burned black. Maw's cigarette glows. She spreads her hands over her hips, the nail polish glinting against her white smock. She says nothing. Romeo zips his fly. Maw turns sideways in the door, so that he has to face her as he leaves.

"You okay, kid?" she asks me.

"Sure." I go on cleaning basins, knowing she is too short of workers to fire him. When the boats come in, full of herring, pilchards, salmon, she has to have a crew to unload, can, or smoke the fish.

"The jerk," she says, and leaves.

She transfers me to the bloater house to pack bloater paste into tins with a woman Bev calls Diva.

I find that if you sing, time speeds up. Diva has already discovered that. She sings in monotone, sometimes *I will take you home, Kathleen* or *Old Black Joe*. Mostly it's *Holy, holy, holy*, just the one verse. Must be a member of the United Church. An hour of *Holy, holy, holy* is quite a few tins of bloater paste.

August 25, 1945

Ella from Boeing turned up at the production line. Pretends not to see us. We welcome her at lunch time, and ask her to go to a movie in West Van with us after supper. She agrees, but neglects to take a shower. People in the bus and theatre move away from us.

"They don't like our Nights in Norway perfume," Bev whispers across Ella.

Ella restless. Next day she begins to eat with Diva, with whom she shares a room. Pretends not to see us again.

August 27, 1945

Bev and I in the loft, rolling cans down the conveyor belt for ten hours. Like sorting letters at the post office at Christmas. You achieve so much in one minute repeating a motion that time drags. We roll a hundred cans a minute. I try to figure out how many cans per hour, per day, but my mind staggers. Everywhere I work, I see that the Industrial Revolution didn't free us. It made us into Charlie Chaplin machines. How can that silly economics professor say that industrialization is the answer for the underdeveloped countries? I ask Bev what she is thinking about.

"Sex."

"Sex?"

"What else?"

"The meaning of life. Why we are here."

"Here in this cannery? I thought it was your crazy idea."

"No, the meaning of our individual lives. Are we here in the cannery because we chose it, or were we sent? As part of a pattern or plan?"

"I thought we came here because the money was good?"

"We did, on one level, but . . ."

"How many levels do you want to live on at one time, for Pete's sake? You're unreal, d'you know that?"

Am I unreal? I don't feel so. But I realize, rolling one hundred cans a minute, that Bev and I have grown in different directions. Her whole focus is on Doug. She is quitting the cannery tomorrow to be with him.

August 29, 1945

Yesterday I was alone for ten hours, packing cans hot out of the steamer, which burned through these cheap gloves. My nails are brown, the skin of my hands is rough and scaling.

Today Maw put me to work with Mrs. Petra, who gets the easy jobs and is not popular. The others say she is a stool pigeon, because she does housework for the owners. But she's okay. She has a scrubbed look, skin hanging loose on her face. She says a few words of Chinese to the Chinamen. I'm impressed, ask how come. She trained as some kind of mission worker, learned Chinese to go to China, then the war.

"Oh, are you going now the war is over?"

"Oh no! I met my husband meantime."

Would I do that? Given the choice of vocation or marriage, would I choose marriage?

August 30, 1945

Well, what do you know? Today I made money doing piecework. Eighty-two cents an hour instead of fifty-two. But oh, my back is bent out of shape. Maw put me to work with Roberta, the fastest worker in the cannery. She doesn't look forty-five, with her shiny store teeth, her mashed-carrots hair worn with a pomp of curls in front, braids around her ears, a purple kerchief. She jokes about her smock barely containing her large breasts. "I had five kids. Breast-fed 'em all. Should have been a Guernsey cow. Had a cup of yellow cream left after feeding each one."

September 2, 1945

This week when thirty-five tons of my allergy came in, I worked with the men for two days in the warehouse. The men, some unfamiliar with English, watched that I did no heavy lifting. People are by nature kind, particularly when you are accepted as one of them.

Yesterday Brenda and I washed cans in the alkali bath. Brenda has a tilted nose and gentle brown eyes. She is saving for a washing machine for the bungalow she and John are building in North Vancouver. They keep chickens in the backyard, her pets, his food.

John? She points to Romeo, of the open shirt and loopy belly.

He sees her point to him and comes over. Eyeing my breasts, he leans too close.

"I'm not coming home for supper," he says to Brenda. "The Number 3 boat is coming in."

Maw looks over at him. He goes back to his job.

"That means he is going to a beer parlour with the crew after they unload."

This is outrageous. What can Brenda be thinking of, this gentle soul, allying herself with that crude man? Romeo never eats with her in the cannery, has never treated her as special.

When I work with Roberta again, I ask if Brenda and John are married. I wish I hadn't. She roars at me.

"Kid, I can't believe you. How old do you say you are? What do they teach you in that university anyway?"

Her voice is resounding, yet when she chitters to the Chinamen, I can't hear what she is saying.

She did tell me her favourite male is Barney from the Number 5 boat. Favourite. I bet she services them all. No wonder Bev called her "our lady of the fish boats." No wonder she laughs at me.

September 7, 1945

My farewell to Great Pacific. On Marine Drive, waiting for the bus from Horseshoe Bay, I can look back at this little community with its green lawns, gray cedar buildings, grey smoke rising.

Tonight at supper, except for Ella and Diva, there was lots of chatter, and I was part of it. When Maw came up behind me, I captured her warm hands pressed on my shoulders.

"Well, kid, will we see you back here next summer?"

"I hope so," I lied.

She walked away. And I walk away. I am able to.

~

Julia van Gorder was born in 1923 in Regina, where her father was with the Saskatchewan Provincial Police. The family also lived in Yorkton and Winnipeg before moving to Vancouver in 1938. Julia was married for thirty years to the philosopher D. G. Brown and has two children. A graduate of the University of British Columbia and Simon Fraser University, Julia was a social worker and school counsellor before retiring and becoming a full-time writer. She is active in the Federation of B. C. Writers and in mental health promotion. She lives in the sky by Stanley Park and shares her balcony with a family of finches.

Motherhood, Eh?

Carolyn Pogue

*O*NE DAY WHEN MY KIDS WERE little I visited a neighbour and said I'd lost my sense of humour. I told her that motherhood started off all right, but it was getting too complicated. People were coming and going and staying overnight or not being home and having appointments and dance lessons and scout meetings and teachers I didn't know and friends I didn't know, and what the hell was going on, anyway? And do I have to do all this by myself? Is this what motherhood is?

She was wise, that mother. She'd raised two children and fostered more than twenty-five. She told me two things that helped: When the kids get out of line, serve liver for dinner. The second thing she told me was to rush out and buy Erma Bombeck books. Erma had a good perspective, she said.

Erma Bombeck's titles include *If Life is a Bowl of Cherries, What am I Doing in the Pits?* and *The Grass is always Greener over the Septic Tank.* She understood me.

Actually, we didn't have a septic tank in Yellowknife, but my neighbour was right. Liver helped. And I read Erma's books and went one further. I wrote her letters.

"Dear Erma," I wrote in 1979, "I adore Christmas. The old carols, the little boys in bathrobes, the little girls with Saran-Wrap wings make me feel weepy and happy. Making Christmas cards with kids, however, just makes me feel weepy.

"It's my sister's fault. For years we've received kid-made cards.

Pretty green Christmas trees decorated with sparkles, stars, Marys and Josephs, lovingly made by dear nieces and nephews. You know.

"Now, my children are old enough to draw scribbles and dots, we sit at *our* table and I say enthusiastically, 'Let's make a nice card for dear Aunt Marty.' I smile and look quite Christmassy. Michael says he's tired. Andrea wants a drink. We do two cards. Then Andrea gets glue all over her dress and hair. I pretend to smile because it's Christmas and I'm happy and it's all for love and peace and joy and all those relatives waiting at mailboxes.

"I remain calm. I help. I cut, Andrea glues, and Michael sticks on stars. That works for one card. Then Andrea gets mad because she wants to stick on the stars, but Michael says it's still his turn. They are fighting over the star that shone on the Prince of Peace. I am a failed mother."

In 1981 I wrote Erma again:

"Michael is ten, Andrea is eight, and Kathryn is two. I'm fairly certain that Kathryn will have decided to use the potty by the time she graduates as a doctor.

"I am working as a researcher for a priest. That means that Kathryn has a babysitter. I don't get to hear all the funny things she's saying. Maybe there's something funny about that, Erma, but I doubt it.

"Today I'm working at home. A flock of neighbour kids is running in the yard. The phone rings seven times in ten minutes.

"Andrea had a bad day at school. To cheer herself, she decides to burn some chocolate syrup on the stove, and while she's doing that, in comes the priest. He brings me some more work. He wants to know how I'm doing. 'Okay on the research,' I say, 'but you know that slide-tape presentation we're doing? When I was editing it, I made a hole in the tape.'

"He doesn't say anything, just shakes his head. And Andrea, who'd gone outside again, returns. Crying. The priest hears the crying, smells the burning syrup and looks at me. He leaves. He lives alone.

"I run down the street to Kathryn's babysitter who tells me

she's leaving town and no, she doesn't know another babysitter. Kathryn and I trudge home; she is tired and miserable. As soon as we get home she starts to cry and it's twenty to six and the kids' father, who's been hiding in his study, has to eat and go out within an hour. I try to tell him that Michael's teacher wants to meet with us, but the competition is too fierce. Everyone is hungry. Everyone is mad.

"Kathryn puts milk in her dinner and plays in it with her hands and her father looks like he's about to leave. Michael isn't hungry because his teacher got her cast off her broken leg today and bought the class pizza to celebrate. Andrea doesn't like hers and her friend, Monique, is the only one who finishes. The kids' father takes a phone call, so his dinner gets cold and when he hangs up he leaves for his meeting. By this time, my appetite isn't all that great either.

"Michael sits at the table to do his homework and Andrea and Monique go next door to help a neighbour feed the goats. Andrea promises she'll feed her cat later, but she never does. I do.

"I ask her when she's going to bury the dead bird that's sitting in a box on top of the refrigerator, the one she rescued from the cat three days ago, that had enough spunk to fly around the house pooping before dying during the first night. It's still up there when she goes to bed.

"When the stories are read and the teeth are clean, when the dishes are done and the laundry is folded, when I have typed the research needed for tomorrow, I sit alone in the quiet living room and think about being a working mother."

In 1982 I apply to be a secretary in an elementary school. The principal interviews me. He asks me if I can deal with confusion. *"I'm a mother!"* I practically shout. After we talk for twenty minutes we shake hands and he tells me I have the job. As he is leaving he says, "By the way, can you type?" That fall I am a school secretary. That is, Mother times six hundred.

I run the office, look after the budget, practise first aid, and write songs for the school choir. I am a mother at home. I am a mother at work. There are children whose parents are getting divorced. There are children whose parents beat them. There are children who fall off the monkey bars and need to go to the hospital. There are always children needing hugs, and Band-Aids, and laughter, and hope. There are too many children in need. I love this job. They pay me money to be a mother. I do it for four years.

In 1988 I am a member of Rundle United Church in Banff, Alberta. It is the first year since 1970 that I am not a Northerner. I suffer culture shock. I am a participant in the music theatre program at the Banff Centre. I hear the word "profound" at least thirty thousand times. I am the mother of two teenagers and one seven year old. I am separated from their father.

On Mother's Day the minister asks me to say a prayer in church. Out loud. On Mother's Day I am not living in the same house as my children. I sit in my one-room log house in the mountains and stare not at elk or the Bow River, but at my silent typewriter. I try to conjure up Erma, but she will not come and I am left alone to contemplate what I will say to God on behalf of the congregation. I'm scared.

I think about the miscarriage I had at Christmas twenty years ago. I type "women who have miscarriages" on the page. I will pray for women who want to become mothers, but cannot.

I think about becoming a foster mother to a beautiful six-week-old baby, who became my own adopted son Michael, now fifteen. I remember another foster child, Robert, and a teenager full of rage who stayed with us for two months and then went somewhere, I don't know where. I remember the Christmas we became house parents in a group home in Yellowknife: a girl baked cookies with me one day and freaked out on LSD the next; a boy, brimming with hopelessness, ran away twice in two weeks; two sisters sought asylum from their parents. I will pray for foster mothers.

I think about the birth mothers of children placed for adoption. Two of my children are adopted. I often think of their birth mothers, knowing that a piece of their hearts is with my children, knowing they must think of them each birthday with pain and hope, knowing they must think of them on the first days of school. I add birth mothers to the list.

I think about the first time I felt Andrea move inside me. Michael and I were visiting my parents in Ontario. I rushed into the kitchen to tell mom what I'd felt, but there was no need for words. I remember the doctor shouting, "She's here!" as if it was his first birth, too. I remember the warm, milky smell of her breath after our first experience of a second miracle, breast feeding. I will pray for mothers giving birth.

I think about my daughter Ruth Ann. She lived for five days. I will pray for mothers whose children are ill or have died.

I think about the first time I saw Kathryn, four months old and with a belly laugh already. She crawled into my heart and stayed there, loving and joyous and always surprising. I remember the social worker bringing Michael, six weeks old, a bundle of blue fluff, bright, easy to love. I will pray for adoptive mothers.

I think about not living full time with my children, not giving them a kiss every night, not looking at them when they sleep, not knowing if they had a tough time on the playground or at the school dance. I will pray for mothers separated from their children.

If I knew then what I know now, I'd have included stepmothers, too. They are the ones who do motherings for people without the deep memories that keep mothers warm.

I will never forget that Mother's Day. Maybe it's when I started thinking about Mary, Jesus' mom. Since then, I've thought of her often. There must have been many times she wanted to write to Erma. Did she have a friend who would listen to her when she was ready to scream?

"He wanders off into the hills talking about other worlds. When is he going to get organized?" She must have said that to someone. Him hanging around with friends she didn't know, being with people he shouldn't. Hearing voices, talking to people who weren't there. Why couldn't he just be normal? She must have felt the distance, being on the outside of the ever-widening circle of his life.

When Michael got sick, I didn't write to Erma anymore. I was too scared. I didn't want to write about street drugs. I didn't want to believe it when they said he had schizophrenia. I didn't even know how to spell it. When I found out, I called the Schizophrenia Society of Alberta. I called our family doctor. I called the psychiatrist. I thought about Mary.

Schizophrenia is a biological illness, they told me. Something in the brain misfires, causing auditory and visual hallucinations. Sometimes it can be controlled by medication. Sometimes not. It strikes one in a hundred, mostly young people in their late teens and early twenties. Their families generally live in fear.

"What is it you're afraid of?" my new husband lovingly asked last fall. "That he will die," I answered. Three months later, we held his hands and stroked his poor body at the Royal Alexandra Hospital in Edmonton while Michael died. He was twenty years old.

Motherhood can be a catchword for pain and joy. It is not for the faint of heart. Nor is life, really.

I am standing now, at the threshold of the third and final part of the lifedance: menopause. It is said that in menopause a woman becomes pregnant with herself, at last. I am sure that Erma is not only a good dancer, but is also experienced at midwifery. I will write her.

~

Carolyn Pogue has written a wide range of work for children and adults. In addition to stints as a newspaper reporter and book editor, she has written a youth musical, film, poetry, songs, short stories, and nonfiction. Caroline has written two books of nonfiction: *Yellowknife* (1981), *The Weekend Parent: Learning to Live Without Fulltime Kids* (1992). She is a founding member of *Yellowknife Writers, Eh?* Raised in rural Ontario, she has also lived in Quebec and the NWT. She and her husband Bill Phipps call Calgary home. Parts of this essay first appeared in *Topic, Newsmagazine,* and *The Weekend Parent.*

Carpenter's Apprentice
Vera de Jong

"HMYGODOHMYGOD . . . "
Inside I am a mass of nerves while on the outside I put on my best "tough broad" look — the stern, capable, I-don't-even-*feel*-pain sort of look that is a must for every woman in my shoes — or boots, rather. I am an apprentice carpenter and I am about to begin my very first job.

I curse the icy sidewalk. I curse my heavy, embarrassingly new toolbox and curse again as I walk onto the job site and steel myself to try to locate my new boss, asking myself why in hell I am always starting over.

I summon my courage, fix my face into its mask, and stride up to the man nearest me. He smiles patronizingly at my question like I'm a kid playing dress-up and I want to smack his face. I curse again, conscious that the depth of my hostility matches my fear.

Finally I locate my employer, thrust out my hand and tell him who I am, careful to suppress my natural tendency to smile pleasantly. Take me seriously, buster, I warn him silently . . . , please, I feel myself adding. He tells me to come with him and proceeds to cover ground at a pace that I, needing to stop every twenty feet or so to shift my toolbox to the other hand, cannot hope to maintain. Again I curse, but this time I have an urge to laugh as well, as I detach myself for a moment and observe this scene. I have borrowed the laughter from my women friends who will enjoy my tale later, as I will, when it has become funny.

"Ever done formwork?" he asks me over his shoulder, as I struggle to maintain both my pace and my dignity. I say no and he continues his conversation with a co-worker who has accompanied us. I am rapidly falling behind.

Finally we round a corner and approach a group of men gathered around a snack truck. Ten pairs of eyes focus on me with the same question: "What can she *possibly* be doing here??" I am a Martian among Earthlings. I have three eyes and horns among two-eyed, hornless people. I am a woman. Here. To do a job.

So begins my acquaintance with the men with whom I will spend ten months, almost seventeen hundred hours, 420 coffee breaks. With whom I will laugh but towards whom I will direct a largely unexpressed rage of an intensity that until then I had never found within myself; the men who will teach me about my trade and among whom I will learn much about myself.

I spend that first coffee break being observed but not addressed, feigning nonchalance as I sit sipping my coffee. Finally the men begin to drift away and I am assigned to one of them and follow him down a slope slippery with mud into an even muddier hole. A few concrete walls are standing already stripped of their metal panels. Others are being built. Everyone busies himself at his task. I follow my partner and catch myself as I stumble over an object half-hidden in the mud. "Watch yourself there," I hear from the top of a wall. I ignore it because behind the words is a sneer.

Coffee breaks are spent in a tiny cluttered trailer. The floor is caked with mud, the walls are plastered with large glossy pictures of bikini-clad women. For the entire first day no one addresses me, but by now I have rallied my resources and sit self-contained and cynical. I sense that they are ignoring me at least partly because they have no idea how to talk to a tall, muddy, hard-hatted woman who is not doing the work of providing conversational openings. (I am not their mother or their lover or a cute girl in a bar: they are at a loss.) I sip my coffee, I draw on my cigarette, and I observe them.

What is the "glue" here? I wonder, noting the absence of anything recognizable to me as communication. How can they bear to spend their days like this? I listen to the WASP guys harass the Portuguese labourers ("Hey, speak English or die!"), and the mainlanders insult the Newfoundlander. I almost feel a bond with the labourers as they ignore the taunts and continue chatting, but I also feel something like shame. I am intensely nostalgic for other "first days" when settling into the job was usually accompanied by lots of talking, information sharing, story telling, helpful hints, the inside scoop on the boss. I feel myself in a dry, barren place. I survey the postered walls, silently daring the men to comment. A svelte, black-haired, scantily-clad woman holds a power tool seductively at crotch level, the shiny black cord wound enticingly around her thighs. Three women in bikinis arch forward, smiling from the upraised buckets of three yellow backhoes. Tammy, a voluptuous "Sunshine Girl" from the local paper, is in a pink bikini and smiles out from under tousled blond hair — she is a waitress, we are told in the caption, and loves Caribbean vacations. Other "Sunshine Girls" simply gaze out alluringly, deprived of even their two-line personalities. On one wall the pictures overlap so that heads are covered and only almost-naked torsos and thighs are displayed. I observe as if from a great distance and with a certain numbness.

We go back out into the muck and the February cold. Now it is raining but even rain jackets do not prevent the icy drip down one's back. I do as I'm told, carrying heavy metal panels, buckets of steel pins, four by fours up and down the muddy slope until I am beyond exhaustion. This, I know, is a test. As I listen to the grumbling and cursing at the rain I let not one word of complaint pass my lips. Several of the men come up to me out of what I sense is real curiosity and ask the same question: how do I like the rain? Each time I smile, responding carefully and somewhat inanely that I do prefer sunshine, and return to my work. Yes, folks, I think drily, I do believe that we are experiencing conversation. But I find myself appreciating the contact.

At the end of the week I am called into the trailer by my boss to fill out forms to do with my employment, and I am triumphant. I know then that I have passed the test. He enquires chattily as to what I worked at before this and is satisfied by my vague reply. "Social work," I think with irony, does not quite cover almost two years at an abortion clinic dealing with insults and taunts from picketers outside, with tense, often frightened women inside and with tension that at times invaded my entire body, depriving me of sleep and appetite. But "social work" is as close as I'm going to get in this environment; I can in no way let myself be vulnerable. I must keep my other life locked firmly away because to give them information is to open myself to verbal violation. Welcome to schizophrenia.

I soon realize that there are rules that set strict limits on intimacy. It is acceptable to refer to one's spouse as "the wife" but almost too personal to call her by name. One can complain on Monday that "the wife" was nagging all weekend to have chores done around the house, but to reveal gladness that she was finally back from visiting her family out east would be much too dangerous. A pregnancy is announced by saying that "the wife" is "whining for two." Armour is always on. I proceed slowly, carefully, tentatively. My armour is constructed rapidly in those first weeks, built of humour and quick comebacks from safely behind my protective shell.

The weeks slip into months. My strength grows and I am no longer utterly exhausted at the end of the day. Gradually I become hooked on certain aspects of this new world. Every day I am outside. The changing seasons and day-to-day variations in temperature become real, to be observed and enjoyed.

My brain must accept an expanded sense of scale. With delight I watch the prefab tunnel sections that I have helped build being lifted high over our heads and over hydro wires, trying to grasp that I am watching thirty-four thousand pounds of concrete moving through the air. All the previous day my boss and I had worked with small hydraulic pumps to separate these three sections of tunnel and slide them the necessary two feet apart so that they could be prepared for placement. We tried every possibility, every combination of blocking and steel pipe, till finally we saw a tiny shift. We were jubilant — he because he was experimenting with a new method of his own design and the stakes were rather high; I because of my wonderment that this small hydraulic device could translate our effortless arm movements into a force that could move tens of thousands of pounds of concrete.

The months slip by. My body changes, toughens, strengthens. I feel myself striding around with easy, fluid movements. I no longer feel in my movements that implicit apology for being a large woman. I am learning to take up space. I am proud of my five feet ten inches and my muscles that enable me to carry full-sized sheets of form plywood with less and less difficulty and to swing a sledge hammer in long smooth arcs.

But as time passes and my confidence grows, so does my rage. Several times a day I feel it surging up in response to comments or behaviour of my co-workers. I have no outlet for this anger but a quick retort, an insult clothed in humour. The depth of the misogyny in those around me constantly makes me an alien. The posters on the walls begin to cause a fury and a pain that I can barely contain. They become a reference point for me, symbols of the hostility towards women that manifests itself in the daily conversation of my co-workers. I try to lobby for the removal of the posters. I do not dare to take them down myself because I am alone and not sure I can deal with the backlash, whatever that might be. Occasionally my anger can find no outlet but to go into the trailer and tear one of them down, and the consequences be damned. "Did you take the picture of my girlfriend down?" I am asked the next day. "She's not your girlfriend, Jack, and yes I did take it down," I answer tightly, overwhelmed, depressed, at the chasm that separates me from the people I spend eight hours a day with — my "brothers" in the union.

It is an environment that does not sustain, but rather exhausts. I receive no support, no encouragement. When a personal problem leaves me distraught and near tears for days, I hide it completely, only allowing the tears to fall when I am safely hidden behind a wall cutting steel. I am desperately lonely, then, for women co-workers with whom one can shed tears and share troubles. The energy I receive in my other life is spent sustaining me through my days.

And my co-workers bore me. Before long I categorize their stories under two headings: 1) Dominance Display Stories: ". . . so I get out of the car and I go up to his car and I say through the window 'You wanna get out and talk about this, Bud?' and I show him my fist. So he rolls up the window and takes off like a shot. Ha ha ha." Endless tedious variations on a theme. 2) Personal Excellence Stories: I am regaled by numerous accounts of my boss's former prowess in competitive skiing and swimming, by accounts from others about the speed of their cars, their superhuman capacity for consumption of liquor. . . .

I find myself challenging their racism and homophobia even though it alienates me further. "Jesus, this is hard work — we should get some nigger to do it" must feel a lot like ". . . and there were two guys holding hands. Ugh. It made me feel sick" must feel a lot like "I could go for that — look at those tits." The men insult or tease by calling each other "faggot" or "woman" or — worse yet — "old woman," and think they are complimenting me when they tell me I am "just like one of the guys." ("This is my dream," I tell them drily, but I don't think they get it.)

That I respect their skill as tradespeople is a given. Often when I watch them work I feel a hum, a fluidness in the relationship to wood, to machines, to practical physics that leaves me awed and envious. I pick up the excitement of the rush towards completion of a form before concrete trucks arrive. It becomes a dance, a calm but urgent coordination of tasks that flows out of a wordless understanding of a common purpose. Electrical and plumbing conduits and steel rods are put in place inside the walls by men who appear on schedule, perform their tasks rapidly and efficiently, and disappear again, leaving us to close up the walls, straighten them, support them. . . . And so I learn the steps of the dance, learn to watch closely, anticipate the next step, have the appropriate tool or piece of material already waiting when my partner turns to ask for it. I allow myself to be taught. When I am teased about my mistakes, I laugh. I swallow my pride and devote myself to becoming a good apprentice, which, especially in one's first year, is a necessary prelude to, but quite aside from, becoming a good carpenter. As my skill grows, I begin to work a little more independently, a little more equally, enough so that now and again I am able to glimpse the satisfaction that it will give me when I am finally competent. Sometimes this vision is the only thing that keeps me going.

My boss is a fair man and takes his obligation towards me as an apprentice fairly seriously. In this I am fortunate. Mistakes do not draw his anger or ridicule — it is sufficient that the person is aware of his/her error and willing to put up with teasing. Only outsiders — the deliverers of materials or the hired crane operator — receive the heat of his anger. I interpret this as a kind of loyalty and relax within it, confident that my willingness to work hard and to learn is obvious and, in that context, my best is good enough.

Personalities emerge. There is Joe, the Portuguese labourer. Within the construction site hierarchy Joe and other labourers perform the unskilled tasks — shovelling sand, stripping the forms of their wooden or metal panels, moving lumber, pouring concrete. Joe and the other ethnic labourers mostly keep to themselves, but because I am a woman and somehow outside the hierarchy (not needing to prove the same things), I talk with Joe. Gradually, in response to my questions, he opens up a little. He knows I will not mock him and that I am the child of immigrants and proud of it. Joe, too, lives something of a schizophrenic life. On the job each day he is a labourer: without status, without skills, depended on but not respected, taunted about his ethnic background, unhappy, quiet, thirty-eight but carrying himself like one much older. Yet in Portugal, where he and his wife and their two children spend every other summer, he is the cherished son of aging parents, owner of a beautiful home near a sparkling sea (he brings in photos to show me), proudly regarded as having made good in far away Canada. He, I'm sure, shows photos there of his house here, his modern car. I picture him walking proud and straight, perhaps boasting a little. He has become, as did my parents, caught between two worlds — one is "home" in the true sense; the other, in Canada, is where his children have put down roots and where he can have some economic security. He chain smokes and dreams of Portugal, holding out for some kind of joining of the two worlds which will probably never come. He chain smokes and coughs, and clings to the thought of the better life his children will have. I remind myself not to make assumptions about these men — everyone has their intensely lived story.

Then there is Danny, from Newfoundland. We soon develop a fast-paced repartee which includes frequent references to his talent as a singer and his regret at turning down the Rolling Stones. (He was needed here, he told the Stones, and was devoted to being a labourer.) Danny, like Joe, dreams of another life. After his wife leaves him, taking their child, he tells me often that he is "not too pleased with my gender these days," and wonders aloud whether he *should* give me a lift to the subway, since he's not in a mood to do anyone of "my gender" any favours. It is said jokingly and I respond on the same note, but I sense his confusion and pain and am not unsympathetic. But I have no desire to cast myself in the role of confidante. I do not provide openings and feel good that I am aware of this as a choice and am not being forced by a sense of obligation to spend my energy this way. One day as we are leaving the trailer I point to a particularly offensive poster of a woman naked except for two strips of yellow plastic "Caution" tape across breasts and crotch and ask Danny would he do that. "What do you mean?" He is used to me by now but not willing to risk an answer till he's sure what I'm getting at. "Would you stand around wearing only Caution tape and let people take pictures of you?" He considers for a moment and says thoughtfully that no, he guesses he wouldn't. I leave it at that, suddenly too tired of it all to pursue the matter. When, another time, he asks what is my problem with the pictures anyway, "They're just pictures of pretty girls and they *are* sort of dressed," it becomes obvious to me that he really does not know.

And then there's Steve who, without question, hates me because I am a woman who refuses the traditional categories. He is also titillated in a way that makes me uncomfortable. He dares not express it except through constant references to my clothing, the new patch on my jeans, the colour of my shirt, the rip in my jacket: none of them direct or offensive enough to be labelled harassment. Mornings when anything is different about my appearance I brace myself to enter the trailer, filled with disproportionate dread of his half-sneered observations. In fact, he seems to have difficulty saying anything to me without a sneer in his voice, except when he launches into a string of dominance display stories: then he is safe, confident, in his element. And he says things like, "yeah, I used to date girls from the shelter, but it was hard to find one that wasn't too bruised up. Ha ha." Ignore him, I tell myself, he is immature and not going to change so forget it. But this is where I work, this is my *work place!* I want to scream.

It requires enormous self-discipline, on many days, to perform my obedient-apprentice role. Having spent a good part of my adult life struggling to rediscover my power as a woman, I find myself in a totally powerless position, and some of those who have power over me in my working life represent everything I have struggled against. One day I am told that it is good for me to have to take orders, that it will make me more humble, and I am stopped short, simply stunned at the idea. You, sir, I want to tell him, are looking at someone who is still learning not to apologize for taking up space on the planet — humility is one thing I do not need to learn! Again I am overwhelmed at the chasm that separates us and intrigued, too, at the difference between how he must see me and how I see myself.

And so I maintain my armour, always guarded, always careful, often lonely, but some days it is almost more than I am willing to stand, and I hum a favourite women's song as I work, in order to create a connection to my other life and an island of calm in which to rest. Whenever possible I slip away at noon for a precious half-hour of recharging. I am aware that leaving at lunch time increases my alienation but day after day I succumb to the temptation to avoid that half hour. I feel unequal to the risk: although there are periods when the conversation is inoffensive enough — occasionally I even share a genuine laugh with them — at any moment a joke or comment can leave me feeling stunned and violated: a female politician taking a stand who "just needs to get laid"; a woman whose appearance from the picture makes it "surprising that anybody would even want to rape her"; a comment that the women who underwent drug experimentation in Montreal in the forties were "good people to practice on. Ha ha." The words draw appreciative chuckles from the other men, reinforcing their sense of belonging through their common misogyny, and I am left torn between wanting to respond from the anger, the hurt and the aloneness that I feel, and longing only to be far, far away. Usually I bury myself deeper in my newspaper (my shield, my refuge during almost all of the time I sat with them as a group) and pretend to ignore them. And I burn, knowing that inside me is a wish to hurt them back as their attitudes and the attitudes of those like them hurt me and other women. One can reason logically and sensibly about how this culture teaches misogyny and acknowledge that these men too are victims who speak from their fear. But what, still, does a woman do with her rage? A few of the men do not participate in the woman-hating (black-hating, gay-hating) conversation, but I long for them to once — just once — take a stand in opposition to it. I wait in vain.

I become a fortress. I hold out stubbornly because I want to learn carpentry, and because I have set myself a challenge that I am not ready to give up on, and because, in the current weak economy, my alternative would be unemployment. And I hold out because I feel myself growing stronger and I like the new strength.

This story has no conclusion, no resolution. At noon one day, as the snow falls so heavily it piles on our shoulders and buries tools in minutes, my boss tells me he must lay me off. I have half expected this: a sagging economy threatens the very existence of the company. In his own way this man has been good to me and I find myself wishing him well. In line with usual practice, I and a few others, also laid off, have received one hour's notice. Because that last hour's pay is free, within minutes we have collected our tools and are climbing into cars. A co-worker drops me at my door and, as we shake hands he says, unoriginally but not unkindly, "Don't take any wooden nickels, eh."

I smile and bend to pick up my battered tool box. "Yeah, you either."

~

In her own words: After this first year of working in construction in Toronto, I moved to Vancouver and began working in renovations, which largely escapes this "construction site culture." I am currently in the third year of my apprenticeship but am taking time off to teach in Japan and travel in Asia. I look forward to continuing my trade upon my return to Canada.

In the Bleak Midwinter

Dianne Linden

*J*FELL IN LOVE WITH A BARI-
tone at the Pro Coro Christmas Concert last year: stayed in, love
with him for at least ten minutes because of his face. He bore the
burden of homeliness, and I wanted to share it with him. I saw he
had poor posture, thin shoulders, a slight paunch and that made
me love him more. I was sure his appearance was caused by some
difficulty in his life which could have been prevented by the love
of a good woman, like me.

He had a real hangdog face: the kind of face that would look
morosely at me over the breakfast table because the newspaper
had gotten a little wet when it lay out on the porch steps in the
snow, or because the three minute egg I cooked him was really
a seven. (Let's say I was thinking about knitting a new silver
hat or a cobwebby pair of wings or a black, sequined hat band,
tasteful, in case someone I knew died and I had to go to the
funeral: and I lost track of time.) He'd look at me over the
newspaper, and I'd feel his disappointment that my control over
time and the world in general was less significant than he'd
expected.

He and I had never spoken, never looked deeply into each other's eyes, sighed, searched each other's mouths with tongues as
eager to communicate as newly uncapped pens, yet I can say with
sad certainty that if we were to meet and become lovers, one day
his eyes would complain to me of my imperfections over the

newspaper at breakfast, which I hardly ever eat, and I would have to ask him to leave.

He'd probably have brought two or three pipes with him to keep by the chair my cat slept in before he moved in with us on nonconcert evenings: maybe a second tuxedo in case his awful need of me made it necessary for us to be together just before he went off to sing. He'd have shaving things, of course: a mug of soap, an old badger-hair shaving brush, a silver-handled razor engraved with someone else's initials, hair tonic, silk shorts: all those frugal accoutrements a man brings along with him when he means to stay a while, and I'd have to ask him to leave. (He would have left me anyway, when the next potentially omnipotent person came along.) I wouldn't like asking him to go. But I'd do it anyway.

It would be traumatic for me, watching him walk out my door with his threadbare carpet bags, and wait on the porch for a taxi cab he probably couldn't afford, so instead of sending him a little note at the end of the concert saying, "I loved your small, modest solo at the end of the Schütz piece. I was the tall woman in the purple parka who waved at you repeatedly from the front row. My name is Dianne. Please phone me at 455-6693 if you feel as lonely and nostalgic over Christmas as I do," I put my boots on and went out for a caesar salad with a friend of mine who's gay. He already knows I'm not in control of anything much, and he apparently doesn't care.

~

Dianne Linden is an educator and writer based in Edmonton. Her poetry and short stories have previously appeared in such publications as *Dandelion, Grain, Other Voices,* and *Wascana Review,* as well as on CBC Radio's "Alberta Anthology." She has also published *Faux Paws,* a book of poetry in comic book form with Edmonton artist Jerry Dotto. She believes, along with Dorothy Parker, that the saddest words in the English language are: *it might have been.* Having experienced a number of these in her life, Dianne has resorted to humour as a form of self-defence, it being less life-threatening than new relationships, alcohol, sun tanning, or late night walks over the High Level Bridge.

Chicken and Fingers

Mary Maxwell

S OPHIE'S RIGHT HAND HAS
tightened into a permanent claw. Olga has developed a chronic
misalignment of her spine and Florence now has one hand that's
significantly larger than the other. Mildred's grip will never be
normal again. As for Sonya, her wrists have literally worn out.
These are just some of the exploited women I came to know when
I was hired to open a health office in a meat-packing plant outside
a prairie city.

The workers I met there belong to a silent majority numbering
many thousands; women who are violated daily by the crippling
work they must do to make a living. Despite permanent injury,
daily pain, and frequent harassment at work, they rarely complain
aloud for fear of losing their jobs.

This packing plant was opened in the late eighties, and management claimed its design and equipment was "state of the art."
Production moved here from an older plant in the downtown
area. Now, it was in the suburbs.

When the new plant opened, the company reasoned that hiring a nurse like me to work on the premises would help control
absenteeism, rising compensation claims, and resulting fines. The
legally required assessment of employees who worked directly
with the product would be done at the plant rather than giving
workers time off to seek treatment elsewhere.

For years the meat-packing industry has been at the top of the

Department of Labour's list of hazardous industries. As an article in the *New York Times* described a few years ago, workers in a packing plant toil in extreme heat or refrigerated cold; they stand shoulder to shoulder on assembly lines for hours wielding honed knives and power saws. Grease and blood make the floor slippery and the roar of machines is constant. There is an overpowering stench from the offal. I saw the workers cut themselves, slip, fall. They wore out their insides doing repetitive-motion jobs. In this plant the annual statistics showed that out of every one hundred workers there were about thirty work-related injuries and illnesses. This is roughly four times the average in private industry.

The plant manager told me part of my job would be to tour the work site regularly and watch the workers do their jobs so I would better understand the problems brought to the health office. When I advised him that part of my duty as a health professional was to guard a person's confidentiality about health findings or personal problems, he said "Of course," and so I should. However, if a person's problem interfered with her work, he reminded me, there were a lot of others out there who could replace her.

The plant tour began at the receiving area, where trucks stacked high with crates of live poultry waited to be unloaded. On the platform, two men lifted crates of ten to fifteen live chickens on a moving belt that led to the "live hangers" who opened the crates and hung each of the chickens by one foot on a moving chain, which then carried them to the "sticker," who slit the chickens' throats after they had been electrocuted in a water bath. The chain carried the dead chickens through machines that plucked and singed feathers, cut off the heads and feet. Then two men, the "dead hangers," hung them on another chain that carried them into the eviscerating room. Here the entrails were removed by a combination of machines and human labour.

Fifteen people worked in this room, which swirled with steam so thick you could not see across it; the temperature was roughly 29° Celsius and the noise was deafening. An overwhelming stench hung in the hot, heavy air. Ten of the people in this room were women, all of them over fifty.

As I interviewed each person in my office during the health assessments, I was struck with the number of these women whose extremities had become permanently disabled from their work on the assembly line. At first glance, they appeared normal; that is, they could walk and use their limbs in most activities of daily living. However, their hands in particular were visibly distorted, raw, and work-worn.

Sophie had worked in the eviscerating room for twenty-one years, pulling guts with her right hand; it had become larger than her left and had tightened into a permanent claw because of the repetitive nature of this job. This made it impossible for her to wear gloves — a change I attempted to introduce in this area. She could not straighten her fingers nor could she touch each finger with her thumb. It was as if her hand was frozen in this position: when she removed her glasses to clean off the spatters of blood, she grabbed them with her claw-like hand and pulled them sideways off her face. Sophie stood on a metal platform and yanked the chicken's guts, which had been mechanically pulled to the outside of the carcass before it reached her. Her back had grown a hump of muscle between her shoulders from twenty years of leaning forward to pull guts. Her fingernails were embedded with fungus, cracked and misshapen. The skin on her hands was thin and broken in several places, and there was evidence of many old wounds. She had tortuous varicose veins in her swollen legs from standing, her ankles bulging over her shoes.

When I saw Sophie in my office she was quiet, speaking little of her family or about the sure ache in her hands and legs. She was short and rotund — her hair bleach-blonde — and when she smiled her plump cheeks framed a nearly toothless grin. Sophie was not interested in trying another job to give her back and hands a rest. She said she was not long from retirement and besides, she was used to her job and thought she did it well.

Olga, known as Ollie, had worked on the gizzard-harvesting machine for nineteen years. She sat on a metal stool hunched over a table, sweat dripping down from her glasses. With her right hand she grabbed the mechanically removed gizzard fed to her by an auger, snipped it in half, peeled it and then pushed it through a hole on her table that carried the gizzards to another part of the plant. Her left hand was covered with warts and several cuts in various stages of healing. The warts were caused by bacteria from the chickens, the cuts from the scissors slipping. Because of the design of her work station, she was required to sit on a high stool with no back support so she walked with a permanent forward stoop. She had headaches daily from the chronic misalignment of her spine and neck. Her vision had deteriorated because of the close work and poor lighting. She had a significant hearing loss from the years of working in noise without proper hearing protection.

Ollie visited me daily, always with a cheerful message and a wink even when asking for an aspirin. In her calm, rather resigned manner she expressed concern for some of the younger women's work-related health problems but minimized her own. Ollie talked about her sixteen grandchildren, of frequent weddings and birthdays, and how she regularly knitted clothing and made perogies for them. I wondered how she could smoothly roll out the perogy dough with such misshapen hands.

Florence had worked on the line for twelve years as a checker. It was her job to examine the eviscerated birds for any bruises or obvious malformations before they reached the inspectors from Agriculture Canada. She stood for the entire shift and wore a wire mesh glove on her left hand to grab the bird by the leg. With her right hand she slashed a large sharp knife through the diseased or bruised bone or muscle, marking it as unfit. The line moved at 42 birds a minute or 2,520 an hour. Some days the kill was twenty-four thousand. On a busy day, Florence made over seven thousand slashing movements with her right hand; consequently, it was significantly larger than her left. She had an unusual muscle mass just above the wrist on her right arm from the repetitive motion; across her shoulders and up into her neck was a thick ledge of knotted muscle that caused her constant pain.

When I tried to massage her shoulders, it felt like kneading cement. After two sessions, Florence said she could not stand the pain during and after the massage. Her normal posture was to keep her shoulders hunched up around her ears rather than relax them; consequently any relaxation induced by the massage was painful. She also had a persistent problem with fungus growing in her outer ear. One day on the line, she had scratched the ear with her gloved hand and even though she'd had a course of antibiotics, it still bothered her.

It took time to win Florence's confidence, as she was extremely suspicious of me. I had to prove I was not a spy for management. When I had, she would come in after her shift and in a deep and serious voice, sometimes almost whispering for fear of being overheard, she would lean toward me and tell me some of the problems she saw as a worker at the plant. She believed management was slowly replacing women with men because, as she put it, men don't wear out so quickly; she said the soap at the hand-washing stations was watered down (to save money), so workers never really felt their hands were clean; she said the knives were cheap and never sharpened properly and it was easier to cut yourself because of this. Flo suggested her back might not hurt so much — especially after the roasters went through (they were larger than the small fryers usually processed) — if she and the other workers could have one metal stool to take turns sitting down. All of her concerns had been brought to the attention of her foreman, she said, but he just told her to stop complaining.

Florence's husband was a trucker, so she had raised her family on her own and spoke with great pride about her children. She talked of someday quitting the job and applying to shelter homeless, retarded adults. She said she just loved those people.

Mildred was a checker too, there for about the same number of years. Both of her wrists had gone, as she put it, again from the repetitive motion required by her job. And even though she had had surgery on them in order to free the nerve, her grip was that of a child. Millie wondered if she could get them "done again" so she could continue her job. I told her the details about carpal tunnel syndrome, explaining her wrists would never be the same again, even after surgery. As with many others who had to miss time because of a work-related injury or illness, Millie was docked sick time when she was off for surgery instead of being covered by Workers' Compensation.

The exact date of a repetitive strain injury is difficult to ascertain and to be awarded compensation benefits, the date and time of injury has to be given and supported by the employers. Workers' claims were repeatedly refuted by management; thus the person was denied benefits and had to use sick time for an injury very clearly caused at and by work. (Although this was five years ago, both management and this policy remain unchanged.)

Mildred played bingo almost every night, hoping to win someday so she could quit her job.

During the working day at coffee or lunch break the women would sit together in groups in the coffee room, pass around pictures of recent family events, play a hand or two of rummy while they absentmindedly rubbed their hurting parts, wipe the smear of chicken blood and bile from their glasses and tell jokes. One would warble hymns such as "Amazing Grace" and "Rock of Ages" in sweet soprano while another hummed country and western ballads. They exchanged endless stories about bingo, wondering aloud when they might win the big one.

Next to the eviscerating room was the pack room. Out of the thirty people who worked there, twenty were women. Here the eviscerated chicken was cooled in large refrigerated tanks and then dismembered with a series of cuts either by machine or by hand, each person performing the same motion over and over again for up to twelve hours a day. The temperature was kept cool at 10° Celsius to discourage bacteria from growing on the raw chicken. Most of the people worked with felt liners inside their hard hats and double wool socks inside rubber boots to insulate them from the cold concrete floor. Here the women were younger, most in their twenties, single, and with young children.

Sonya had worked at the plant for four years on the electric saw, cutting the chicken into nine pieces. Soon after I arrived she was unable to work in this area because her wrists had literally worn out. She was twenty-two. After her doctor demanded she be taken off the saw, Sonya was constantly harassed by the packroom foreman, who verbally abused and humiliated her because he did not believe she was really disabled. He was convinced she just did not want to work. The jobs he assigned her, even though they were supposed to be easier, required her to keep flexing her wrists, which had caused her problems in the first place. He also cut her hours and would not allow her to leave the floor to go to the washroom.

Two older women, Lizzie and Ann, were both close to retirement and had disabling medical problems as a result of their jobs. They had grown bitter from years of abuse and poor working conditions, despite the efforts of the union and promises from management that things would change after they moved to the new plant. Ann's husband had a brain tumour and was in a chronic care home. She was trying to put her son through university. Lizzie's husband had to quit his job at the plant after thirty-two years as he was unable to work on the vacuum machine because of a frozen left shoulder caused by overuse in this very job. He was denied Worker's Compensation because he had been in an accident about the same time he was experiencing problems with his shoulder, and the plant claimed he had never complained about his shoulder before the accident. They had difficulty making it on Lizzie's salary.

Some days when the foreman had been chewed out by the production manager because efficiency rates and production quotas were down, he would speed up the line and cause an increase in accidents and injuries. The people on the line would plead with him to slow it down but he would just stare at them, almost threatening to increase it some more. He was in the middle of a divorce and had just found out that he had lost custody of his son because of his drinking.

Most of the people at the plant were poorly educated and had come up the hard way. Their identities were tied to their jobs; they were grateful for work and had an unswerving loyalty to the company. They put up with the poor working conditions, mistreatment, and abuse because they did not believe they could get another job. They said they got used to going home hurting.

I found the conditions in this new plant to be outdated and horrifying. All my attempts to negotiate with management to change some of the more grisly conditions failed. I learned that the business of packing meat was a brutal industry whose dominant corporate ideology was to blame the victim. I saw the worker set up as culprit, seen as careless or accident-prone, freeing the company or work environment from responsibility. Often the poor equipment design, inadequate ventilation, and lack of management directives (such as job rotation) caused accidents and resulted in the company paying fines for having compensation costs that were far higher than in other industries.

I heard management say, "If she hadn't been so careless," and "I told her to wear a mesh glove; she wouldn't listen, so she was asking for it." But there were no mesh gloves to fit her because someone forgot to order them. And her so-called carelessness was caused by cheap knives that could not keep an edge. It was disturbing that management's statements echoed what we often hear in rape cases.

For the first few weeks working in this plant I was in a state of shock. I had never seen people used up and abused on such a large scale. At first I found their complacency and powerlessness contemptible, but slowly I began to understand that if they kept quiet the abuse would not escalate as it did when someone asked for change. I was not able to change any of the abominable conditions for these people but by taking the time to listen and by believing what they were saying about the horror in their lives, I was able to validate their experience and some of them actually came to believe they deserved a better place to work and left.

Working women are on the lowest rung of the job ladder. This, in addition to their poverty, low self-image, and poor education, is exploited in workplaces such as this one. Unlike their articulate sisters in business, the professions, and academia, they have yet to find their public voice. Yet their plight demands to be heard.

Ever since I worked in this packing plant, I have wanted to describe what I saw and heard. I hope this story will encourage others to tell the truth about what is happening in many working environments across Canada. The conditions I encountered in one plant — and comparable conditions in who knows how many other similar workplaces — are not all that different from the barbaric conditions Upton Sinclair exposed in his epic novel of Chicago meat-packing plants, *The Jungle.* That book was written almost one hundred years ago.

~

Mary Maxwell is a writer living on the prairies. The names of the women she writes about have been changed because of the content of the material and the very real threat to the employees of losing their jobs. Ms. Maxwell writes poetry and short stories as well as social justice journalism. She hopes to contribute to the effort of giving working-class women a voice so that they will no longer be "mute figures in our cultural landscape." Her essay was first published in *This Magazine*, August 1992.

Forbidden Knowledge

$\mathcal{J}$N THE JUDEO-CHRISTIAN TRA-
dition, the power of knowledge, and its danger, is encapsulated in
the myth of Adam and Eve. In the story of the Fall, as in so many
other stories, woman's desire for knowledge is linked with sexuality. Because of the presumed nature of their sex — or their sexual
nature — women have historically been deemed unfit for certain
kinds of knowledge — the religious knowledge that would allow
them to be rabbis and priests, the academic knowledge that would
permit them to take part in the intellectual life of their society, the
practical knowledge that would enable them to lead independent
lives without a man's protection. And as women who lack these
kinds of knowledge have often been denied a place in the larger
social world, so women who possess forbidden knowledge have
had their truths denied.

The knowledge forbidden to women still has strong links with
sexuality. Paula Johanson's exclusion from "A Modern Ritual" has
no serious consequences, and Rose DeShaw presents young girls'
ignorance of their bodies comically in "New Dress." But R. M.
Thompson's "Remembering Red Rosebuds" reminds us of the
painful consequences of such ignorance.

Other writers emphasize the struggle to know fully the reality
of their own experience in the face of strong pressures to deny it.
In "Interrupting Memory," Apryl Babcock seeks the sense of biological and cultural identity she lost with her Cree mother. Jan

Semeer finds "A Safe Place" in which to reexperience childhood traumas long denied by her family and by herself. In "Once Upon a Time [. . . and it hurts . . .]" Sarah Murphy suggests another means by which women's truths may be concealed — through the "fictions" about women constructed by male writers and subscribed to by some women.

By claiming women's right to knowledge once forbidden, these writers free themselves — and other women — to become whole human beings.

A Modern Ritual

Paula Johanson

I SAW A MODERN RITUAL ONCE.
It won't make the *National Geographic* like the cargo cults, and it won't make the little ads in the back of men's porn magazines, but it was the damnedest thing to see a circle of men stroking off a salmon.

It wasn't something as dirty as that sounds, or at least I don't think it was. I'd been helping these conservationists harvest salmon from the spawning run all day, and they seemed like a plain bunch of old fishermen. They spent that morning up to their hip waders in cold water at the downstream side of the pool in Goldstream River. At the upstream end of the pool a young guy in a wet suit complained bitterly that it wasn't his turn, dammit, he froze his ass last year, and chased the salmon into their nets. The fish were then dumped one at a time into a plastic garbage bag with a little water and chloroform mixed in the bottom.

They told me and my friend Linda to carry the fish up the bank to tanks waiting in the back of a pick-up truck. It wasn't easy to climb a dirt cliff one-handed while carrying a struggling salmon bigger than my arm, until the fish had sucked up a little of the chloroform. Gradually the fish would quit beating its tail against my thighs and then rest its bony head along my side.

I have to admit that it was a good dodge for the old fishermen to invite us, so we could do the scrambling up and down the cliff a dozen times each while they stood in the river freezing their feet off, debating whether they had enough males for all the females, and whether a three-year "jack" salmon was really comparable to the mature four-year-olds. The last fish I staggered up the bank with must have been five years old; it was solid meat and as big as my leg. No wonder they chose that one for the incubator stock.

Linda and I had peeled off our heavy wool shirts and were sweating in our T-shirts, but the fishermen and diver were blue with cold when the old men decided they had enough salmon. Then they took the fish to the holding stream and the incubator, kept in the watershed area, behind locked gates to keep out curious vandals.

By the time Linda and I found the gravelled yard past the gate, the fishermen were milling about getting salmon in the holding nets in the stream and checking the incubator's pump. One of the men took time to explain to us how the fresh water would keep running up from the bottom of the incubator, through the layers of gravel and eggs that he would lay out, and flow out the top, carrying away stale water until the fry hatched and were released in early spring. With his next breath, he told me and Linda to go over to the pick-up and get the coffee made. He spoke pleasantly enough in dismissal, but this was the first thing that hit me as beginning to get strange: girls make coffee, men get to pick which fish get harvested.

Now, I had never yet met up with a sexist attitude that actually succeeded in cutting me out of doing anything. I knew by then that anyone in a crew does whatever work is useful, and that beginners make coffee, fetch, and carry. Still, it stuck a little in my liberated craw to be shut out of the more symbolic job of fertilizing the eggs and layering them in the incubator. Linda and I went ahead and made coffee, knowing we couldn't be cut out of something unless we let ourselves be; after all, we'd worked hard all day with these guys. The pair of us probably reeked of fish and chloroform, sweaty wool and the loamy clay we'd been clambering on, but I can remember only the smell of the coffee perking and wood smoke coming from somewhere.

When I came up to the circle clustered near the incubator, with a cup of black coffee in one hand and one with sugar and cream in the other, no one noticed me. All those fishermen stood shoulder-to-shoulder in a tight circle around some activity in the centre. I thought they were still discussing which of the fish to use, until I saw the red-and-silver flash of the salmon somebody was holding.

Maybe they had gathered together to hide what they were doing from us, or to be closer to their leader, the oldest fisherman. He had the head trapped under his left elbow and was restraining the tail in his free hand, while someone carefully slit the vent with a wickedly sharp knife. Another pair of hands held a bucket below the gutted female, to catch the eggs that streamed forth. I assumed that they'd stunned her, but she jerked in the big knotted hands as one of the men reached into her body with cold fingers, pulling out the last of the roe. I spilled a little coffee then, outside the circle. There was less blood than when I'd cleaned fish myself.

It was a three-man job, no need for the dozen of them crowded into this pack. Yet, when the emptied female stopped shuddering and I nudged a cold shoulder to offer coffee, no one turned for a steaming cup. The dead fish was laid outside the circle with two or three others, leaking body fluids underfoot, forgotten. A second glance told me the bucket was perhaps a quarter filled with salmon roe.

The fishermen wouldn't look me in the eye, or take coffee for their cold hands. It was like they wouldn't let me be there at all. All attention was on the oldest fisherman as he held a big male. The hooked jaw scraped against the elbow pinning it to the fisherman's right hip; the ruddy body needed both hands to restrain it. The circle of men pressed closer, standing hip to hip in two tight ranks. I couldn't see past them until I ducked down like a kid peeking through a fence.

They didn't use a knife this time. When the bucket was held ready, the man gripped the fish in both hands near its tail and just back of its pectoral fins. He made a curious motion with his hands, pressing his thumbs down hard and stroking them together, towards the vent. The male jerked, and the bucket caught his white spray of milt. Another pass of the big-knuckled hands brought a few more drops from him as he quivered. Then the man relaxed his grip, and gently carried the exhausted fish back to the holding net in the stream a few steps away.

Everyone was shifting his weight, stamping blood back into cold feet as I offered the coffee cups again. There were no takers; one or two seemed angry at my being there. The diver came up to me from where he'd been busy checking his equipment a few yards away.

"I'll take cream and sugar," he said, looking into the cups and taking the black one. "It's over at the pick-up, eh, come on and show me." He steered me back to the truck, saying quietly: "They won't want any coffee for a while. They'll come and get it when they're ready. Don't worry, it isn't you they're shutting out. They just don't like anyone else around while they're doing that."

I muttered something to the effect that I wasn't making fun of them, and anyway we'd been invited to help today. Were they shutting us out just because we were young women?

He had a crooked smile for us, half patronizing, half sheepish. Linda and I sat on the tailgate on either side of the coffee maker, listening. "Oh, I know you're not a couple of gigglers," he said quickly, "but they wouldn't feel comfortable doing that with younger people around. I mean, you couldn't imagine a woman involved in that."

Linda asked what they did with the fish afterwards, and he looked away, face gone cold. "Well, the females are dead," he said shortly. "Can't take the eggs without gutting them. No, they don't eat them. Anyways, salmon don't taste good when they've been in fresh water."

He drank from the coffee cup that had gone cold in his hands, and hesitated before going on. "They put the males back because in a couple of days they'll be ready to milk again, maybe two or three times in a week or two before they die anyway like the ones in the river. They'll be out there a couple of times next week."

I wondered if maybe we could help them, but he shook his head. "No," he said automatically, then in a more detached way, from his twenty-three years to our sixteen: "It isn't just you girls. I've been doing this three years now, and they still won't let me in on it yet."

He asked for more coffee, but we said it was time for us to go. As we drove away, the circle closed in again, the young man closed the tailgate of the truck, and behind our car the gate swung shut.

~

Paula Johanson recently moved from Victoria, B.C., to a farm north of Edmonton, Alberta, where she writes science fiction stories and novels, poems, and freelance articles while helping her family in the market garden. "Blood Turn" won *The Edmonton Journal* Literary Contest for 1991. Another of her stories was nominated for an Aurora, the national science fiction award. Paula has been known to do poetry readings at the drop of a hat.

Remembering Red Rosebuds

R. M. Thompson

*T*HEY CARRY PLACARDS WITH messages dripping blood. They march across my TV screen. I spot them in newspaper photos. I hear them on radio talk shows.

"Who would have formulated Einstein's theory of relativity?"

"Who would have painted da Vinci's *Mona Lisa*?"

"Who would have written Schubert's *Unfinished Symphony*?"

How I yearn to show them; take them back; give them a glimpse of life before birth control tablets, IUD's and "Life Skills" courses in schools.

Physicians, legally, could not dispense birth control information without the knowledge and consent of a young woman's parents.

"Safes" were available, if a young man could muster up enough courage to ask for them at the corner pharmacy.

Condom dispensers were not available in schools nor did roving health professionals provide graphic demonstrations on how to apply condoms to erect organs.

Organs!

A joke from that era . . .

A man with a particularly fecund wife seeks counsel from the family doctor following the birth of the couple's sixth child. The doctor listens, then advises, "Place a rubber on the organ." A few months pass and the physician receives a call from the man who says that his wife is pregnant, yet again. "Did you put a rubber on the organ?" asks the doctor. "No," responds the frantic father, "I didn't have any rubbers so I put my overshoes on the piano."

And that about says it all!

It was a time when a thirteen-year-old farm girl was sent away to high school with the advice, "Never do anything in the back seat of a car that you wouldn't do on the living room couch."

Now, I as you would wonder, what the hell *was* that?

Let the placard carriers travel back to a Calgary drugstore.

Let's "get real," as the young people say.

Sixteen-ounce bottles of rubbing alcohol are ordered — twelve cases of twelve bottles each — every week. Fifty cents a bottle to the general public for chicken-pox itching and ear-piercing and dabbing; one dollar a bottle, no questions asked, to the young/old men in stinking overcoats who visit daily, then one night freeze to death in a boxcar down by the railway tracks.

"Hell! If they don't get it from us they'll get it from someone else or they'll drink shaving lotion or melted shoe polish," says the pharmacist. "It's the lesser of two evils." His fat cheeks suck lungfuls of Chesterfield cigarette smoke and his red-veined nose bespeaks thousands of twenty-sixes of summer-time gin and winter season rum.

"Name your poison," as they say.

He exhales a cloud of smoke and turns his attention to a new product, just arrived. Three dozen condoms to the package in a drop shipment of Ramses and Sheiks. I price the condoms with a grease pencil and place them in the lowest check-out counter drawer, beneath the cash register.

"When one of these young bucks asks for some Sheiks, ask him if he wants a 'weekend pack.' He'll say 'Sure.' Then, you plop one of these thirty-sixes on the counter. He'll be too damned embarrassed to say it's more than he needs. Six dollars! Damn good sale!" he chuckles and wheezes.

There's nothing he isn't — if it isn't a master of merchandising.

And so I did. And they did. But, sometimes, they didn't. Then came another type of customer. Gaunt girl/women, with eyes suffering from fear and shame.

"Is there anything you can recommend if your period's late?" they'd whisper, as if a period was an end to a sentence, which it sometimes was, the sentence of being an unwed mother. And for those too we had merchandise: black capsules, as big as footballs, for the restoration of menses; snowy grains of quinine sulfate, encapsulated in gelatin; double-ended syringes; castile soap (for purity) and Hygeol (for disinfecting); and then there was always the old apothecary jar filled with slippery elm bark, used for centuries by wise old women in countries much older than ours. When all of these, or none of them, produced the desired results, the fearful, shameful, and by now, terribly frightened girl/women slipped into a dingy bathroom with a length of straightened wire clothes hanger.

Some bled to death. Some died of blood-poisoning. Some aborted. Others completed their sentences.

And then one day it happened.

The thirteen-year-old farm girl is seventeen and she works in that pharmacy. She's bright-eyed and beautiful and doing things in the back seat of a car that she wouldn't do on her parents' living room couch.

And her boyfriend, twice her age and "worldly," assuages her fears of pregnancy. "It's all right. I wouldn't let anything happen to you," he whispers as his excitement mounts.

But he does, and she is, and all the pills and potions in that pharmacy are to no avail.

"Not to worry," he soothes, when she has missed her second period. (She is beginning to see how *this* sentence reads.) "I know someone who can make everything all right."

So, it's down an alley between Eighth and Ninth avenues, where the stench of urine and garbage bespoil the summer air. He opens the back door leading to the "Men's" parlour of the King Edward Hotel, and the stale beer smell mingles with the alley stink. "I'm going to be sick again," she thinks, as she stifles a gag.

The "someone" who "can make everything all right" is a bartender named "Doc." Funny name for a bartender. Arrangements are made for the following night and $250 changes hands.

Her lover and protector coasts the wine-coloured Buick to a stop near a curb in Riverside, at precisely 2 A.M. "I'm not allowed to come in with you. Here's the other $250 for 'Doc' and some money for a taxi home . . . after . . ." and he kisses her lightly on the cheek as he reaches across to open the car door.

A gentleman to the end.

On legs of rubber she crosses the sidewalk as the Buick's taillights disappear around the corner. Up the darkened walk. A timid knock at the scabby door.

Light from a 150-watt bulb, dangling from a twisted, cream-coloured electrical cord, reflects off "Doc's" head. His sharp nose casts a lengthy shadow down his salt and pepper moustache. When he opens his mouth to speak, beer and tobacco fumes escape in a whoosh from between weasel teeth.

"Come in sweetheart, I've been waiting for you."

He riffles the $250, not really looking at it all, then leads the way down the wall-papered hall to the kitchen, where an oilcloth covered table dominates the room.

"Might as well get to it. Take your clothes off, get up on the table and make yourself comfortable." And, as she positions her clammy bottom on the oilcloth, "Doc" unbuckles his belt, unbuttons his waistband and unzips his fly.

Softly, he says, "This won't hurt a bit, not in your condition."

"Doc's" pants drop to his ankles and he slides her towards him across the sticky oilcloth with its pattern of tiny red rosebuds.

~

Born and raised in Alberta, **R. M. Thompson** first began her writing career as a member of the Flagstaff Creative Writers group headquartered in Killam, Alberta. Her profiles, nonfiction articles and humorous short stories have appeared in magazines in both Canada and the U.S. Her work has also been published in the anthology *Crocuses and Buffalo Beans*. She presently resides in the Cowichan Valley on Vancouver Island where she is working on a book of humour.

Interrupting Memory
a procedure for understanding

Apryl Babcock

1

Mᴇᴍᴏʀʏ
upon memory wraps itself
around our lives like the bark on a tree
each remembrance, each member branching out with a different
pain
Lil, mother of John and Iva, grandmother of Heather and Roan
Sawyer, husband of Lil
John and Violet and their children, Heather and Roan
Iva and David, childless, rootless

Grandmother in her kitchen heard voices. Straining to listen, she could not hear. She knew John was outside his house. These are my children, you get out.

Violet walking away.

2

This is where memory begins, with a loss. I lost the story of my mother that day.

3

Three. I began writing when I was three years old. Writing became a way of interrupting memory, a procedure for understanding. I had to understand that she was gone. I had to stand under her absence.

History wrote itself, but she never came back. Grandfather, Roan, and I lived in Grandmother's house. She watched like a deer watches. I had to understand a grandmother who was also mother.

And John went out one day and brought home his Angel(a). He also brought another son. I had to understand a stepmother. A stepfamily. A step up?

And there was a death and Iva was alone, with two children. I had to understand a mother without a man.

4

I got a notebook for Christmas and in italics I wrote the things I didn't understand. Very soon I couldn't see the story for the words. So I played hangman with my brother and wondered why it wasn't hangwoman. I whispered and asked him if he remembered Violet? He didn't answer, just made a hole in the wall and played with his Tonka trucks. Even though she was gone and we were not allowed to mention her name, we grew up in the shadow of her memory.

5

Dear God. Grandmother hung up the phone. Dear God, she said, what does she want? So wicked, phoning all the time. Reaching her hand under my fence, past the no-trespassing signs. It's my place here, and I know my place. No person's got a right to keep phoning. To keep phoning when I got the right papers.

I raised up them kids. Under the law. She got no right.

She never sent any presents, no birthday cards. She just knows how to phone and call me dirty names. What kind of mother is that?

When I came to this country people had to take care of themselves. These two are my own flesh and blood. I got things to give them.

6

Angela felt her there in that country. The country of her husband, John. In the house that was hers and not hers. Do I have to share you, she said, with your mother and her?

7

What, besides their fears, did my mothers have to offer me? Trying to write my memories like their own. I rejected the wordrobes they tried to clothe me with. I listened for the telling silences and tried to understand with my own orphaned words.

8

I felt the fear. Fear skulking around. A great bear of fear in my Grandmother's cupboards. In this version of my life, fear walks in the shape of my mother.

Do you want to grow up like her?

I just(ly) want to see her, I said, with my own two eyes.

She turned to me. I didn't move. Look at who raised you, she said.

If I don't find anything good in her, I said, I can't find anything good in myself.

A tree needs its roots to survive.

9

But I didn't know then that Grandmother sat in another's doom. Question: how can I tell your memories, Grandmother? Answer: the story never forgets.

10

Lil, on the eve of her story. She had come with Sawyer over the sea. Had come into the wilderness, into another war. She had been judged. Eyes looking from between the spruce. Disapproval. There's murder in Sawyer's eyes, her mother-in-law said. You put it there. You dirty Catholic. You worked heavy like a stone on my Protestant son. Go back to your netherworld of windmills.

11

Grandmother and Grandfather lived in the house where he was born, in the house with his mother. Grandmother gave up her god to please her mother-in-law. But she still practised her own rituals, she set up her own boundaries. Telling only the stories she herself wanted to hear.

12

Build me a house Sawyer, she said. (Sawyer was Lil's carpenter.) There's not room enough here. Not for her always (s)mothering you. My house will be built with the trees of my own choosing. Dear God, she said, she doesn't own you.

13

My grandmother put up signs on her own land. No hunting. No fishing. Stay out. My mother's story was never allowed to become a story. And when she finally told it to me, I read my own loneliness and confusion into it.

14

Violet lived in a different world. She felt the earth shake more than once.

She was taken from her family at the age of two. Taken from her mother. Her roots ripped out like so many weeds. Savages, they said.

Her mother heard them come in the dawn of day. She turned to look and tasted the dust of the prairie. Bitter it was in her brown mouth. The last thing she heard: we will educate her like a whiteman.

She flipped her braids at them. I have four more born in the heart of this country. She went back into her lodging.

15

There are no heroes in this story which is not a romance.

16

So she was schooled. She took up residence in the house that wasn't a house. Watched over by a god she never understood, a god she never wanted. The same god Grandmother never wanted to lose.

Violet learned suffering and put on fear like a jacket. She took their lessons and in return they took her words.

In the time before healing, her days were not sweet and the grass she burned was bitter. In a stupor she would call out *muther*. No one would answer.

Then she found the country with John. Here the earth was quiet and did not shake. For a while. She and John had children. One with carrot hair and one a different colour. She hardly had time to be a mother before she remembered her lessons. She thought, because of me the whole world's wrecked.

So she grew herself like stone and wouldn't let anyone touch her.

You dirty Indian, he said.

She knew there was no use crying, no use crying at all.

17

Who carries the dirt? The dirt from the mothers is visited on the children. Where would you be if we hadn't taken you, (grand)mother often says. What is the difference between owing and owning but one letter?

18

My grandmother's story is her house. She inherited it from all the mothers before her. Between her walls my love is held captive.

My own mother has no house of her own. I found my place in a different version of history. Her signs read welcome. My love is free to walk with her.

I walk a line now along the different coloured memories of my past.

19

Too much has happened, too many memories. I am root-bound with memories. All my mothers wear their mothering like a hood, I don't remember their real faces. Where does memory end? Now that I'm

20

twenty. The twentieth chapter. I saw clearly for a moment my simple hope. Maybe it's not time for remembering.

There are too many words here, there are not enough. The story is mocking me now. Trying to erase me. I must see things with my own two eyes. I must begin my own story, under the shade of my own tree. No more interruptions.

~

Apryl Babcock was raised on her grandparents' farm in northern Alberta and currently resides in the neighbouring town of High Prairie. She is of mixed ancestry — Cree and English/Dutch. She holds an Honours B.A. in English from the University of Alberta and occasionally writes book reviews for *The Edmonton Journal*. She has travelled in Canada and Europe and published an article on the Soviet education system in the *Alberta Teachers' Association Magazine*. "Interrupting Memory" is her first published piece of creative writing.

A Safe Place

Jan Semeer

$\mathcal{T}$HERE ARE FOUR BEDS IN MY room but I'm lucky because the other three are empty, so I have the room all to myself. Perhaps tomorrow someone will move in but for now I'm on my own. I brush my teeth and apply lipstick so that I look well-groomed for my first session. Having some minutes, I lie down, hoping that now I have taken the sedative my shaking will stop, so that I can go there in a calmer state of mind.

As I walk around the corner of our house to enter by the back door I stop, horrified to see a police car parked in the driveway. That can mean only one thing: they have found out I am thirteen, a very new thirteen at that, and do not go to school, have in fact never gone to school in Canada.

I was twelve and had just finished grade six when my father decided to leave Holland. When we first arrived at our destination I had taken for granted that I would go to school. But my parents had decided otherwise.

My father, called by a newly founded small Dutch church in Canada, had felt obliged to leave his large congregation in Holland. When the letter came he had said, "It is a cry for help. And what an opportunity to bring the Word of God, the true Word of God to Canada."

We came, the six of us, my parents and their four children.

My father earns eighty dollars a month and the house in which we live is rent-free, but my parents can barely make ends meet. My mother, who is not always in good health and has been used to live-in help in Holland, finds it extremely difficult to cope with the new life here. These circumstances have made them decide not to send me to school. They know it is against the law, but feel my mother's needs are more pressing than my need for an education or the threat of discovery, and have instructed me to keep my mouth shut. I must not tell anyone my age because if I do we will all be in trouble.

So for months now I have cleaned house for my mother in the morning and for other people in the afternoon. These people pay me thirty cents an hour. The $1.20 I have made this afternoon is safely tucked away in my coat pocket, ready to hand over to my parents.

"Can any one tell me where the kitchen is, what it is used for and by whom?" a beautiful young woman asks. I'm told her name is Ann and that she is a recreational therapy university student, working on the psych ward for the summer under the supervision of an experienced therapist. "Yes Amy, that's right. Very good. It's great you remembered it all so well. Now, can anyone tell me what we need if we want to leave the hospital premises? Very clever of you, George; you're absolutely right."

On and on go the questions. I shake my head in disbelief. It is as if I'm part of a kindergarten class. Too bad I don't know all the answers yet; just wait until tomorrow, then I'll get a pat on my head as well.

I review the work I had done that very afternoon. When I arrived I had found a list of instructions. Since I read English almost as poorly as I speak it, I had great difficulty deciphering the note. It read: vacuum and dust living, dining, and bedrooms, clean bathrooms thoroughly, wash kitchen walls and ceiling, wash out kitchen cupboards (I'd puzzled over the word "cupboards," what were they, boards for cups? I had been unable to find such boards so could not clean them) and iron the clothes in the laundry basket. But no matter how hard I'd tried I had been unable to finish it all.

After I washed out the kitchen it was transformed from a dull brownish grey to a lovely light blue — unreal! What a job it had been. The ceiling was the toughest: the dirty water running along my arms into my armpits and from there down to my waist. I could not stand it and yearned for escape but there was nowhere to go. Only my mind could roam free and it wandered to earlier days, to fun-filled times in Holland, all of them involving friends: cycle trips in the country, having fun on the way to and from school, climbing trees, playing hide and seek in the inner part of the old city, playing ball against the big blank wall of the church at the end of our street, playing hopscotch in the school yard, just playing.

Next — crafts. I don't want to go but the nurse tells me I have no choice. "Everyone goes to the craft sessions," she says. "Perhaps you'd like to make a leather belt for your husband?"

A bag full of little pieces of leather; somehow I have to fit these together. Pick up one, and another, push the second through the loop of the first, then a third to go through the loop of the second, and so on, again and again and again. I'm getting there, I can see results — a belt in the making.

"Ann, I have to leave. My son is here from out of town to visit me. I just saw him on the ward," an elderly patient says.

"We have another ten minutes to go, Jane; sit down and finish what you are doing. You can leave soon enough."

"Then he'll be gone, I know he will be," Jane whimpers. She walks to the door crying. "How come she can come and go and I can't," she says pointing at Judy, who has been walking in and out of the room the whole time the craft session has been in progress.

"She should sit down too and stick to her work; won't you sit next to Jane here, Judy dear?"

Jane cries, "I want to see my son, I know he is here, I saw him talking to my doctor."

"Jane, you know your son is not here. He only picks you up for the weekends, never during the week. Now please be quiet, sit down, and see to your cross-stitching," the supervisor says firmly. Jane sits down but continues to sob.

I would love to put my arms around Jane, but do not dare since she sits across the table from me. I'd have to get up and that's not allowed.

I must not feel — it hurts.

Here I have no friends. Most of the Dutch families belonging to

*our church live on farms miles away from our small city. I've made
no friends in town because my life is so different from that of the
neighbourhood children. Besides, I do not dare to approach them
because I do not speak their language.*

*It is a good thing I'm tall, otherwise my parents and I would have
been caught much sooner, I think as I stand on the back steps, not
daring as yet to go in. How has it been detected though? As far as I
know I have never breathed a word of my age to anyone, or have I
after all let something slip? I could easily have misunderstood someone's question and exposed the lie.*

*Oh, if I could only be like my eighteen-year-old sister. She fin-
ished high school in Holland and therefore speaks English fairly well.
She's already building up a circle of acquaintances. Only this morning I saw her jump into a car, waving at me as they drove off, her
cheeks flushed and her eyes sparkling with excitement. The driver
was probably someone she works with at the local supermarket. She
sure has all the luck — a nice job and exciting friends.*

*Well, there is nothing I can do about it so I might as well go in.
All that can happen is that I will be sent to school and then my cleaning days are over. I should feel relief but don't. Surely my parents will
blame me for it. The day seems to blacken even more and as I stand
on the steps I shiver not only because I'm cold, but because I am terrified of my parents' anger. They'll blame me, saying that they can't
do without the money I earn, and that it was I who gave them away.*

Over lunch with Barb, a young patient, we discuss her E.C.T.
Neither one of us eats much, but she does talk and tells me of her
frequent deep black depressions and how they are cured for short
periods by E.C.T. She laughingly relates that when first back at
home she does not know where many of her things are. "Such a
nuisance! but I have survived so far and will again. Tomorrow I
hope to go home, then the cycle starts all over." Suddenly her eyes
are full of tears. I don't know what to say and just touch her hand.
So we sit silently, side by side.

*With a heavy heart I finally push open the door and step into the
kitchen. No one is there, but I hear voices coming from my father's
study. Exhausted, I sit down. Usually I go straight for the bathroom*

to scrub the dirt, other people's dirt, off me, but today I sit and wait.

A door opens, voices, then a man's voice. "We can't do much right now. We'll wait until your daughter gets home; then we'll question her."

A door slams and they are gone. I'm paralyzed with fear and cannot move. "Thank goodness," I breathe, "they did not know that I was home."

As we leave the dining area I see Jane walking down the hall holding on to the arm of a man. Barb says, "Her son is here; she was right after all." Then she adds softly, "She is schizophrenic and often sees strange images, so was not taken seriously this morning."

When I get back to my room, there is a note on my bed informing me that I'm expected in the television room for group psychotherapy at one-thirty.

I've been told that I'll have to talk about feelings there, even though I don't know what my feelings are. All I know is that I'm sad, incredibly sad. But I have no idea why I'm so sad, no idea at all. My teeth are chattering and I want to run away.

I can think but it hurts.

My mother's voice. "How can she do this to us, how can she be so stupid. Oh the shame of it! What are we going to do?"

My father does not reply. The kitchen door opens and they see me.

I stammer, "What happened; how did they find out?"

My mother, now crying, "Your sister got raped and instead of coming home she went to the house of a friend."

I feel weak suddenly. Is it relief, is it disappointment, is it terror for my sister? I do not know.

Later that day my sister comes home. She is a changed person — *her face numb, her eyes dull and lifeless. And I can give her no comfort. I have my own burden to bear.*

There are five other patients besides myself. The therapist introduces us to one another. It makes me feel better that I sit close to the door. If need be I can flee quite easily. Would Rose have placed me here on purpose? she seems like a very nice person.

Relaxing a little, I try to listen to the discussion.

"My cat died last week," a woman suddenly sobs, "she meant everything to me. I'm so alone, I have no family, nobody loves me or has ever loved me."

"That's very tough, Linda," Rose responds, "perhaps we can talk about that; what are you willing to do?"

I look at the crying woman with more interest; she must be the one I heard about, the one who threw the chair through the window. I wonder whether Rose will mention it. She doesn't. She gently leads the conversation in such a way that Linda never feels threatened. Then Linda herself talks about her extreme anger during the night, how she felt she was not in control of her life any more but that after she had thrown the furniture she felt worse than ever.

"So, that was not the answer," Rose says. "Does anyone want to respond to Linda?"

The talk becomes general for a while then zeros in on some others. One woman has been beaten by her husband and shows us her black and blue arms, another has given up a daughter for adoption some years ago and has severe guilt feelings. "Does she know I did it out of love for her?" she asks, her voice full of anguish.

My head reels, I hear many voices, what are they saying? My arms are tingling, my fingers feel dead, I have to get away from here.

A sad teenaged girl stands at her Grandpa's coffin. She loved him. He was always kind to her. The small country church is packed with people who want to pay their last respects. The atmosphere is stifling to the girl; she thinks, I can't breathe, I can't breathe. Her hands are wet and sticky.

She stumbles out of the church saying, "I've got to wash my hands! I've got to wash my hands!"

"Jan, are you okay?"

Is that Rose's voice?

"No, I can see you're in trouble. Don't take such big breaths, try breathing quite shallow. Good, that's better. Now I want you to breathe into this paper bag, you are getting too much oxygen. You are doing just fine, now try to relax, good!"

My head feels so strange, so very strange, but I am aware of my surroundings again. I am holding on to someone's hand, tightly. It's Linda's hand.

"I'm sorry," I gasp.

"That's all right," she says, "tomorrow I might hold on to yours."

I am still shaking.

The family has just arrived home from the morning service at church. There is a lot of activity. Removing coats, taking off shoes, putting on slippers, standing in line for the one bathroom in Grandpa and Grandma's house. The girl is allowed to go first, because she is only little and can't hold up her pee as well as the grown-ups, but "hurry, hurry," they all say.

Grandma adds, "Don't forget to wash your hands, sweetheart."

The girl's mother laughingly replies, "She won't forget, she is forever washing them."

The little girl nods solemnly, she will hurry, she knows about hurrying, and her hands will be washed, she hates dirty hands.

Then there is the rush to get the coffee ready. All the women pile into the small kitchen; one whips up the cream, another cuts the homemade cake, a third puts out the cups and saucers. Grandma is already busy with lunch so that when coffee is finished lunch can be eaten promptly, then no precious time will be lost.

The men are discussing the morning service. "Good sermon," says one uncle. Another replies, "Yes, but I wish he would have emphasized the first point more." Grandpa disagrees. "It was a good Biblical sermon," he says, and on goes the talk, with some of the women joining in now that the coffee is served.

The little girl has wandered from kitchen to living room to decide which scene is the more interesting. Her father and Grandpa both spot her and vie for her attention. She stops to consider. If she sits on her father's lap she will have to sit still, otherwise he will get angry. He will not give her any of his cake. Grandpa, on the other hand, will let her wiggle as much as she likes and better still, will share his cake with her, even though she has had some of her own already in the kitchen. She climbs on Grandpa's lap.

Lunch is served in the kitchen where the big walnut table with six matching chairs takes up nearly all the space. Somehow room is found for the additional chairs which are needed when everyone is home. The little girl sits squashed between her mom and one of her aunts. She feels safe there and eats her soup happily, already anticipating the dessert, her favourite — ice cream.

"Hurry, hurry sweetheart," Grandma says as the little girl is playing with her ice cream. "You need a nap, as do some of the others here; the afternoon church service is not far off."

To close the meal Grandpa reads aloud from the Bible and thanks the Lord for His goodness to them all.

The women get up quickly to wash dishes while the men disperse looking for a quiet spot to nap.

Grandpa takes the little girl by the hand and says, "We are going to nap together."

Everyone smiles, thinking how sweet it is that those two are so fond of one another.

Rose says gently as she takes the paper bag away, "It's all right to cry here Jan; this is a safe place."

I look at her mutely, and shake my head.

"Why not Jan, can you tell us why you don't want to cry?"

"Because," I say and stop. Trying once more I say, "Because, I'm terrified that once I start I will never ever be able to stop again."

The door closes behind the little girl. She is now all alone with Grandpa. They share a secret, a real secret! She is not supposed to tell anyone ever; and he has promised, "Neither will I." This is their secret, just between the two of them. She loves her Grandpa; he is always very kind to her. Because he is kind and pays a lot of attention to her, always has some little gift for her and takes her on long walks, she does things for him in return. Strange and exciting things. At least they are exciting for Grandpa. She yawns and curls up into a ball on the bed ready for her nap. However, now it is her turn to play with Grandpa.

"Hurry, hurry," he says, "it is church time soon, we do need our nap, otherwise we'll sleep in church and that will never do."

So she hurries and accomplishes her task. Her hands are wet; she does not like that.

She whimpers, "I want to wash my hands."

"Ssh," says Grandpa, "we don't want anyone to hear now, do we? You can wash your hands later, let's have our nap first."

The little girl goes to sleep. Her hands are sticky. She hates dirty hands. She hates her dirty hands.

After Grandpa suffers a heart attack later that year, there are no more Sunday afternoon naps with him. The little girl tucks the "secret" away, far away. She does not remember it. She does not like eating sticky foods. Her hands are scrubbed clean all the time.

"Jan, your doctor is here and wants to see you," a nurse says to me as I walk to my room, holding on to the wall for support. I'm so tired — so incredibly tired.

Sagging into a chair I wait for him to start. When he does, I'm too tired to respond. I hear his voice but the words do not make any sense to me. He expects an answer, but to what?

"Jan, I was saying that if all else fails we can try e.c.t. It might work for you."

But I'm not that bad, am I? am I? Surely I'm not that crazy? — Oh God, oh God, I am, I am!

"Jan, listen to me, this is just another option available to you. I'm not saying you will get that treatment, only if it is your own choice. Do you understand?"

My head is empty, completely empty, I can't think. Yes, I am crazy, really crazy. There is no hope, no light, there's nothing, nothing at all.

Stumbling into my room, I draw the curtains around my bed, shutting out the sunlight, and lie down. That is how my daughter finds me and her tears drip on our intertwined fingers.

I must think I must hurt I must feel I must cry.

~

Jan Semeer is a Dutch-Canadian who finally remembered in her fiftieth year that as a child she dreamed of becoming a writer. She began writing and has not stopped since. "A Safe Place" is her second publication.

Once Upon a Time
[...and it hurts...]

by Sarah Murphy

S HE WANTS YOU TO KNOW THAT
this is not a fiction. Is not. Is not. This is a telling. A way to the
telling. Important: the way to be able to tell. She can tell
because she can tell it this way. As if she were the author. Only
the author. (That fiction.) As if she had the authority. The
authority of the telling. (That other fiction.) Something she
can hide behind if she wishes. Or hide in. A maze. A labyrinth.
Of images or pain. In which to play hide and seek. The way
she always does. Through changing, changing. By moments
mute, by moments screaming. Always soft-coloured. Blurred.
A Victorian garden. Or pastel drawings. With fiction the condition of the text. Because she lies sometimes, and sometimes
lies are the clearest way to the truth, to the meaning of the
telling. Because even when she lies the pain is real. And this
time she wants you to know it. The way she wants you to
know the details are real. And I will be her witness. Swearing
to the truth of what she tells because no matter how she tells
it what she tells me in my mind appears in detail in my body.
In detail on my body. Some days is my body.]

There is a story someone tells. That Julio Cortazar wrote. It's a story I keep hearing. A lot, actually. Sometimes I think they tell it to me. Sometimes I think I just hear it. Over and over. That I listen for it. For that particular story. Among all the stories that they tell.

Once upon a time there was a rapist, this story begins.

Or maybe it's a bit different. Maybe it doesn't begin that way at all. And maybe it's about a rape-murderer. I do know it's a mysterious and magical story. At least that's what they say. Because Julio Cortazar is a very great writer.

The story tells about this man who rapes this girl by a road and then she dies. Rape is when a man puts his penis inside a woman even if she doesn't want him to. The story says this rape took place somewhere in France. And they say it really happened. Some of them are quite sure about that. That he raped her and then she died.

Only I don't know how it happened. If he kills her or if he just hurts her

[and hurts her]

so bad that he doesn't know how bad and then he leaves her there by herself and then she dies. She's so sad she just dies. Like that.

And then maybe police find him and maybe they know what he's done so maybe they execute him. Or maybe it's not like that at all because it takes a long long time or he has an accident or something. But then he's dead too.

And he meets the same girl over there on the other side of death and she forgives him, and she makes love to him. That's when a man does the same thing to a woman with his penis only she wants him to. Maybe she even asks him to. Because the rapist needed her and he felt so sorry

[so sorry]

and she had beautiful hair and he reached out his hand.

And everyone was happy ever after even if they weren't alive.

I don't think I believe that story. I don't believe it at all. I don't think it's a true story even if they all repeat it and Julio Cortazar wrote it and they say he was such a great writer. I don't think it would happen like that, not at all, not even after death. I'm quite sure it wouldn't. That's something I'm really sure about. Because I know I wouldn't forgive anything like that. It wouldn't even matter to me if he reached out his hand. I wouldn't care.

And I certainly wouldn't forgive him before he died the way some people say they would. If the police didn't catch him and they didn't get to execute him I know I wouldn't do that. The way this woman Carolyn says she did when something like that happened to her. When this rapist who had raped a lot of women came and raped her too. Only he didn't hurt her so bad she died, he just hurt her

**[and hurt her
and hurt her]**

while her four-year-old son stood outside the door screaming and crying because he didn't understand what was happening to Mommy and she had to tell him to go back to sleep, just to save his life and he was only four years old and so sad and that's even younger than I've been all this time sitting on my stair listening. And the rapist cut Carolyn with a little knife little tiny cuts and she bled a lot and still she forgave him. Even if she didn't die she forgave him anyway and told her son he had to forgive the rapist too. Even if they were both so sad for the longest time still they were alive to forgive him. And they could live happily even if it wasn't ever after. And that was that.

I know that story's true because Carolyn still cries when she tells it only she's not sad any more because it makes her feel so good to know she didn't kill him, she didn't even try to kill him she forgave him and she's sure that makes her a good person. And so is everyone else. Only I still don't think I would do it and it wouldn't matter if I died or I didn't or if he died either. Or even if they would tell me what a good person I was and give me great big hugs the way Carolyn gave her son great big hugs after the rapist went away and the police came. It wouldn't even matter if they asked me to come down from my stair and gave me ice cream.

Not if he got up on top of me and he grabbed my shoulders and he held me still and I couldn't move and I could hardly breathe and then he grabbed my chest and it didn't matter if I wasn't a woman at all because I had no breasts and what he pulled at was handfuls of skin or if he stuck his penis in from behind and it hurt

[and it hurt and it hurt
and it hurt and it hurt
and it hurt and it hurt]

and that's all I can tell

you about it: it hurt

[and it hurt
and it hurt]

so bad with him holding

on and pushing in and grabbing at me with his hands digging into my shoulders and pulling at the skin on my chest while it hurt

[and it hurt and it hurt
and it hurt and it hurt]

just like that one two

three four one two three four in and out and it hurt

[and it hurt
and it hurt]

so bad that I sometimes

get stuck in it and I can't hardly stop saying it. Telling how it hurt

[and it hurt and it hurt
and it hurt and it hurt
and it hurt and it hurt]

and the pain was all

yellow and blue and red mostly red hitting me and hitting me like the waves at the shore hitting me and hitting me until I can't feel anything else but how it hurt

[and it hurt]

until I'm all lost in how

it hurt

[and it hurt and it hurt
and it hurt and it hurt]

                    and there is nothing else

but how it hurt
        [and it hurt and it hurt
        and it hurt and it hurt]

                    and I don't know if I'm

alive or if I'm dead because it hurts
        [and it hurts and it hurts
        and it hurts and it hurts]

                    until it doesn't matter

anyway. Any of it.

I'm just walking in a field of pain and I'm still lost and I don't know where to go because it hurts
        [and it hurts and it hurts]

                    but it doesn't matter

because even if it hurts
        [and it hurts and it hurts and it hurts]

                    and he grabs onto my

shoulders and pulls at my chest: still, I won't forgive him.

Even if I'm lost and I can't find my stair where I like to sit and play with my dolls and my little toy tea set stamped made in China on the bottom of every cup while I listen to their stories, there's still a little light that I can always find. And it's sort of like a firefly and sort of like Tinkerbell in *Peter Pan*. That's a book that I read sometimes too when I sit on my stair, especially if their stories aren't very interesting.

Only this is the light that reminds me that I won't forgive him no matter what. No matter if I hurt
        [and I hurt and I hurt]

                    still I won't forgive him

not even if I'm dead and I can't ever come back not even as far as my stair still I will hold onto that one light and I won't forgive him. Not ever.

No matter if I float away the way she did in that story the soft hair billowing out all around her like in an ad for Breck shampoo, the one I used to see on TV. While I look down on him the way she did on that rapist so far away and sorry. Still I won't forgive him no matter how far away I get or how long I wait or how beautifully my hair billows out. Or even if I'm very close and he reaches out his hand and calls my name.

And says please

[please please please please please]

and touches my hair, I did have beautiful hair, still it wouldn't matter. Even if the hurting seemed to stop it wouldn't matter. Because no matter how much it seemed to stop hurting it would still hurt. Deep inside it would still hurt

[still hurt still hurt]

and I still wouldn't know how to find my way back from the field of pain and I wouldn't know who I was except that I am the one who won't forgive him.

Even if he said I'm sorry

[I'm sorry I'm sorry]

still I wouldn't forgive him. No matter how long he kept saying I'm sorry

[I'm sorry I'm sorry]

how could I do this to you I'm sorry

[I'm sorry]

and he reached out his hand and he cleaned off my tears and he said it again I'm sorry

[I'm sorry I'm sorry I'm sorry I'm sorry]

it wouldn't matter at all. No matter what I said right then it wouldn't matter at all.

Even if I let him bathe me and he was so gentle and he smiled his gentlest smile and he wiped away my tears still it wouldn't matter at all. Not even after he went away and he got married and he smiled at that girl just like that his gentlest smile, the one he had always saved for me, as I looked at him lift the veil she wore, so much like one of my dolls. Whether I could already see from the way she looked at him how easily she would forgive him all the things I knew he was going to do, even then it wouldn't matter. Even if he died after a terrible accident it wouldn't matter. It wouldn't matter at all.

Because even if he kept saying I'm sorry how could I do this to you you're so beautiful

      [so beautiful so beautiful so beautiful]

                      you're so beautiful and good, one two three four in and out

      [in and out in and out
      in and out in and out
      in and out in and out]

                      you're so beautiful and good how could I do this to you how could I do this to anything so beautiful and good

      [and good and good and good and good]

                      while he went in and out

      [in and out in and out
      in and out in and out]

                      it wouldn't matter at all.

Even if he bathed me and I didn't bite his hand and he washed away my tears and I still didn't bite his hand it wouldn't matter. Whether he promised me he would always love me and he would come back and he would marry me and not that girl at all, he would never marry her, because he was so sorry that he would do anything if I forgave him. Anything at all if I would just forgive him.

Still I wouldn't forgive him no matter what I said I wouldn't forgive him

      [forgive him]

                      even if I said I forgave him

      [forgave him forgave him forgave him forgave him]

                      even if I said I had forgiven him

           [forgiven him forgiven him forgiven him forgiven him]

                            even if I said I would

forgive him

           [forgive him]

                            even if I said I was all

right

           [all right all right all right all right all right]

                            even if I said it was all

right

           [all right all right all right all right all right]

                            even if I said I loved

him too

           [loved him too]

                            and that he could do it

again

           [again again   again again   again again]

                            push in and out

          [in and out

          in and out

          in and out

          in and out]

                                again

          [again

          again

          again]

                       he could, as much as he

liked. If he really wanted to. And if he would reach out and touch
my hair.

That's a lie. What I said was a lie. It's not nearly even as true as
Julio Cortazar. That's right: I was lying. Even if I said all that right
then I was lying. Because I know that if he died and I died and it
was after death and we were right there together like those two
people in that story and he reached out for me and he touched my
hair I wouldn't forgive him. And I would never let him do anything like that to me. Not ever again.

ONCE UPON A TIME [...AND IT HURTS...] ~ 85

Because I could go away. And it wouldn't even matter if it was into that field of pain because I wouldn't have to listen to him. And I would never invite him to make love to me

[love to me]

no matter what I wouldn't even if I had breasts like that other girl he married and he could touch my hair. And it wouldn't even matter that they say I'm just a little girl who has never grown up because I know now that I don't have to say those things. And I especially wouldn't have to say all those things if I was already dead and there was nothing he could take away from me. Not ice cream. Or big hugs. And it's been so long since anybody touched my hair.

So I just know I wouldn't say anything like that. I wouldn't at all. I would just turn into that little place inside me inside that field of pain where I always went with all its bright colours and nya nya nyanyanya

[nya nya nyanyanya]

I would say: nya nya nyanyanya

[nya nya nyanyanya nya nya nyanyanya]

I'll never forgive you.

**[never forgive you
never forgive you]**

Even if all those other people forgive you

I'll never forgive you.

**[never forgive you
never forgive you]**

Even if the whole world forgives you I still won't. Not ever.

**[not ever not ever not ever not ever
not ever not ever not ever not ever]**

I'll be just like the wicked witch in that other story I was told. The one who wouldn't ask for Baldur to come back from hell no matter how happily ever after she would get to live or he would get to live or you would get to live or I would get to live, still I wouldn't forgive you or ask you to come back from your field of pain.

Not ever no matter what even if I'm the only one who won't do it
I won't do it.

> **[won't do it won't do it**
> **won't do it won't do it]**

>> I won't do it.

Because you can stay in hell forever for all I care. Just stay
there.

> **[and stay there and stay there**
> **and stay there and stay there**
> **and stay there and stay there]**

>> Because that's where

you belong. That's where you deserve to be where you deserve to
be forever even if I have to stay there too, right by the door, to
make sure you don't get out. You never get out of hell.

And it won't matter at all if no one ever hugs me or invites me
down for ice cream.

That's still where you deserve to stay. Because no one should
ever hold anyone by the shoulders and the skin on the chest while
he pushes

> **[and pushes and pushes and pushes]**

>> in and out

> **[in and out in and out in and out]**

>> so that it hurts

> **[and it hurts and it hurts and it hurts**
> **and it hurts and it hurts and it hurts**
> **and it hurts and it hurts and it hurts]**

>> and they have to go

away and they don't know if they're dead or they're alive or even
where they are and they have to walk through a field of pain and it
hurts.

> **[and it hurts and it hurts**
> **and it hurts and it hurts**
> **and it hurts and it hurts**
> **and it hurts and it hurts]**

>> And it never stops

hurting. And they get so sad that they die they just die.

So that's what I'm going to tell you: you can just stay in hell as far as I'm concerned. Even if you're not dead you can stay in hell because I won't forgive you

[forgive you
forgive you]

I never forgave you

[never forgave you
never forgave you
never forgave you
never forgave you]

no matter how many times you said you were sorry or you wiped away my tears still I never forgave you

[never forgave you
never forgave you]

and you deserve to be in hell and that's that. Because I didn't deserve to die or hurt like that

[hurt like that
hurt like that
hurt like that]

even if you washed me and said you were sorry I didn't deserve to be hurt like that.

[hurt like that
hurt like that
hurt like that
hurt like that]

And I certainly didn't want to be so sad that I died.

No. I don't want to be so sad that I'll die forever while it hurts

[and it hurts and it hurts and it hurts
and it hurts and it hurts and it hurts
and it hurts and it hurts and it hurts
and it hurts and it hurts and it hurts
and it hurts and it hurts and it hurts
and it hurts and it hurts and it hurts]

and I'll never be happy like Sleeping Beauty or Cinderella or Snow White or even Carolyn and her son who got lots of ice cream. While all I'll get to do is listen to them talk about that woman who forgave that man when he reached out his hand. And I don't want to listen to that any more, certainly not for forty more years, you can just bet on that, I've made up my mind what to say.

To that rapist and to Julio Cortazar and to that hand reaching out and to that hand washing all the tears off that face and to that man holding onto those shoulders. Go to hell I say go to hell.

[go to hell go to hell
go to hell go to hell
go to hell go to hell
go to hell go to hell
go to hell go to hell]

Go to hell.

Only it doesn't matter what I say. They never listen to what I say when they tell those stories they just tell me to go away. Go away

[go away
go away
go away
go away
go away]

they say. Nothing ever happened to you they say what can you tell us about it they say you're always making up stories. How would you know

[would you know
would you know
would you know]

what to do how would you know

[would you know
would you know
would you know]

anything about it you're just a little girl who's never grown up you just keep saying the same thing over and over,

    [over and over
    over and over
    over and over]

you always repeat yourself you're not even interesting, you've never been to any place like that where it hurt

    [and it hurt and it hurt
    and it hurt and it hurt
    and it hurt and it hurt
    and it hurt and it hurt
    and it hurt and it hurt]

so why don't you just play with your dolls, you know that you don't know anything about it. And besides that, you're not like Julio Cortazar, you're not a great writer.

And that's when I think about how to fool them. They think I'm still listening to them but I'm hardly listening at all. I have other games besides my dolls and my tea set, I've learned a lot from all those books he left me, that's why I'm sure I can figure out how to do it. And it won't make any difference how long I've sat here or how often I repeat myself because even if I've waited for so many years and even if they don't think they want to listen still I'm going to tell them. I'm going to find a way to trick them into listening to me.

Then pretty soon they'll want to hear how it hurt.

    [and it hurt and it hurt
    and it hurt and it hurt
    and it hurt and it hurt
    and it hurt and it hurt]

Because I'm going to walk back into that field of pain and I'm not going to get lost in the blue and the red and the yellow and the pounding waves I'm going to learn the differences between all those colours and all those patterns I'm going to learn all about them. About red and yellow and blue and pain

[and pain and pain and pain
and pain and pain and pain
and pain and pain and pain
and pain and pain and pain
and pain and pain and pain
and pain and pain and pain]

until I won't have to repeat myself at all. Because it won't be all the same any more it will be all different. A beautiful marvellous magical different field of pain and mountain of pain and ocean of pain and earth of pain

[of pain
of pain
of pain]

and cave of pain

[of pain
of pain]

and I'll be the Pied Piper.

That's another favourite story I read over and over, only I won't have a flute, I'll invite them all in with my words. My red and blue and green and magical mysterious words. I'll lure them into my cave of pain where it hurts

[and it hurts and it hurts
and it hurts and it hurts
and it hurts and it hurts
and it hurts and it hurts
and it hurts and it hurts
and it hurts and it hurts
and it hurts and it hurts]

and I won't let them out again.

Until they listen for the longest time and they tell me they believe me and that my story is just as magical and just as mysterious and just as beautiful as Julio Cortazar even if it only begins:

Once Upon a Time There Was a Little Girl. A little girl so little that she believed everything she was told.

Even when he said how sorry he was and how he would never do it again. And he reached out and he touched her hair. And told her how he loved her and how she was beautiful and how he was sorry and how she should forgive him. And how he would come back to marry her when she grew up.

Then, after they listen, they'll ask me what I would do and I'll tell them. About how you never forgive people who hurt you.

[and hurt you and hurt you
and hurt you and hurt you
and hurt you and hurt you
and hurt you and hurt you
and hurt you and hurt you
and hurt you and hurt you]

You send them to hell
and that's that.

And they'll all nod and say how true it is, how true my story is, even that woman Carolyn will say that, how it's so much truer than Julio Cortazar. And then I'll let them out for ice cream and it won't matter at all if nothing like that ever happened to me. If no one ever held me down and grabbed my shoulders and the skin on my chest and forced his penis into me. And it never hurt.

[never hurt
never hurt
never hurt]

No, it never did. And no
one told me that I was good and I was beautiful and that he loved me and he didn't understand how he could do this to me he was so sorry.

[so sorry
so sorry]

And I was never so sad that I died.

I've just been here listening all along. And playing with my dolls and sipping tea out of my little china tea set with my pinky finger raised while I look at those books that he gave me with all their pretty pictures while I sit on my stair right above his door where I've been ever since he went away waiting for him to come back just the way he said he would because nothing like that happened to me nothing at all not ever even if I'll never forgive him and it hurt so much

    [so much

    so much]

                                  he deserves to go to hell, you understand?

~

In her own words: I was born in New York City in 1946 and raised there in an interracial home. My studies have included Latin American literature at the University of Toronto and visual arts training in Mexico City and Parson's School of Design, New York. Since my move to Calgary in 1979, I have published three books of fiction, *The Measure of Miranda* (1987), *Comic Book Heroine* (1990), and *The Deconstruction of Wesley Smithson* (1992), as well as numerous short stories and occasional writings in Canada, the United Kingdom, and Australia. The present work is part of a cycle of documentary parafictions collected under the title, *The Child . . . in the End.* It also includes an interdisciplinary work "Scrapbook" which was shown at the Alberta College of Art in 1994. My work in Calgary outside the arts has included the teaching of English as a second language, creative writing, Spanish and art, as well as extensive support work with the Latin American immigrant and refugee community. I am also the mother of three children.

New Dress

Rose DeShaw

$\mathcal{J}$N THE LAST FEW DAYS BEFORE my aunt succumbed to the demons in her mind, she bought two lots of red and blue border-printed material to be made into skirts for her daughter and us three cousins. Doll skirts, we called them, since the design was silhouettes of women in eighteenth century ball gowns, holding hands and dancing all around the hemline.

My mother made ours, throwing them together on the sewing machine with a quick elastic gather at the top, in something under an hour. Our cousin's was handstitched with a zipper and a carefully measured waistband that buttoned into a beautifully-crafted buttonhole.

My cousin and I were just starting junior high school, my younger sister two years behind us and my older sister a year ahead. I felt pleased that all four of us had something alike, marking us out as family, especially with my cousin whom we didn't see much. With the skirts, we would be recognized as a unit anywhere. My sisters didn't see this as any advantage and my cousin wasn't talking, as usual, but I bonded to that skirt like a lone gosling preparing for the feuds of the duck pond. I wore it proudly downtown to J. C. Penney's with my mother one of the only times I remember the two of us going anywhere alone, considering our large family.

Usually she drove the dented brown Ford my father had fixed up in exchange for her promise to quit teaching school, stay home, and take care of the family. She always kept a paperback detective novel in the glove box, most often featuring a scantily-clad woman on the cover, stabbed with a knife in her chest or back, from which bright red blood oozed onto a background heavy in the yellows and purples. Whenever we hit a red light, my mother would yank the book out of the glove box and read, resulting in a lot of honking behind us and ensuring that any excursions with my mother were always accompanied by a volley of curses from other drivers, trying to make out what the woman was up to.

My father was an unemployed miner with damaged lungs who couldn't go back underground. We were living off his savings while he tried to decide what to do. Being supported by what my mother could make as a teacher was not one of the options in his 1950s world.

This particular day, however, Mother's Ford was at the garage on the corner, having the dents from one of the numerous things she had run into beaten out of the front fenders. So we took the bus to Penney's where more grey wool socks for my father were on the agenda. While she browsed, I twirled away to the men's suit section where the triple mirror afforded the opportunity to see yourself in multiples.

I was admiring the doll skirt from every direction when I noticed suddenly that there were stains on the front. Bloodstains. "Hey!" I bellowed, racing back to my mother. "Look at all this blood on my skirt! Where did it come from? Do you suppose I brushed up against somebody on the bus who was hurt and bleeding? Maybe we should go and try to find out?" Yeah, I was almost thirteen, but ignorant in the way that could only have been possible then, in those days before Kotex ads in magazines, "light day" demonstrations on television and sex education in rural schools like ours. We had health education classes, and they were about teeth.

My mother's jaw dropped, and she threw the grey socks she was holding towards the counter. "Shut up!" she said, grabbing me by the arm as though I had just announced I had leprosy. She was nearly six feet tall and well on her way to 300 pounds, a volatile, brooding woman with her hair like Bette Davis in *Dark Victory*. Then she yanked me along to the ladies' room, like a beagle negligently trailing a bit of dandelion fluff, and hauled a handful of paper towels from the metal dispenser over the sinks, her heavy jaw set tight.

"Stick these in your underpants," she said, pointing to a toilet cubicle.

"Why?" I began, "what's it all about anyhow? Where'd the blood come from? Who got killed? Is it like those books you have in the glove box? Will it come out of my skirt? Besides, these aren't my underpants, they're my brother's." I thought that settled the matter. Clothes among the four of us had been wearing out rapidly and the first one up got the best selection. I was never the first one up but I could always beat my brother. Even today, I wonder if he ever got any underwear. . . .

"*Go in there and stuff!*" bellowed my mother and I leaped for one of the doors in the long line. Outside I could hear my mother pacing heavily in her worn, high-heeled black lace-up shoes.

"Hey!" I shrieked at her. "There's blood on my underpants too! Does this mean I'm dying? Am I bleeding to death? What's this all about anyway? What happened on that bus?"

"*Shut up!*" articulated my mother. She never used language like this. My mother was a school teacher even though my father wouldn't let her teach anymore. She practised such a high standard of refinement that I couldn't recall anyone in our house ever having said "shut up" before. Maybe she got it from those books she kept in her car.

Obviously we were having some sort of crisis here and I was undoubtedly going to have to go along with whatever it was, as long as it didn't kill me, although I was far from sure that it wouldn't. I came out of the cubicle walking funny, the paper towels in my brother's underpants making some kind of herniated bulge in a strategic place on my bloodied skirt.

More arm grabbing. With her jaw set, my mother whisked me up the escalator to the Misses Department. (She *never* took the escalator, believing that men stood around below for the sole purpose of peeking up your dress as you ascended.)

There were some nice pink cotton frocks with little lacy collars and big full skirts hanging tantalizingly where we got off. Over on another counter were socks to match and white patent leather pumps and little wicker purses with bunches of flowers on the clasp. Mother propelled me grimly to the extreme end of the department till she found the only black dress on the premises.

It was a lint-picking-up green and orange cotton plaid on a black background under a section called "school dresses" and it had six orange buttons down the front. It might have been a good dress for a cleaning lady, maybe, mopping out office buildings at night. When she held it up against my skinny frame, a sort of stick-figure build, on the order of a hall coat rack, the dress looked like a shroud, its baggy length travelling well past my scarred, skinny knees.

Not loosening her grip on my arm, my mother grabbed the dress with her free hand and marched me to the counter. "She'll wear it," she told the clerk, indicating the tags.

"In public?" I squawked. "What's the matter with what I've got on now?" But I knew what was the matter. It had something to do with the blood that had mysteriously appeared on my adored doll skirt and now seemed to be bubbling merrily from deep inside me like Old Faithful. Only this time, none of the tourists seemed at all delighted.

"Go put it on." My mother propelled me towards the dressing rooms with one brawny arm that could wring a chicken's neck with a single twist or throw a pitchfork of manure over her head like a salute at Ascot.

I dragged my feet, and the dress, along the expensive grey department store rug, aware of my mother watching anxiously lest a little trail of blood should follow in my wake. It wasn't fair. This was the very first time in my entire life I or any one of the children in our family had gotten a brand-new, store-bought dress. Not a hand-me-down or one of Mother's inventions, usually cut from an old curtain. And did I have any say in what it looked like? Was I being listened to at all on the weirdest day in my life? Nobody else was bleeding all over the place. This was something spectacular, a centre-of-attention sort of thing. Obviously it was holding my mother's attention. But she didn't seem to be rushing off to the hospital any time soon.

I stuck my head through the huge ugly cotton thing, pulled my arms through the raglan sleeves, each decorated with a big orange button, and tried to pull its cloth-covered belt tight, but I had run out of notches. There was room for a whole other person in it with me. I took the pink barrette out of my hair and tried to see if I could make a notch with the prongs.

"Come out of there!" my mother bellowed. I reclasped the barrette and lovingly cradled the doll skirt in my arms as I pulled the curtain back. The saleslady stifled a gasp of dismay, bringing a bright-nailed hand convulsively to her mouth as she peered over my mother's shoulder. "It looks a trifle . . . big," she said weakly.

My mother grabbed the doll skirt from me and stuffed it in a shopping bag she had acquired from somewhere, totally ignoring the saleslady. Then she grabbed my arm and shifted her big black worn leather purse so she could carry the shopping bag in her other hand.

We went down the escalator, squashed onto the same step, my mother glaring at all the men standing below. She pushed me ahead of her, down the centre aisle and out the big brass-handled front doors where she took the final extraordinary measure of hailing a taxi!

I had never ridden in a taxi. Nobody in our family had ever ridden in a taxi. By now, I knew it was all connected with the blood on my skirt. Was I going to die and my mother knew it, and this was the dress she had picked out for me to be buried in? It was probably suitable. I had heard somewhere that black was what you wore to funerals, although I wasn't sure what you wore if you were the corpse.

She didn't say anything going home, just counted the change in her purse and looked out the window, her lips pressed tightly together as though she had tasted something sour.

"We forgot Daddy's *socks!*" I bellowed as the cab drew up

before our house in the sparsely-settled section a mile beyond the city limits.

"Shut up!" said my mother for the last time, paying the cab driver something that didn't seem to make him very happy. We walked down the driveway soberly, side by side, two travellers abruptly come to the end of a nightmare journey. My sisters, who had gone on some sort of trip with my mad aunt, were peering out our living room window at the cab. I was never included by this aunt since the time I had convinced my sisters and my cousin to paint their faces green and blue with food coloring that didn't come off for several days and convinced my aunt that she was losing her mind much sooner than was strictly true.

"Where'd you get that dress?" my younger sister was on it like a flash. First I'd gotten a ride in a taxi and *now* I came home in a brand-new outfit. "And why on earth, if you were going to get a new dress, would you pick *that* one?"

"I dunno," I told her. There must be some way I could show off my superior status here, especially now that I was probably going to die soon. I looked at my mother out of the corner of my eye but she wasn't looking at me anymore.

"Where's your doll skirt?" asked my older sister, the practical one. She kept a little hidden cache of odd supplies that a person might suddenly develop a need for. Canned milk was one of the items, after a memorable fight my parents had once when they ran out of milk for coffee. She supplemented her stock from time to time from money she earned from babysitting. She also had all her Halloween and Christmas candy which she attempted to sell to us, for additional funds. She was a gentle, nonassertive person with big brown eyes and a quick brain which she kept well-concealed. My younger sister, a fat little redhead, ran her like a bingo game. One of my fiercest objections to this second sister was her habit of eating everyone's share of whatever bag of cookies my parents tried hard to include in the groceries they brought home once a month. Now she was picking up on the absence of my doll skirt. "We're going to wear ours tomorrow. Where's yours?"

I wheeled on my mother who had sat down in the old green

rocker in the corner and was easing her bunion-covered size tens out of the tight black shoes. Where was the shopping bag? The old leather purse lay on the floor beside her, entirely alone.

"*You left it in the taxi!*" I screamed. "You lost my doll skirt!" My mother looked up from the darkness of that corner, perhaps the last time she ever looked me in the eyes and all at once I knew she had done it on purpose. She had gotten rid of my doll skirt because of the blood.

"Ask your sister about it," she said, her long, leathery face flushing as though she was bending over the wood stove in the kitchen.

I knew which sister she meant. I went on into the bedroom I shared with my brother who was at cub scouts, found yesterday's underwear and substituted one of my father's socks for the paper towels. Then I wrapped the bloody underpants in newspaper and buried them in a far corner of my personal garden by the root cellar, deep enough so the neighbour's dog wouldn't dig them up.

When I went to bed after supper it was not to sleep but to die. Lying there stiffly in the darkness, trying to figure out what my body was doing, I was convinced that an experience like this must be what that line in the children's prayer was written for, "If I should die before I wake."

When the murmur of my parents' voices finally stopped coming from their room at the end of the hall, I got out of my lower bunk and tiptoed into my sisters' adjoining room, where my older sister lay quiet and peaceful on the bottom bunk, her long black hair fanned out across her pillow. She always woke right up when you called, without smacking you around or screaming like the redhead. She'd never had any opportunity to behave like that. She was the one designated to look after the problems of the rest of us and her brown eyes opened quiet and unsurprised as I whispered all the amazing events of the day and the reason for the new dress and the lost doll skirt and the taxi. "And I'm still bleeding!" I informed her dramatically, expecting to see shock on that placid face. "What on earth *is* it?"

She sighed and sat up, swinging her feet primly out of the covers, smoothing down her long, flower-sprigged nightdress and looking over towards her little cache of supplies as though she had something there that could help me.

"I don't know what it is either," she said softly. "It goes away in about a week but it comes back again over and over for the rest of your life. Don't ask Mother anything about it," she added, pulling out a long, soft pad like the middle of a giant's bandage. "It makes her too angry." As I started away, she said, almost to herself, "I think maybe it's something that happens when you've been bad. It isn't something that's ever happened to Mother."

～

In her own words: A long time ago I wrote up my honeymoon and sold it to *True Confessions* but I hadn't written anything that I considered risk-taking (outside the "nice girl" genre) in my entire life. Somehow the idea of your anthology got me thinking about what kinds of things might be in it; what stories can only be told by women because they only belong to women. I had read quite enough of the miracle of birth and I haven't yet figured out menopause so "New Dress" was all that remained.

Relative Knowledge

Knowledge that springs from juxtaposing two ways of seeing is relative. There are no absolutes, no eternities. We change: we see, we feel — differently. Emotions transmute understanding, and understanding redraws our emotional map. This entire section could have aptly taken its title from Anna Mioduchowska's lyrical and elegiac essay "Adjusting the Lenses," for all the essays are concerned with the discovery of a new perspective.

This change in perspective is most dramatic — and most literal — in Holly Quan's "The Eyes Have It." With joy, Quan tells us how an operation that changed her physical sight changed her mentally, in fact, changed her very self. For others, the shift in perspective comes with a shift in roles, or the perception of roles. Susan Sharpe moves from certainty to uncertainty after she marries and women whose views she had once shared deny the truth of her experience. In Kathryn Fraser's "And When They Are Gone," the expected roles do not fit, and that realization plunges Fraser into a confusion of love and hate, need, and resentment. Elizabeth Entrup views aging as a demeaning and fearful process until she writes the biography of an opinionated and lively woman of ninety-one, and aging becomes seasoning. Death, that final change, also calls forth reassessment and affirmation. Taking part in the burial rites for her fiancé's mother brings Debra Purdy Kong new understanding and respect for cultural differences —

and human limitations. Mioduchowska's new perspective comes after the long illness and death of her father. Her struggle between family responsibility and personal needs is made more difficult by a clash of cultural values. Mioduchowska earns herself a new vision which encompasses both Canadian and Polish ways.

Events less personal may be equally enlightening. A high school reunion leads Shirley Serviss to contrast teenage hopes and fears with middle-age realities, with sometimes surprising results. Graffiti scrawled on an office door resolve Stewart's ambivalence about abusive behaviour. And, in overcoming the self-doubt created by economic failure, Maxine Hancock discovers the generous kindness of friends.

We adjust the lenses, and see the world anew.

The Eyes Have It

Holly Quan

$\mathcal{T}$HIS IS HOLLY: QUITE ORDInary. A breezy, sometimes cynical sense of humour. Curly brown hair that develops blond streaks in summer. Ragged smile (crooked teeth). Generally enthusiastic about life although prone to worry. Has many close friends but sees them seldom. Tends to be solitary, private, reads a lot.

Holly lives in a two-storey house with a man she loves dearly. Holly and her man are not married. They like it that way; they say "It ain't broke, why fix it?" They laugh frequently. They are content.

Holly's professional life is similarly satisfactory. She has worked at the same place for many years and likes her job and her co-workers. After all this time, you might think she'd be bored and looking for advancement or change. None of that. She's fine where she is.

She is fit and healthy. Holly eats sensibly and does not usually indulge in desserts, Coke, or junk food. She drinks wine and Scotch, in moderation. She does not wear makeup. (There is a good reason for her fresh-facedness, but she usually doesn't give people that reason. Instead, she is flippant. She says, "There are better things to spend money on than eye shadow. Wine, for instance." And who would argue with her?)

Holly enjoys the outdoors. Hiking, gardening, but especially skiing. She is passionate about skiing. This is not to say she is an excellent skier, in fact she is just average. But she loves it! Holly lives to ski.

This is also Holly: legally blind.

Holly *gets by* in life, you know? She appreciates her good fortune in finding a position where her co-workers don't mind looking after her to a certain extent. She isn't seeking another job, because who would take her? Her vision is awful, and getting worse. She can't drive (this has caused some major logistical problems in her career) but generally she shrugs and says, "Where there's a will, there's a taxi." She finds a way. She manages. And she is never shy about begging a ride.

With contact lenses Holly can see some detail to about five or six feet. Beyond that, it's all just shapes and colours. She depends on intuition and familiarity to find things, to figure out where she is and what is happening around her. New places, crowded places, make her very nervous. At home, she depends on putting things away, arranging, running a tight ship; everything has its *proper spot.* Otherwise, she would be lost, and so would everything around her. She doesn't recognize friends or family on the street until they are practically on top of her. (They don't mind. They're used to it now. And they know better than to tease her about it.)

Poor vision is the real reason that Holly faces the world each day without eye liner, blush, mascara. She can't see her own face in the mirror well enough to apply makeup accurately. If she doesn't give you her jokey reason — the one about buying wine instead of eye shadow — Holly will say she'd rather go without makeup than do it clumsily and look like a clown.

Poor vision is the reason that Holly is only an average skier. She might be better except that it's stupid to ski aggressively when you can only see six feet in front of your face. She and her man have worked out a satisfactory arrangement, though. He stops at the top of a pitch and describes to her any hazards, moguls, ice. Then he starts down and she follows, keeping close behind him. They do the same run several times until she learns the terrain. Then she can ski beside him. If it's a sunny day and the light is good, she can see shadows and undulations in the snow. On such days she can even ski ahead of him. To watch her on such a day, you'd never know she had a problem at all.

In fact she likes to conduct her entire life that way — so you'd never know. It irks Holly to admit defeat because of her eyesight, to say "I can't do that" or "I can't see it." When her man sees geese flying in the fall he'll point them out and Holly will say she sees them even though she doesn't. She figures things out. She uses context. She has good hearing.

Holly gets by. You'd never know.

Here is what happened to Holly one day: having problems with a contact lens, she makes an appointment to see her ophthalmologist. (She likes to call him My Eye Guy. "I'll be in late tomorrow. I'm going to see My Eye Guy.") She sits in his darkened office, her chin on the little tissue-paper pad of his slit lamp ophthalmoscope, keeping very still while he looks into her eyes. (She's always wanted to be on *his* side of the slit lamp. She'd like to know what he sees in there.) When he's finished, he turns the machine off but doesn't turn the overhead lights on. He drums his fingers on the table. He sighs.

To Holly sitting tensely in the dimness he says, "There's a new surgical technique available that I think would work really well on you."

He flicks the lights on. He continues: "In the past, surgery for someone with your condition has been extremely risky." (Holly knows this; he has told her so many times: "No surgery is worth the risk. You're doing fine. You've got too much to lose," he has said. She has come to accept that her life will always be dim and circumscribed. No help is on the way. No cavalry is on her horizon.) Today, though, he says, "This technique is different, the risks would be significantly reduced. You could have normal vision."

Picture this: Holly, a self-possessed woman in her midthirties, a woman who *gets by* in life and is proud of it, sitting in an ophthalmologist's office, gasping and trying not to cry.

Holly gropes mentally for something to hang on to. Her ophthalmologist keeps talking, explaining the surgery. She can't hear him. She can hear two words: *normal vision.* They chase one another around her head, barking and creating a fuss. Finally she realizes there is silence in the room. Perhaps she should say something.

Holly blurts, "Could I still ski?"

A little later Holly is riding the bus downtown, going to work. She is still trying not to cry. She feels like a rock in a mountain river, with silty milk-green water pounding her from every direction, pouring over her head and viciously scouring the bottom from beneath her. Her life whirls and spins. Holly consults everyone she can think of for opinions on the subject of possible surgery. Friends, dad, brother, her man, her own heart, are examined and cross-examined for ideas and points of view. They pose sensible questions: "Did you ask what could happen if the surgery fails? How much vision would you be left with? Would he do both eyes at once or one at a time? How much does it cost? Is there a waiting list? How long would you be off work? The Kleenex is over there."

Holly cannot answer these questions. *Normal* and *vision* are still yapping and carrying on. Meanwhile, she gathers opinions. As time passes she comes to divide the opinions into two camps, the *caution* camp and the *go for it* camp. Generally speaking, *caution* has more members, and they make more sense when delivering their opinions. Holly's own heart leans strongly towards taking a flying leap into the rest of her life. She's waited long enough. *Go for it* wins.

And now, picture this: Holly is sitting up in bed on a lovely but cold September morning. There is a plastic shield pasted to her face with strips of white adhesive tape. The shield covers her right eye.

She is listening to the radio, and to the sounds of a routine morning in her neighbourhood. She stretches (carefully! She is not to bend over, lift anything heavy, or exert herself in any way for a few days. Just keep still, read, sleep, listen to "Morningside" and "Gabereau." This is Holly's idea of heaven.). Slowly Holly gets out of bed and steps into the adjoining bathroom, peels the tape away from her right cheek and places the plastic eye shield beside the sink. She washes her face (carefully! She is not to get water into the recently outraged eye) and moves back toward the bed.

There is a copy of *Maclean's* on the bed, open to the last page, Fotheringham's column with the usual headline in large black type and the cartoon in the middle of the page. Holly chuckles as she reads the headline (it is a pun; Holly likes puns). Then she stops smiling and stares at the page.

She has just read the headline from several feet away. Using her new eye. Without glasses, or contacts, or any other mechanical means. It is a most alarming sensation.

The interior chamber of Holly's right eye is now full of blood and other biological detritus, which must slowly be absorbed before her vision is clear enough to resume work. Days go by. The biological scum thins and disappears, leaving dark waving shadows that look to her like seaweed, or like thick curls of oily smoke, slowly evaporating. She spends afternoons sitting anxiously in her easy chair, listening to jazz, fretting her fingernails, checking the progress of her emerging visual clarity every twenty seconds or so.

Weeks go by. Holly's view of the world improves dramatically. She can't believe the change. She had no clue, no inkling about how things really look. How could she? Holly is ecstatic.

Holly and her man go grocery shopping. Customarily, Holly takes a hand basket and charges around the store like a honeybee, grabbing whatever she needs and filling the basket until it becomes too heavy or awkward to carry. Then she finds her man, who has the grocery cart somewhere in the vegetable section, dumps off her load of sundries, and is off again in search of more items.

Today, Holly is wandering around the store, grocery list and basket in hand. She is not, however, looking for laundry detergent, pantyhose, bath soap, or cooking sherry. She is not even looking for chocolate chip cookies. Eventually she makes her way to her man in Produce. Her basket is empty. Her man, who is tired and wants to go home, says, "Holly, what are you doing?"

"Faces," Holly replies. "People have faces, now."

Autumn carries on in full colour, complete with warm evening light, and long shadows, and poplar leaves in schoolbus yellow. Holly and her man go hiking. They find three mountain bluebirds playing in the sharp cool air. "Birds," she once said, "are a waste of time. They look like flies to me, black blots." Holly can see the bluebirds now. They are not black dots. They are brilliant blue. Holly sees other birds, too. In her backyard, waxwings with saffron bars on their tails. In the air, magpies like long-tailed kites. In formation, geese.

Before surgery, Holly never considered that *normal vision* could have drawbacks. She is startled to see things formerly invisible — dust, threads, hairs, lint. She says, "A black skirt used to be a black skirt." Holly spends a considerable amount of time looking at her reflection in the bathroom mirror. This is not conceit, but education. Holly has never seen her own face in such detail. She decides to have her teeth straightened. She embarks on a new initiative: *self improvement.* She begins weight training, swimming. She brings her guitar up from the basement and buys new strings. She takes Italian cooking lessons. She buys knee-high riding boots and signs up for English saddle lessons. Holly has always wanted to do this.

She goes skiing by herself. This is incredible, audacious. She rides the chair lift and watches her solitary shadow bounce from tree to tree, then slide over blue-shadowed snow, then leap into the trees again. She gets off the lift, snowplows to the edge of the run, adjusts her boots, and launches. She skis fast. She skis moguls. She avoids rocks and ice. They are perfectly clear and obvious to her now. Holly meets people in the lift lines, takes up conversation while riding the chairs or eating lunch. She laughs at people's concern about her skiing solo. They don't understand.

Holly is currently somewhat self-absorbed.

Holly is given to making analogies. Here are some of the things she says about improved vision: She says there were once many closed doors in her life, but recently there's a fresh stiff breeze blowing them open. She is sure everyone else can hear the doors swinging and banging in the wind. The breeze ruffles her hair, tickles her nose and makes her think of travel and adventure. But she also says that a wind like that can pick up garbage and blow it around, plastering it to fences until it looks like self-supporting graffiti. So is this gale good or bad? She's not sure yet.

Holly observes to her man one day that improved vision is like finishing a good book. "The outcome is satisfying but it leaves you a bit empty. You're on your own. You have to stop living in your head and start living in your life."

Holly's man is concerned. She is showing a side of her character hitherto unseen: *independent*. He misses the former Holly — competent but a trifle timid. The old Holly made him feel needed, worthwhile. She talks now about strength, possibilities, power. The new Holly is a bit threatening. He says, "It is a striking difference, you know. You're much more confident now. You dress differently — bright colours, reds and blues. You even walk differently — your head is high, you're looking at the world head-on. It's quite remarkable."

Holly hopes that she and her man can find their way through this surprising maze. She likes her life with him, but right now it needs some adjustment. *Normal vision* has certainly complicated things. She is amazed, a little resentful, curious to see what will happen. Meanwhile, she's taking driving lessons.

Her man thinks the surgery has changed her, but Holly disagrees. Surgery has allowed what was in her head already an opportunity to speak up. She always knew she could ski better. She always knew she could do more than *get by*. She says, "This change in my life isn't really a change at all. It's just an old song in a new key. It's just the Doppler Effect: the whistle only appears to change when you're standing still and the train goes by. I'm on the train now, and I know that the whistle sounds the same — but the scenery's fantastic."

Good analogy, Holly. Good luck.

~

In her own words: Born in Edmonton, I've lived in Calgary since I was six (long enough to be a Flames fan). I've published several magazine articles; "The Eyes Have It" is my first creative piece to see the light of print. I came into the world with an eye condition called *octopia lentis*, which was cured by surgery in September 1990 and May 1991. I now drive, ride horseback, and ski like Jack the Bear!

Adjusting the Lenses

Anna Mioduchowska

THE BRANCHES OF THE MOUN-
tain ash in front of my house, heavy with berries, stream low
towards the ground, like so many braids. Braids not so much of
hair as onions, braids of garlic. September thoughts.

"It's been a good year for berries," I remember an old man at
the farmers' market pronounce to a customer last Saturday.
"Raspberries, gooseberries. . . ." Earlier in the summer, there had
been handfuls of indecently large wild strawberries along the
cutlines in the Rockies. Of huckleberries. Tonight, the matt red
fruit of the mountain ash pulsate contentedly against one another
and against the still green leaves. As do the stars in the anaemic
city sky.

"Geese," my son explains and points to the thin silver line
moving high above our heads. My father's newly released spirit, I
can't help thinking.

It's an unusually warm night and neither of us wants to go
back into the house. Geese, in such a hurry to get away from here
before the first snow that they skip their usual noisy introductions
and farewells.

Two weeks ago we had swathed his coffin with mountain ash
branches for the funeral service. Cut from the tree in his front yard,
identical to this one, and from the one in the back. Their remains
are indistinct from his now in the ridiculously small mahogany
box that sits on his old dresser, awaiting burial. Surrounded by

vases full of gladioli my mother tends with as much determination as she had tended his sick body, of carnations, last sweet peas of the season, marigolds that are able to emanate warmth even in this room.

I breathe in deeply, careful to taste the soft night with my lips, with the whole length of my tongue.

Refusing to be ordinary to the end, my father. Demanding special arrangements even after death. Not for him the neighbourhood cemetery, crowded, like any city, with so many bodies competing for the necessarily limited amount of good, clean air. Father disliked the city for as long as I remember, taking every opportunity to either go camping in the mountains or spend a day at one of the nearby lakes. We have even eaten Christmas and Easter dinners at a picnic table — always the same one — at Wabamun Lake.

"You can take my ashes out of the city when I die," he reminded us regularly. "Find a good canyon, with a river at the bottom, and drop them in."

An amusing enough request when the subject is sitting back in a comfortable chair, in the midst of his strong, smiling children, his skin glowing like a ripe crab apple. That glow is the first thing death snatches away from the body. As the heart stops and the blood drains, quickly, a flat, waxy hue spreads over the forehead, the cheeks, the lips . . . fingers. . . .

Those fingers were Father's most sad/funny feature in the end. Twisted beyond all use by rheumatoid arthritis, they were artfully intertwined in the funeral home, and the hands placed on Father's chest to give his body a devout, serene expression. Father was not a serene man. Quite the contrary. Haunted by visions of perfection, he treated every aspect of life as a climb up a tortuous path. Nothing anyone did was ever up to his severe standards. A man with a convoluted lifeline, many unfulfilled dreams, both difficult to live with and to be. A man so ill, helpless, and lonely in the end, that he feared the proximity of people other than his family even after death. How ironic, and unfair, that he should be the first one of our family to die in Canada. A most unwilling pioneer — he had fought to stay alive for so long that we had finally stopped believing in the possibility of his death. Unhappy, unwelcome thoughts. I stand still, tense, and wait for the flood of tears that must come in their wake.

They don't.

The truth is, I am not capable of sadness tonight. I don't miss my father. Not yet. Maybe I never will.

He had been sick for twenty years. I, the whole family, have the words "rheumatoid arthritis" etched deeply into our brains. It's an insidious little disease, classified as an "autoimmune disorder," meaning that the body directs its defence mechanisms against its own tissues.

How neat, comfortingly efficient that sounds.

What really happens is messy and beyond comfort. The joints in the hands of the affected person, in the feet, knees, hips, elbows, neck, swell and become stiff, deformed. Little by little that person becomes, well all right, my father became a twisted stump that could not be touched anywhere without causing him pain. The process was accompanied by attacks of fever, anaemia, temporary deafness, "general malaise." Meaning, again, that he felt terrible all the time. In severe cases, the sinuses and saliva slowly dry up, making it impossible to swallow solid food and breathe through the nose, and the body devours its own eyes before attacking the lungs and finally the heart. My father was an exemplary case, attracting the attention of many specialists, because he exhibited all the possible symptoms before dying.

Except that he did not stop walking. One of his uncles, affected with the same arthritis, had spent fifteen years in bed, with his wife and children, but mostly his wife, in constant attendance. I am convinced it was his ghost that kept Father in motion — exercising daily in spite of the pain, walking as soon as he was finished with the next operation, demanding to be taken around the block when he couldn't see any more, then around the house in the last few months, days.

How does this translate into the everyday life of an ordinary family?

Somehow, all I can think of at this moment is the spiel we received from the funeral director in the coffin display room, and smile, in spite of myself.

"Solid brass . . . Solid copper . . . Solid oak. . . ." Asked for something less solid, price-wise, the soft-spoken, obliging man showed us a simple plywood coffin. "But," he quickly added, ignoring the inappropriate expressions on our faces and lifting the white sheet to reveal shredded newspaper stuffing underneath, "it has no spring mattress, like the better ones. Now if you care to look over here. . . ."

Father would have celebrated this bit of absurdity with a fitting poem; he had entertained us with occasional facetious verses for as long as I remember. Towards the end, the only subject of his poems was his failing body; he made light of its infirmities, ridiculed humiliating accidents.

How we used to giggle at those verses! He wrote them down at first, and then, when blindness did not allow it any more, he composed and recited them from memory. We giggled hysterically, grateful to deny again and again our own pain, and fear, at the sight of the slow-motion tragedy being played out in front of us. Just as we argued, or shouted, when he annoyed us with his harsh judgements, criticisms, and unreasonable demands. Or we pouted and withdrew, taking away with us what he needed most: our physical expression of tenderness. Maybe even our love. All natural stages that occur whenever there is prolonged, incurable illness in a family, I found written in the many wise books I read. And read and read. . . .

"What are you going to do with your father?" the more action-oriented of my friends asked objectively when, bursting at the seams, I confided my frustrations to them.

"Crate and ship him off to Peru," I wanted to answer but didn't, disgusted with myself for the resentful reaction to their well-meant words. "Plant him in a flower pot and put him outside to freeze in the snow, as I have done with other bedraggled plants I didn't want to look at any more."

Except that he lived under my mother's watchful protection. . . .

Well-skilled in the arcana of North American culture, I knew very well my father should have been in a nursing home for the last two years, or at least since he fell, six months before his death, and began to require complete, around the clock nursing. Preferably with his eighty-three-year-old wife installed in the wing designed for the healthier spouses, so she could visit him at leisure. So the rest of us could visit them both on Sundays, maybe bring them home to dinner. It would have been much more civilised than what did happen instead. Much more . . . nice. We live in the kingdom of nice, the land of fine, how are you, fine, forever fine, thank you, and here's a nice smile to prove it. . . . Thoroughly ashamed of us all, my whole progressively more confused and angry but unfailingly devoted family, my mother, my brother, I used a lot of smiling bluster to cover up our inadequacies.

"He is my responsibility and I would rather work myself to death than let him rot in any institution," my eighty-three-year-old mother told me calmly and succinctly, when I suggested improvements to her utterly miserable situation. She almost succeeded, earning herself great respect among her elderly neighbours, who faithfully inquired about my father, and devoutly raised their eyes, saying "your mother is a saint" whenever I met them in the street. My father's family echoed the sentiments, offering continuous support and encouragement in letters.

Saint.

I found my role defined with a more up-beat term. Enabler.

"If you count the stars that make up Cassiopeia, and look towards four o'clock from the fourth star, you'll just be able to see Andromeda," my son tells me. "It's the only galaxy visible to the naked eye."

His voice startles me. I have forgotten about him. I wonder, guiltily, how many times over the last years I had done just that. Forgotten about my son, as my father and his needs, my mother's needs, gradually expanded to take over so much of my consciousness.

Gratefully, for I don't want bitter thoughts to spoil what

remains of tonight's magic, I count the stars and look towards four o'clock. I can't see Andromeda. My tall, almost grown-up son hands me his field glasses and I put them to my eyes. Adjusting the lenses, I skip back and forth among the confusing dots to find the elusive galaxy. There it is, like a flash of understanding, lost almost immediately. My eyes become comfortable with the distance, and I find it again, but the back of my neck begins to throb.

Immediately, as if responding to a prearranged signal it has been waiting for, my whole body begins to throb.

Such a long time. A lifetime of careful orchestration of thoughts and feelings. In order to carry on as normally as possible. In order to be of maximum help without total self-annihilation. A most delicate balance to maintain, impossible at times in the best of times.

There had been moments of late, during sleepless nights especially, when even the smallest problems tend to glitter with a grim, unredeeming light, that I had wished Father dead. Writhing in a bed turned to swamp full of vicious thoughts, I desired nothing of life but his nonbeing. Except that the next day, he would ask me, ever so humbly, to pluck out his ingrown eyelashes, or I would feed him his boring, puréed food — how he complained about my mother's cooking! — or take him to the doctor, where we both heard from the receptionist how well he was looking, how glad she was he felt better, and the balance would swing back to fierce tenderness and a desire to shield him from the understandably but nonetheless cruelly indifferent world. The anger that had almost succeeded in killing compassion in my heart the night before would turn upon that world. I even understood his fear of being nursed by strangers. Until the return of darkness. . . .

I am too tired to miss him.

It is becoming chilly. The sky is a shade darker, the stars brighter. I don't even try any more to imagine not being able to open my eyes at will and see all that I can see at this very moment.

He must have dreaded the coming of death the same way he came to dread injections.

I had watched him die. With disbelief — surely he would come through again — with wonder, shameless fascination. I held his shoulders and watched the stubborn, rock-solid life disintegrate quietly.

With the binoculars hanging around my sore neck, I step back towards the mountain ash. The branches part, rest, languorous on my shoulders. The leaves, the cool, firm moist-with-dew berries brush against my face. Next weekend we — our complete tiny tribe — are going to look for a burial place. My son, who has already sharpened a thick nail in order to carve his grandfather's name on a rock, has asked that we do not drop him into a river. We will find a small crack in the earth somewhere instead, a mini-cave, deposit the ashes and the flowers and, following an appropriate ceremony, pile the entrance shut with rocks. Discreetly, so that no accidental passers-by, human or animal, will be able to associate the spot with a grave. An intensely private grave to please an intensely private person, to make up for the indignities he had suffered in life, for our lack of patience with him, for our wandering affections and, in my case, for the ability to smile, and enjoy the night so only two weeks after his death. With plenty of good, clean air around him, with birds and stars as his only companions.

Our first grave. . . .

~

In her own words: I was born in Poland and have lived in Edmonton for the past thirty-two years. Since books have always been my most tolerant and steady friends, it seemed natural to choose English and later Comparative Literature as my fields of study at the University of Alberta. I wrote my first story in 1987. Since then my short stories, essays, and poems have been published in *Prairie Fire, Canadian Women Studies, OnSpec, Other Voices,* and others. My work has also been accepted for publication in *Places of the Heart* and *Kitchen Talk* anthologies, and performed at "Womanstrength." I was coeditor of *Other Voices* for four years. One very supportive husband, one tall lovable kid, and one yellow dog complete the picture of my life at this moment.

Uncertainties

Susan Sharpe

*I*N 1985 I WAS ON FACULTY IN A
speech communication department in a small western U.S.
university — teaching too many courses I cared little about, with
too little time for the research I cared much about, and too little
salary to make any of it worth the drain of time and energy. That
spring I said "No more!" and resigned, with no idea of what to do
instead. I finished the term and then took a temporary adminis-
trative position with the university because it gave me an extra
year to figure out what to do next.

I knew I would have to move to a larger city in order to
find nonacademic alternatives. But which one? Seattle? Or San
Francisco?

The solution to my dilemma seemed obvious to the man I was
newly involved with — he was thinking of accepting a job offer in
Canada.

"How about moving to Edmonton?" Norm asked.

No, no, no, no, no, no.

"Why not? We love each other. We want to stay together.
Right?"

Yes, yes, yes, yes, yes, yes.

"Do you want me to turn down the job so we can stay here?"

No, no, no, no, no, no.

"Then why not come with me to Edmonton?"

Because I am a feminist. A staunch, public feminist. A role

model for my students. I cannot pick up and follow a man when he moves to take a job. It simply is not done.

It was a tough year, as I went 'round and 'round, sometimes with Norm but more often with my feminist principles: *You must not sacrifice yourself for a man's career.*

Right.

But what if my own career has foundered, and I have to move away in order to get it going again? *No excuse. You have to find your own way. You cannot carve out a new identity or build a new life by piggy-backing on what a man does.*

Right. Okay.

But what if I have no career-related criteria for choosing a place to live, and one city is as good as another for what I'll be doing? Shouldn't I at least work around the one good thing in my life? At least have a relationship going for me when I carve out a new life? *Hah! Don't fall for it. The choices women make always appear to be logical, reasonable, at the start. Women don't get trapped because they are stupid; they get trapped because they think they can sneak through the territory without being caught. But the whole territory is booby-trapped. If you walk into this now, you'll lose your self in the relationship, and may never get it back.*

Right. Damn.

And how could you face people if you did this?!

"People" in this case referred to my feminist colleagues at the university and the students I had taught when occasionally seconded to teach a women's studies course. The young women who told me I had opened their eyes and irreversibly changed their lives. The ones who, under my tutelage, saw for the first time the delicately woven net that restricts women's movements. Saw the veil that draws close around a woman's intimate relationship with a man. The one that tightens and seals around her — paralysing and choking her if she tries to move — when she makes that relationship legal, that is, validated by the patriarchy.

Wide-eyed with alarm, my students had challenged this vision.

"Always?" they asked. "I mean, yes, we can see now the dangers we didn't see before, but is it always that way? It's *possible* to have a good relationship, isn't it? Isn't it?"

"Well," I had said, cautiously, patiently, "I am sure it is. Will be. Once we change the patterns, replace the patriarchy. . . ."

But in fact I could not imagine a time when the patterns would be different, when women and men could create truly healthy relationships. Experience and observation — my own early, short marriage, and what I saw of others' relationships — both made me sceptical of what was possible with men. I had lived happily alone for more than a dozen years, and saw any other state as dangerous.

Yet the picture was muddying. I had begun to hear a challenge whispered from somewhere inside, a tiny current of dissent beneath my convictions.

Living alone those dozen years, I had been living in a wide zone of freedom where I did not have to share my activities or coordinate schedules or turn out the light so someone else could sleep. A place where I could retreat from the world without walking into another set of demands. With no serious involvements, my own time and space were both mine to control. I needed the safety of that freedom, and it allowed me to relax into a certain amount of happiness.

That zone also gave my relationships a wide safety margin. I had a network of friends, colleagues, associates, acquaintances; I shared activities with a wide range of people, connecting on the basis of shared interests and similar styles. I sometimes wished I had a best friend to fight with, but no one in my circle seemed to be a candidate. My friends and I sought relationships that were interesting, maintained them as long as they were comfortable, and disengaged if they became less satisfying. Life as a single person was stimulating, fun, easy.

Much too easy. There was no one to watch me live out the dailiness of my life and call me on my hypocrisies. There was no one to see the ranges of my boorishness and generosity and tell me when I carried them too far. No one to hear me rant about someone else's boorishness and tell me I was being unfair. No one to do their own share of being hard to live with, pushing me to do the harder work of loving. Living alone gave me the path of least resistance, and I began to realise it was time to take on more.

So I started dating again and was discouraged more often than not. A couple of men did seem to be different from the rest, but they too turned out to be traditionalists in disguise. They did not try to control me, and even supported my having an independent life — as long as I kept it out of their way. They wanted me to stay in their orbit, rounding out their lives without touching their centres. It was during this period that I taught the women's studies courses, wishing I could support my students' hopes about what was possible, but having only pessimism to offer.

Then I met Norm and fell in . . . well, "in love," yes, but also into remarkable care. He did not at that point call himself a feminist, but he willingly accommodated himself to me in our relationship. He loved me generously, and what he loved was me, not something he wanted me to be. There was much about me he did not understand, but instead of dismissing it, he opened himself to the adventure of seeing what I would do with it. And when we ran into traditional troubles and I nearly left, he said, "Help me to learn," rather than lose the relationship.

I still felt considerable fear and scepticism, but I saw real potential here.

My politics said it was dangerous to follow him north to Canada, but my spirit said it was dangerous not to. This relationship offered me much of what I needed — a place where I could be myself and also be safe, where I was nourished enough to grow stronger, where I was loved enough to risk facing myself. I wasn't sure I was up to all that this gift would demand of me, but I was sure I would pay a great penalty for turning my back on it.

The problem was that I could not just go with Norm to Edmonton, to live and work in the same place he did. The only way I could immigrate was as a dependant. As a wife.

I agonised, I worried, I went more rounds with my principles. Finally I committed myself — to the importance of choosing what is right over what is safe, to the reading of my gut that said this relationship was right, and thus, at the courthouse, to whatever life with Norm might bring.

It was a leap of faith, not a step I could justify, and telling people about it became an exercise in defensiveness. No simple statements of the news, no excited bubblings of the joy I felt. Certainly no articulations of what I was choosing with the commitment. Just stammering efforts to make it sound like a sensible choice: "I had decided to move away anyway . . . the timing . . . the immigration requirements . . . so you see. . . ."

One friend still remembers how I broke the news to her. "I couldn't understand why you kept explaining and explaining," she said, "as if I would be anything but happy for you. I couldn't see why you would be anything except elated to have found and married such a wonderful man."

Ah, but she was my friend. As others were. "Of course," they all said. "Good for you."

I desperately hoped it would be.

We moved to Edmonton, unpacked our boxes, and Norm went off to the new life waiting for him at work. I looked around me and took some deep breaths — nowhere to go, no one to meet, no work to do. Fearful and still defensive, I went looking for my own new life.

It was a long search, and I often came home bruised. "I have no friends here," I would wail to Norm. I meant that I felt rootless, disconnected, suspended in a sea of interactions that had form but no substance. I was meeting new people, but continued to feel disconnected.

"But I am your friend," Norm would say to my wail, and it is true, he was. But I needed women friends.

I looked in logical places. I went to the Women's Resource Centre on campus to find out about programs and other organisations. I stuffed envelopes for the province's feminist political lobbying group. I enroled in an extension course on feminist theory in order to learn about Canadians' work in this area and, I hoped, to find the people and the time for some of the connected talk I yearned for.

In all these places I found a gracious reception. People were friendly, they were kind, they included me in lunches and told me about meetings, conferences, marches. They expressed friendly interest: "So, what brought you to Edmonton?"

The question choked me every time. Sure of how they would interpret a simple "my husband got a job here," I would fall to stammering again. "Well, um, you see, ah . . . I was teaching . . . but I was going to leave anyway . . . and my friend got this job . . . it seemed to me that . . . and so. . . ."

Generally this met with a small pause and an "Oh?" and then a carrying on to other topics. The pause always seemed to me to hold the censure I feared, but in passing conversations I could not be sure of the reaction; I could not tell what people thought or whether they heard my worry.

In the course on feminist theory, however, the judgement seemed very clear. No one criticised my choice in particular, but discussions of patriarchy and its institutions led repeatedly to the position that marriage is a dangerous state for women. The conclusion was soft-pedalled a bit, as a third to half of us were married; the position was clear nonetheless, and none of us challenged its accuracy.

Certainly I was in no shape to mount a serious challenge; the source of my defensive panic was my own belief that the conclusion was right. But now I was committed also to believing it could be wrong, and the dissonance was painful.

So was my fall from certainty. It was jarring to find myself in the role of my former students, tentatively suggesting that my case was an exception, and then hearing the instructor and others take what used to be my lines: "It may seem that way now, but you haven't been married long, have you?"

As I said, "No, but . . ." I felt the gulf between us, knew intimately the certainty they felt, and realised there would be no convincing them. Taking a husband had put me out of their circle, banished to otherness. It was irrelevant that I knew their arguments, that I had shared their experience, that I had recruited others to their ranks. Also irrelevant was the reason for my lapse — perhaps I had never really understood the issues, or had been blinded by love, or just had poor judgement; all they could see was that I had made an error.

The realisation shocked me. Much as I had feared their censure, it hurt to have it come this way. I was fully aware that time might prove me wrong, and I was fully prepared to admit it. But I was not prepared to be dismissed with an assumption that I did not know what I was doing. I knew down to my bones the kind of risk I was taking, and I took it soberly. Precisely because of the risk, I needed guides and supporters.

These women, I thought, were the ones best suited to the task. They were smart and experienced. They knew the dangers I faced, and would understand why I was afraid. I knew they would be surprised that I had set off down this path, but I thought they would still be willing to help me find ways to make it safe.

They could have done that. They could have tried to find out who I was, and why I had undertaken this. They could have asked questions: "How interesting that someone with your history would make this decision. What is it you see as being worth this risk?" Or "This man must be quite unusual. What gives you such confidence in him?" Or "Have you safeguarded yourself against . . . and . . . ?"

They could have helped me weave my feminism into the new cloth of my life, instead of excluding me for choosing a pattern they did not like. They could have discerned that I was one of them, and trusted me because of it. They could have found out where I was before they told me I was in the wrong place. They could have just been there: "You must be frightened. How is it going?"

They would have none of it. When I said, "I think this one may work differently . . . ," their silence felt heavy with condescension: *Sure it will, honey. Whatever you say.*

Perhaps I am too hard on these women. It may very well be that the dismissal I perceived was not at all what they meant. All I know is they did not ask me any of those questions. They told me what was true, so I would know my own experience was false.

Perhaps it's just as well they did. They showed me what I had done to other women with my own certainties of truth. It's a lesson I hope I'll never forget.

~

Eight years after the move described in her essay, **Susan Sharpe** is still in Edmonton, and still glad of all the lessons it brought her. Now a Canadian citizen, she earns her living as a freelance writer.

And When They Are Gone

Kathryn Fraser

*I*T WASN'T THAT THE SHOES WERE particularly offensive, they weren't. They were a tad bourgeois, burgundy leather, and well made. No, you see, it was that they were set next to my shoes, as if they belonged there. Now, you may be asking why I didn't just up and move them away, but there was more to it than that.

I'm not given to one-night stands and this was, indeed, nothing of the sort. Still, there was an illicit sort of atmosphere brewing in my little home that morning. One that seemed very much like the morning after sharing one's bed with a stranger. The safety of my apartment, the very sanctity of it, seemed threatened. A stranger had seen my things, touched them, probably, and had had the audacity to insinuate himself in my life by placing his shoes — not by chance but deliberately — next to my own. Why did I allow his presence at all? I had little choice.

I passed quietly by the bedroom door, hoping to find him gone, but he was still there. The blankets were twisted around his feet, a pillow clutched in his arms. I knew him to be a light sleeper, so I merely watched him for a while. I looked at his balding head, so vulnerable, tucked neatly into his chest. I noticed the tufts of grey hair poking out from his ears. I tried to find something warm and familiar about him, but it was no use.

I went back to the front door and examined the shoes. They were supple, broken in, but the soles were still like new. I tried them on. I walked around the room in them. They were too large, but not much so. I took them off and raised one to my nose, feeling like some primordial creature sniffing out another. They smelled worn but not offensive. I quickly became aware of what I was doing, as if I were watching myself with the disapproving eyes of someone else, and I was embarrassed, but my face didn't colour. His coat hung inside the hall closet. I looked at it, touched it. It was cream-coloured, combed cotton with silk lining. I wanted to try it on but I felt like a hypocrite. I was terribly worried that he might have examined my things with the same curiosity, and yet I wanted to remove his coat from the hanger and feel it next to my skin.

He is a professional man, though he's never really talked to me about what he actually does. His parents were working class and he despised them. He has three children. . . . He loves children — I think — but I'm not so sure about his wife. Once he locked her in the bathroom after a particularly intense argument, and he sat hating her, hating himself, as he listened to her cursing from behind the bathroom door. He drinks too much.

The night before we had gone to a trendy restaurant for dinner. He ordered too much wine. When the flower vendor made his way to our table, he bought out the lot. He gave them to the waitresses. He said carnations and roses were too tacky for me. It cost him $250. At that moment, I despised him, but I was proud that he was with me. He held the hand not holding my wine glass. He told me I was beautiful. I saw that I was a reflection of what he had hoped I would be — his vision of accomplishment. We ate pâté de foie gras, we drank Saint-Emilion, we inhaled fifty-year-old cognac. We talked about nothing in particular outside of my beauty and his love of good food and wine. "I'm an epicure," he told me unapologetically. The waiters thought he was my lover, and they whispered behind cupped hands.

We took a cab back. We sat on the sofa, and in his drunken slur, he told me that no one knew him better than I did. I ignored him, as I always did because I had to. It hurt too much to acknowledge his loneliness, to recognize that I too, felt it. Again, he told me about the early mornings he used to spend with my mother's father. They would eat blue cheese and pickled herrings with sour cream; they would swig thick black coffee and argue politics. These were the times he never had with his own father. For me, they are the times I've never had with mine.

We see each other once every couple of years, but I had never invited him to stay in my home before. I listened to his snoring that night and I put my hands over my ears. He repulsed me. I wandered around anxiously. I thought about asking him to find a hotel. I tried to pretend he was gone. When I finally went to sleep, I had a strange dream.

I was sitting in a high chair — though I was no smaller or younger than I am now — and my feet were dragging on the floor. I was wearing a red dress, and it strained around my neck. I felt choked. I tried to adjust the collar, but I couldn't move. My arms wouldn't reach up. He was there, by the sink, singing in a full, sonorous voice. He was singing "Edelweiss." I tried to join in, but the dress was strangling me. He smiled at me over his shoulder, and I was gesturing to him that I couldn't breathe. He just smiled and nodded and continued with his melody, which he now began to hum in a low, funereal tone. He moved towards the door walking backwards, smiling, waving, humming. I couldn't speak to ask him where he was going or when he'd be back. I didn't know how. I woke up and my night shirt was twisted up around my neck. My arms were beneath me and were tingly numb. It was seven o'clock in the morning. I got up.

I wasn't immediately aware of the shoes, because I was still quite unsettled by my dream. But when I noticed them, finally, and became disgruntled by their presence, I started to realize why.

Then I heard him stir in the other room, and my heart pounded. I could hear him in the bathroom beginning his ritual toilette. He would shower and shave and douse himself with expensive cologne. He would push his cuticles back with lotion and a hand towel and file his fingernails. He would spray his thinning hair with fixative, and blow dry it into place. Then he would come out smiling. In a loud, festive voice he would greet me. He would slap my adult's bottom as if it were a child's, and it would be harder than he intended.

And I would speak in someone else's voice. I would gush and smile and hang onto his every word, and I would feel love for him, but I would hate myself. I would ask him how he'd slept, and I would tell him I'd slept fine. I would pour him thick coffee and offer him breakfast knowing he wouldn't want any. I knew all this. I dreaded it, and yet I was disappointed when it didn't go this way.

But something happened when he came out, something I didn't expect. I felt numb, cold. My heart stopped its furious beating. Instinctively, I stared directly into his eyes. I could see he was afraid, but somehow I couldn't comfort him. My voice was firm, I didn't affect the uncertain tone of a coquette. I looked into his eyes and I saw something that comforted me and wounded me all at the same time. He couldn't look at me. He was acting, as I had been, the part he had thought I expected him to play. I knew then that he would never touch my things. He wouldn't be able to just look at and touch a pair of my earrings or to smell a bottle of my perfume; he wouldn't be able to look at my various photographs or artwork; he wouldn't be able to survey anything I had chosen without having to put them in some kind of context. He would have to think about me as a person, with a life outside of my visits to him, with tastes and desires that might not mirror his own. And then I knew why I touched his things.

"Your shoes," I said, "they're very you." He looked over to them. "They're old," he answered, "but I don't like to waste money on such things. They'll do." "Yes," I answered, "you'd rather spend your money on flowers." We sat in silence, both of us staring intently at the burgundy shoes next to mine by the front door. Then he broke the quiet.

"You really do know me better than anyone." He didn't look at me, and I was glad. I felt that he had known what I was doing while he slept, although he couldn't have, and I was ashamed. I watched his face, the way his eyelids fluttered when he was thinking. I put my fingers up to my thin lips; lips I had inherited from him. I looked for more of myself in him, but I knew that I had been lost. He didn't know where to find me, and he was afraid to look. I wanted to tell him about me, the real me, to make him look. Perversely, I wanted to crawl onto his lap and sit quietly, as we had never done. There is comfort and familiarity in silence, and so we would never maintain it.

I was of this man, and yet I felt no connection to him. I wanted him to stay, yet I could hardly wait until he left. I told him this, I blurted it out in a voice of indifference. He looked hurt. I told him I get further away from myself when he is near, and that I don't like the me that he has created. I told him we never talk, not really. (I considered telling him about my dream and the choking dress and my numb arms, but couldn't.) He said, "You are cold." He picked up his shoes and took his coat from the closet.

I remembered then, with new understanding, my previous visits with him. I remembered that when last he was here, he wanted to buy me a present, but he wouldn't buy me what I really wanted. He insisted on buying me perfume. I remembered that when I started my woman's bleeding I was with him. He wouldn't look at me, or touch me after that. Maybe I had become sexual to him, but I felt desexed. I remembered the early morning/late night phone calls when I would plead with him to put down the gun, never really sure if he even had one. I remembered telling him it wasn't fair, that I was too far away. I remembered him hanging up, and my trying to dial his number but feeling paralyzed; half wanting him to use it, half dreading he might. I remembered introducing him to a man with whom I thought myself to be very much in love, and discovering I would never love another as I loved him. I went to my bedroom and lay down, breathing his essence into my senses, crying dry tears into my pillow.

I knew that eventually he had to come back, at least for now, and that he looked forward to, and dreaded it as much as I. I inhaled his fragrance and felt nausea wash over me. I pressed my palms against my thighs and held my breath, briefly. Behind my closed eyes I saw him walking down the street.

I hated his shoes because they were his, and when they were gone, he would be too.

～

Spawned from a large and complicated prairie family, **Kathryn Fraser** has spent most of her life in Edmonton where she is now completing an M.A. in the Department of Comparative Literature and Film Studies at the University of Alberta. Her areas of research and interest include literature, film, popular culture, and feminist theory.

"He Didn't Mean To"

Kay Stewart

BLUE SKY. CORN STALKS RISING all around. She doesn't tell anyone.

~

"There is a fountain filled with blood," intones the music director. The congregation takes up the familiar hymn. The minister stands in the aisle, waiting for those moved by the spirit to place membership in the church, to rededicate their lives to Christ, to be baptized in the name of the Father, the Son, and the Holy Ghost. "Drawn from Emmanuel's veins." Drawn from the pew where she sits with her family, the young girl makes her way down the aisle. "And sinners plunged beneath that flood." She gives her hand to the minister. She has taken the plunge. "Lose all their guilty stains." Will she?

~

His kiss is wet on her lips. He is her great-uncle, her grandfather's younger brother. He is a carpenter, working at something on their house or her grandparents' house, two doors away. She tries to avoid him, not always successfully. She doesn't tell anyone.

~

In college she sees for the last time the boy she pursued, unsuccessfully, all through high school. He tells her that he almost asked her to marry him the summer they graduated. But now he is in love with a much younger girl, still in junior high, he says, ashamed. He puts his fingers inside her. Don't unless you love me, she says.

~

The young bride comes away from *West Side Story* racked with guilt and tears. She tells her husband about the ex-fiancé (not the high school flame, but the one who, to compensate for the fact that she was smarter, liked to bend her fingers back, trying to make her say uncle). They hadn't had sex, not really, but in fooling around he had broken her hymen. So she had not been a virgin when they married. She tells him about the cornfield, about the fear of damnation. He is tender. He has a confession of his own to make. On a research trip to Mexico his professor, knowing he was about to be married, had seen to his sexual initiation by taking him to a prostitute. "It was like making love to a posthole," he says.

~

The couple's sex life never seems satisfactory. She has read that most couples have sex 2.5 times a week. He studies late. They read sex manuals. After they have sex, he surreptitiously wipes his fingers on the bedsheet. She feels dirty. He suggests Havelock Ellis. Ellis, she reads between the lines, turned his wife into a lesbian. She shivers. It's the sixties. They agree on an open marriage — no, they agree she needs more sex than she's getting from him. They enlist his best friend. They see Bergman's *Wild Strawberries,* most of which she sleeps through, but her husband is shaken by it. The experience with the prostitute, he now realizes, has made him feel as though he is raping his wife every time they make love. But for her it is too late. He has let another man claim her. They separate, divorce.

~

She marries the best friend. They change graduate schools so that he can study under a professor he knows and admires. The professor often kisses her at parties or whenever he finds her alone. His kisses are wet. She can't remember whether she told her husband. She knows she never told the professor to keep his hands off her. She is dissatisfied, starts having affairs. After the divorce she still sees the professor occasionally, because she likes the wife and their children are friends. She tries not to be alone with him.

~

Finally with someone, a married man, she is baptized into sexual pleasure. She begins to learn that pleasure comes from her body, not from what someone does to her. She is shattered when he decides to remain with his wife. Although she does not know that many men have affairs while their wives are pregnant, she has had a premonition that, whatever his wife's shortcomings, he will not abandon his newborn daughter. She dreams about kissing him in a swimming pool, dreams about the high school flame.

~

She eventually finds someone new, available. Disillusioned in her quest for the perfect relationship, she decides to stick this one out despite his not having the commitment to fidelity that she has decided to adopt. She forgives one brief fling, another. He falls in love with someone else and she moves out. His love is short-lived and they continue to see each other. While he is away for several months she is tempted to have an affair but makes a discovery — she does not have to give herself to a man simply because he wants her. Her body is her own.

~

At least sometimes her body is her own. She no longer feels that a man can give her body back to her. But even when she is dry and tight with anger she still gives herself to her husband. Having made sex the issue in two failed marriages, she is wary about doing so a third time. Besides, she is beginning to realize that what she is looking for is not simply sex.

~

Her body is her own, but it is stained by the dust of the cornfield. She has talked about the cornfield in therapy, in her women's group. The picture image she has carried about with her since childhood fades. She writes a semiautobiographical story about a girl whose older brother attempts to force himself on her girl-friend. The setting is autobiographical, the attempted rape is not. Otherwise she never writes about sex.

~

When a younger brother dies, the cornfield, the older brother, return. Not that it was her older brother — it was his friend. But he was there. They were seven, she was three. She reads about childhood sexual abuse. Somehow what happened to her doesn't seem to fit — after all, before she was baptized into the church she and her brother were part of a neighborhood gang where sex was considered all right until you were twelve, when you might make a baby. So why was she making a big deal out of what, in her working class background, was fairly common, a guilty secret you kept from adults and middle-class friends, but little more. Was she focussing on the cornfield, where she was too young to consent, to keep from facing the shame of sexual experimentation when she was eight, nine, ten? She puts the book away.

~

Something frees itself in her. She starts writing fiction again. She is teaching. A student mentions in class that she has been a drug abuser, she has been raped. The students discuss rape, the power men have over women. She, the professor, is silent. The pain of the victim struggles with the politics of the classroom. Politics wins. She remains silent.

~

Why am I so reluctant to say that I was sexually abused as a child? To admit that, until I was in my late thirties, I felt in the power of any man who wanted my body? Who am I protecting?

~

I grew up trying to protect my older brother, and myself, from my dad's anger. We quickly learned not to tattle on each other, because both the culprit and the tattler were likely to get a whipping. Was it fear of punishment that sealed my lips? Or fear of losing my brother as an ally if I told? Whatever the cause, the effect of my not speaking seems to be a pattern of giving up my body, for what? What did I imagine would happen if I said, "I don't like the way Uncle X kisses me," or "You don't want to go out with me, so keep your hands to yourself," or "You're taking advantage of your position as my husband's supervisor and I don't like it," or "I'm angry at you and I don't want to have sex"?

~

What happens now when my father cajoles and threatens a reluctant five-year-old granddaughter into giving him a goodbye kiss? The other adults stand around. The mother says, "Give Papaw a kiss." My stomach churns in anger, but I am silent. What happens now when my father decides that another granddaughter is flagrantly ignoring his repeated warnings to keep her mouth closed when she's eating? He smacks her on the shoulder. My mother, my grandmother, my younger brother, the secretary sit silent. Tears spring to my eyes. I sit silent.

~

The power of men over women. This is not the whole story. This is not the story of men who have been physically abused (as my father was) or sexually abused or psychologically abused by one or both parents. It is not the story of women whose mothers protect or reject them. It is not the story of women whose fathers treat their wives as equals deserving respect, and whose wives claim the respect they deserve. It is not even the whole story of one woman, for my father, who is passionately committed to his family's welfare, passed on to me his belief in the value of education and some of his confidence in his own abilities; and my mother comes closer to loving her children unconditionally than anyone else I know. But she could not protect me from my father's anger, his criticism, his sometimes merciless teasing. When I left the table crying she would say, "He didn't mean to hurt your feelings."

~

He didn't mean to. So the power that men wield over women is unfortunate but unconscious, unintentional. And so I come to rationalize sexual abuse, emotional abuse. Physical abuse I recognize more easily; even as a child I rejected the rationalizations that accompanied punishment: "This is for your own good" and "This hurts me more than it hurts you." So I recognize physical abuse when I see it — but still avoid seeing, avoid naming what is happening when a friend tells me, "The next thing I knew I was on the floor."

~

Emotional abuse takes longer for me to recognize. Just as my body became deadened to its own pleasure, so my heart and soul became wrapped in layers of denial to deaden the pain of cutting remarks, of insensitive behaviour. "He didn't mean to," whispers a voice inside my head. Then the cuts hurt, and I cry. But he didn't mean it, I tell myself. They hurt, and I'm angry. Maybe he did mean it, and if I say something, he'll try to stop. He tries, most of the time. And when he *really* didn't mean to, I can acknowledge it, most of the time. But it's hard: hard for me to release him from my image of the angry Father-God; hard for him to see in me someone other than the Terrible Mother whom it is safe to defy only from ambush.

~

And in the larger world, the power of men over women is not just in our heads. The power to terrorize, to silence. "Nice shooting Lepine," someone scrawls on my office door. "Feminist die." The man who murdered fourteen women and his buddy. My brother and the friend who abused me, standing among the corn stalks. As I try to free myself from the inner voices that keep me powerless, silenced by my early learnings — that a man's word is final, not to be questioned or argued with; that a man's time is more important than my own; that my feelings, opinions, judgements will not be listened to, understood, taken into account — "he didn't mean to" is not enough.

~

Even if he didn't mean to, there are fountains of blood, and guilty stains.

~

Kay Stewart, a native Texan, came to Canada in the late sixties, where, like many of her generation, she held a number of temporary and part-time teaching positions. She now teaches writing and literature courses at the University of Alberta. She has published two short stories and coauthored several widely-used writing textbooks. Her current projects include a series of personal essays and a collection of short stories. Grandmother of two, Kay returned to parenthood when she and her husband became guardians of her young niece.

Seed to the Sower: Dare We Farm Again?

Maxine Hancock

*C*OULD WE START OVER AGAIN? Did we dare? All through the long winter of 1975, we asked ourselves the question. Crop failure, a wipeout on the cattle market and ten years of struggle suddenly seemed to count for nothing. We were back to square zero.

We sold the "home place," the farm we had bought from Cam's father ten years earlier when, full of youth, hope and optimism, we had set out to carry on the tradition of family farming. We paid off all the debts we could, and pleaded for patience on the part of creditors while we tried to decide what to do next.

But even as we attempted to entertain possibilities other than farming, we found ourselves clinging to the country heritage we had been so determined to pass on to our four children, all born since we had "gone farming."

Could we start again? Dare we start again?

We asked the question of each other, of our closest friends, and most of all, we asked it silently of our own hearts. And meanwhile, in ways we scarcely noticed, healing was beginning, gifts were being given.

One day soon after we moved from the house on the home place we had sold into the tiny rented house on another farm, our children pedalled their bicycles to visit Gilda, our nearest neighbour down the road. They returned with a still-warm loaf of bread fresh from her oven. Never had "our daily bread" looked so good or felt so friendly in its brown crustiness.

We had found a piano teacher nearby for our two older children. As I heard them practice, I found myself hungering for music, too. When I asked their teacher if she would take me on, she tucked a free lesson for me into her schedule. I limbered up my hands with scales I hadn't played for fifteen years. And then, with pleasure out of all proportion to my skill, I worked on Bach preludes and Chopin waltzes. In that hour a day I spent at the piano, I couldn't add or subtract. I couldn't talk or think about our problems. In a few months, I was emotionally restored enough to go back to my typewriter to write the manuscript for my second book, *Living on Less and Liking It More.*

On a Saturday when we had company coming for supper, I picked up a few groceries at a village store. We had home-churned butter for our home-baked bread. We had home-grown beef and home-hoed potatoes. But what could we have for dessert? Sugar prices had soared as our income plummeted, and I was eking out a five-pound bag by teaspoonfuls. We had just not been having desserts.

As I finished my spartan shopping, I glanced up to see the grocer's wife blocking my way, holding a big bag of oranges. "Could you use these?" she asked. "They won't keep over the weekend." Sliced oranges, topped with whipped cream, made our dessert that night. Our guests raved: such simplicity! such originality!

On the leeward side of winter, with Christmas and the short, dark days of early January past, we began our ascent into spring. I found a part-time teaching job to give Cam time to complete the sale of assets and make management decisions. My first book, *Love, Honor and Be Free*, was released by Moody Press of Chicago with fanfare and excitement I had never dreamed of.

"We'd like for you to be with us at the Christian Booksellers' Association convention," the voice on the other end of a long distance call explained, and it seemed somewhere I could hear a big brass band playing. "It's in Anaheim in July."

As a farm wife who had written my manuscript at the end of a blown-in winter lane on an Alberta farm, I whispered back, "Where's Anaheim?"

What to wear? With the doors and windows of our little farm home suddenly opening out onto a larger world, the problem was acute. Again, the supply, in love. Elsie, my special friend who lived in a nearby town, sewed me a wardrobe, refusing even the suggestion of payment for her craftsmanship. And that spring, as maple buds were swelling on the trees outside my window, she even bought and paid for the material for my first "going-away outfit" in years.

These tokens of love, these little whispers of "Hang in there" took us through that winter. But still the question loomed. Dare we farm again? It wasn't a decision I could make for Cam. Although I was a city girl, I didn't want Cam to give up his dream short of fulfillment. And I had grown to love the quiet beauty of the country. Above all, I treasured for our children the spaces and the silences, the wonderful and almost unbearable vitality of the seasonal cycle.

And now a few more concrete material signs of hope began to emerge.

For one thing, our major creditor, a local credit union, encouraged us to reinvest a portion of the equity realized from the sale of the family farm. To our amazement, we found ourselves owners of a farm once again. The question now was: a farm — for what? To resell so we could liquidate remaining debt? To rent out to someone else? Or was the land for us to farm? And if so, where could we find the capital for machinery, for fertilizer, for seed?

Part of the answer came one day when Cam's dad offered him a loan of part of the required operating money. And another part of it came the day that Walter stopped by.

Walter and his wife, Jeanne, had been parents of teenagers in Cam's first school class, before we were married. Everything about them said quietly, "Success." Not blatant, showy success. But the kind of accomplishment we dreamed of: healthily developing children, a neat and well-developed farmstead; a big spread of land;

good machinery. Since we had first met, once- or twice-a-year visits with them had become a special tradition.

But the day that Walter stopped by, I wasn't expecting to see him. The look on Walter's face when I answered his knock at the back door told me this was more than a social visit. He seemed a little reticent. Maybe — surprising to me — even a bit nervous.

Cam was away for the day, finding posts for corral repair. I poured coffee and small-talked. We talked about his children, now grown and establishing homes of their own. And about ours. We talked about the weather. I knew there was something more on Walter's mind.

"Well," he said, finally, swallowing his last mouthful of coffee. "I actually came to tell Cam something. But I guess you could pass it on for me."

"Of course." I set the coffeepot back on the stove and sat down.

"We know what it's like to have tough times," he said. "When Jeanne and I first started out, we didn't have two nickels to rub together. Really." He paused.

"An old friend of ours died the other day and that brought it all back. But Charlie was pretty special to us. He'd been a friend of our family's for as long as I can remember." Walter paused, his voice husky.

"I especially remember one time just after my dad died. Things were pretty bad. There were some debts he left we didn't know how to clear. We thought we might have to sell out. And then Charlie called me aside in town one day and pressed a folded twenty dollar bill into my hand. That was like, say, one thousand dollars would be today."

We sat in the silence that fell. Then Walter went on. "We used that twenty dollars to pay off a debt. And, somehow, we inched our way ahead. We finally were able to sell that farm, a little patch of rocks north of the river, and buy better land. . . ."

I was offering coffee again, automatically. Walter covered his mug. "No thanks," he smiled. "I really have to be on my way. Jeanne's expecting me for supper. But what I came to tell Cam is this: I have a bin of cleaned barley seed. Five hundred bushels. It's

Cam's to use this spring. And when he gets his crop off this fall, he can just fill it up again for us." And then Walter lifted his coat off the hook behind the door and was gone.

I found myself sitting, as the afternoon fell grey and cool around me in the little kitchen, tracing around the edges of the checks on the plaid plastic tablecloth. The full impact of the offer hit me only gradually. We were being supplied. All winter we had enjoyed "bread to the eater," but now we also had "seed to the sower." Not only did this mean we could put a crop in, but it also meant someone we trusted and respected thought we *should* put that crop in . . . that we would make it.

Since then, crops have come and gone. We refilled Walter's seed bin that fall and began to pay off debts. Five years later, we were able to buy back the home place, sold in the days of our darkness and despair, and add it to the new land we had purchased to make a good-sized family farm. Our children have watched the seasons, have attended the birth of calves and pigs, have ridden horseback. Cam has seen many of his dreams of farming come true. Our old debts are long paid back.

But there is one debt that remains: the kindness of our friends, their love that gave us hope, their esteem that gave us courage. That is a debt we can never repay. We can only, in our turn, become suppliers — in whatever ways we can — of seed to other sowers.

∼

In the years since **Maxine Hancock** wrote this essay (first published in *Grainews*, 1981 and then in *Plow-Share*, Spring 1982), she and Cam have continued to farm. For Maxine, the biggest deprivation of living remote from a city was the lack of opportunity for further study. When their youngest son was in his last year of high school, Cam and Maxine began commuting from farm to city so that she could study for an M.A. and then complete a Ph.D. in English. To her own surprise, even more than her family's, Maxine was named the winner of the Governor-General's Gold Medal as the most academically outstanding graduate of the University of Alberta at Spring Convocation, 1992. She continues her blend of country living, freelance writing, and lifelong learning.

Parting Gifts

Debra Purdy Kong

D AVID'S MOTHER DIED FIVE
Tuesdays ago. Last night, David invited me to the memorial service, which is how I find myself in the back seat of a station wagon occupied by five sombre men. Although David is driving, the car belongs to his father, Bing, who's scrunched against the passenger door. Bing's youngest son sits between him and David. Periodically, I'm observed by David's other brothers who fidget on either side of me. I pretend not to notice, and instead concentrate on easing the tension in my shoulders.

Despite my reservations about attending this intimate ceremony, I am proud of David's desire to have me here. With his mother gone and his father apathetic to everything but her absence, he sees no reason to hide our long romance. My pregnancy is not yet obvious, and his brothers couldn't care less about keeping their family racially pure.

Bing's apathy could fade, though, once the worst of his grief has passed. Two years ago, at a wedding banquet for an interracial couple, David overheard him say, "Any son who marries a white woman is no son of mine." David knew he meant it, and although he had no intention of breaking with me to please his father, neither had he wanted a battle before it was necessary. Should Bing oppose our marriage, David believes he now has the strength to confront his father, to take a stand for his own happiness — a parting gift from his mother, I think.

~

David learned that his mother had cancer, and that it was terminal, six months ago. His father didn't trust white doctors and modern medical technology, and arranged to take her to China and Hong Kong in search of a miracle cure. David and Bing thought it best to let the rest of the family think ulcers were causing her stomach pain. I didn't understand the secrecy until David explained that traditional Chinese parents don't discuss family crises with their children, and children, regardless of age, are not considered adults until they marry. As the oldest and most responsible son, however, David was privileged with the truth.

He and Bing decided that his mother also wouldn't be told she was dying; they were afraid the truth would exacerbate her illness. I suggested she might want the chance to say good-bye, and to clear up any misunderstandings in her family. Irritated, David remarked that my Western thinking was so narrow I couldn't imagine other points of view. I backed down and shut up until I found out that father and son had also discussed my future.

When Bing mentioned his wife's will and the possibility of an inheritance, David told him about us. Bing's only response was to ask that we postpone any marriage plans until her death. David agreed. Although we hadn't set a wedding date, I was annoyed that he'd made this decision without consulting me. David couldn't believe my selfishness. I could scarcely believe it myself. Since the last thing I wanted was to upset the family, I found myself waiting for a woman I'd never met to die.

~

Bing's fingertips glide along the tips of countless incense sticks protruding from the paper bag in his lap. David calls them joss sticks. He said they're the "wire to the other side," a form of symbolic communication with ancestors. The bag crackles loudly in the silence; the brothers on either side of me are on edge, listening.

Roland sits on my right. His shoulder-length hair is tied back, suit jacket folded over his legs, shirt sleeves rolled up to expose the tattoos. On his left arm, an eagle carries a snake in its beak. The snake is coiled and wriggling to get away; the eagle's eyes are glittering, coy and triumphant.

～

David's parents planned to stay overseas for four months. Two months after they left, a letter announced a change of plans. Apparently, his mother wanted to see her sons. Then, three weeks before she was to come home, she died. His father telephoned from Kowloon to say she'd be taken to his village for a ceremony, then brought back to Canada.

His mother had climbed thirteen flights of stairs the day before she died. The elevator in the complex they were staying at was out of order, and she had wanted to go out. David seemed proud of her stamina. I looked upon this as another example of her stubbornness. She'd experienced stomach pain for two years before consulting a doctor, and only gave up her busy schedule when David's father sold the store; a sign, possibly, that he'd suspected how ill she was.

～

The sweet, spicy aroma of incense glides down my lungs and lies there, dissolving. David's father and brothers reek of it. Chuck, who sits on my left, keeps his head turned toward the window. A long red bag of joss sticks lies across his legs. In the front seat, seventeen-year-old Jamie doesn't move while David and his father quietly speak in Cantonese. The resemblance between David and his father is not strong. David has high cheekbones, seductively arched brows and long brown eyes. Although he too is handsome, Bing is small and squarish. There is pride and quiet strength in the way he moves his head.

In the car, the smell of incense grows stronger; dizzying, intoxicating, nauseating. At the stoplight, David looks at me in the rear view mirror. His brow relaxes, his eyes fill with gratitude and love. Next month we'll move in together. He wants to make wedding plans. Lately, he seems ashamed of his pain and irritability over recent weeks, embarrassed that his mother's death has affected him so profoundly.

～

Aware of David's career pressures, his father said he didn't have to make the trip; but for David there was no choice. He would take Roland, who wanted to see his mother one last time. David had never been close to his mother, and had often complained about her nagging, prying nature, but he felt he should share the burden of funeral arrangements. Guilt was an equally strong motive, I suspect; the trip was his penance for his inability to either understand or accept the bitter, unhappy person his mother had been.

David's mother grew up in China and, before Mao Tse-tung's Communists took control, was attended by maids and servants. An arranged marriage to Bing at age seventeen found her working long days in rice paddy fields and performing household chores in a village without electricity, hot water, or plumbing facilities. Shortly after she became pregnant with David, Bing left for Canada to seek a better life. Four years later, he returned to bring her and David to Vancouver.

Their new home was a cockroach-infested tenement, three blocks from Chinatown, where they shared kitchen and bathroom with other families. Since David's father was juggling three jobs at that time, his mother was often alone and isolated from the world by a language barrier. After Bing bought their first house she had three more babies, cleaned, cooked, sewed, hand-washed her family's clothes, and tended their large vegetable garden. When David's father later moved them to another home with a small convenience store at the front, she also ran the store fourteen hours a day, learning just enough English to manage simple requests. When her sons reached their teens, she often cooked separate suppers to accommodate everyone's schedules and tastes. She rarely took a night off, never ate in a restaurant, saw a movie, or wandered through a department store. She was always too busy, too exhausted and later, too ill.

~

While waiting for his passport and visa, and struggling with grief, guilt, love, and regret, David recalled fragments of his life in China, chasing ducks and riding the backs of baby water buffaloes. Part of him was excited to see the village again, to meet people he hadn't seen in over twenty-five years. Part of him needed to reaffirm his roots while he still could. If he is disowned for marrying me, it will also mean a split with his culture. Since David has few relatives in Canada and most of his Chinese friends are Westernized second- and third-generation Canadians, his father is a crucial link to his heritage and the customs handed down by word of mouth. Only his mother had known his birth date by the Chinese calendar, a date she'd never converted to the Gregorian calendar.

~

At the cemetery we are escorted to a small plot covered by a square patch of grass. I contemplate David's mother's plaque: a gorgeous slab of black marble fifteen inches wide and twenty-four inches long. Brass Chinese characters run vertically down each side; English words sprawl across the centre. David never told me his mother's name was Tsui Jing.

~

The trip overseas lasted five days. David returned pale, exhausted, and shocked because his relatives earned sixty cents a day; because they coveted the Safeway plastic bags he'd been carrying. He showed me photographs of the tiny, cluttered two-room apartment he'd shared with nine other people during his stay in Kowloon. David, his brother and father slept on the floor between paper-thin walls and the noise of a thousand families surrounding them. They left Kowloon by train, crossing the border to reach Canton. From Canton, they travelled to his father's village, completing the last part of the journey on foot. At the village, David was guided through a number of intricate and symbolic rituals that only he, as eldest son, could perform so Tsui Jing's spirit could travel to the "other side." One of his duties was to lead the funeral procession through the village to view her body before cremation. The entire ceremony was photographed for the brothers left behind.

I'd never seen David look so sad, lost, or ill as he did in those pictures. Dark circles punished his eyes; his complexion looked grey and flabby as he led a large group of people past gritty, peeling huts with narrow doorways and small apertures for windows. In his hands, David clutched a foot-high, framed photograph of his mother as a young woman. A white cloth was draped over his raincoat like a sash; a white cap covered his head.

~

David's father carefully opens a plastic bag I hadn't noticed in the car. He removes a black silk jacket, two shawls, and a large tin can. He then removes oranges and other food, four white candles, a small paper house, and what David, whispering in my ear, calls "hell bank notes." One by one, the clothes, paper house and money are set on fire in the tin can. With hands pressed together, the family bows to the plaque. I want to step back, out of their way, but my feet won't move.

~

The photographs of Tsui Jing's body haunt me. Inside the rectangular glass coffin, dozens of brilliantly coloured flowers surrounded her. Her calm, peaceful expression was a poignant contrast to the pained, anguished faces around her. Women were captured with mouths open in silent wails. In one shot, David's hands were outstretched as if wanting to touch her; in another, they were clasped together in despair. Tears streaked his cheeks, his face was twisted with grief. His father stood on his right, dry-eyed, stoic.

After the viewing, Tsui Jing was taken to the crematorium where officials were bribed to ensure her jewelry and clothes wouldn't be stolen, and that the ashes returned to the family would be hers. I wasn't prepared for the photographs of his mother lying before a rusty iron door: the scruples of a Christian religion that intrudes upon Eastern funeral rites. From the crematorium, mourners returned to Bing's ancestral home, a drab, four-hundred-year-old hut, to pay further tribute to Tsui Jing. Inside were photographs and, from earlier days, drawings of deceased family members. In one snapshot, Roland was bowing to his mother's photograph propped on a table below the others.

So that succeeding generations could provide for the spirits of the dead, it was necessary to move Tsui Jing's ashes near her children. As the eldest son, it was David's responsibility. David said this was one reason why his family would be against our marriage. Because I knew little about their culture, I wouldn't be able to provide for David or his ancestors if he died first. I wanted to say that as far as I was concerned Jesus Christ would look after everybody, but by then I had begun to learn.

From the moment David left the village to the moment he arrived at his parents' Canadian home, it was important that he verbally report every change of direction to his mother's ashes so her spirit wouldn't become lost along the way. I joked with him about talking to an urn in the middle of an airport. But David remarked that the ritual was five thousand years old; no one had questioned how it would look in airports.

Once the ashes were placed in his father's house, a small shrine was set up in the dining room. On the last day of official mourning when, according to custom, his mother's spirit was permitted to enter heaven, more ceremonies were performed at the house. The black arm bands they'd been wearing were burned with some of her clothes and an offering of food. When Bing decided to bury her ashes, Tsui Jing's photograph took central place in the shrine and remains there today, surrounded by vases of flowers, a bowl of fruit, and burning joss sticks, or so I'm told; I've never been in the house. I always know when David's been there, though; the odor of incense clings to his hair.

~

As the jacket and shawls turn to ash, David's father opens the paper bag and removes a handful of long yellow joss sticks. Carefully he lights the tips, then begins to plant the burning incense in the ground. With their red and pink joss sticks, his sons follow suit, and soon the whole family is planting sticks around Tsui Jing's plaque. I start to help, but David gently touches my arm, his eyes indicating that I am here to observe and learn, not to participate.

While the family works I gaze at the cemetery grounds, the fragile branches of trees in the distance. Beside us is an empty grave. When the first drop of rain plunks on my forehead David's father lowers his head, then closes his eyes. His expression becomes soft and morose, more vulnerable than in the photographs. David stares at the plaque, his hands clasped together, his expression solemn. The incense burns slowly. Hundreds of wispy spirals rise out of glowing red tips as the fragrant gums and spices dissipate in the air.

As I watch David's family, their grief overtakes me. I'd forgotten how tragedy lingers over graves the way incense lingers in rooms. I regret that Tsui Jing and I never met, that she won't see her son marry, or hold her grandchild. Still, I can't help feeling she is here now, studying my manner and appearance, just as her family has done, just as I have done to them. Nor can I escape the feeling that if David is still welcome in his family after our marriage, part of me always will be looking over my shoulder, stealing glances as we try to accept one another and respect what cannot be changed.

Noises erupt from the other side of the hill; human voices, ringing bells. A hearse glides over the slope followed by what must be a hundred mourners. The leader of the procession wears sandals and a black and orange robe; another man carries a large, opulently framed photograph of a middle-aged Chinese man. As they approach the grave beside us, their feet trample over Tsui Jing's joss sticks. Some of the mourners' eyes meet ours, then look away, uninterested. People walk close to Tsui Jing's plaque. Countless sticks are flattened or broken in half.

David glares at the mourners who rip our privacy apart. Roland's eyes are murderous. He glances at his father, waiting for a signal, but his father remains mute, motionless, watchful. The rain begins to fall. Rage grows inside me as the invaders open umbrellas.

Although our tributes have been paid, rituals performed, David's father does not leave. We stand with heads bowed, eyes on the plaque, the fallen incense sticks smouldering between clipped blades of grass. The rain penetrates my coat. Nearby, a woman sobs and I want to hit her. One of the mourners approaches, looking not the least embarrassed by his intrusion. He points at the tin can and nods quickly, as if to convince us it's all right for him to take the can. Silently, David's father gives the tin can away.

An hour later, the neighbouring ceremony is over, our small group alone again. David's father turns toward the parking lot. His sons follow him, raindrops trickling down their hair and onto their collars. In front of Tsui Jing's black marble plaque, I kneel on the soggy grass, then upright a fallen joss stick.

~

Originally from Toronto, **Debra Purdy Kong** was raised in British Columbia and is a criminology graduate from Douglas College (B.C.). She has been writing since 1980, has completed two murder mystery novels, and after thirteen years of secretarial work is now a full-time mother and writer. She has published work in such periodicals as *Chanticleer 2*, *Green's Magazine*, and *Dandelion*. "Parting Gifts" recently appeared in *Emergence II* (Spring 1994).

Seasoning

Elizabeth Entrup

I. In Which I Come Face to Face with the "Old Age Problem"

MY FIRST CONFRONTATION with the problems of aging occurred when my ninety-four-year-old grandmother suffered a blackout, fell, and broke her hip. She was rushed to the hospital and given an emergency operation the next day. She came through, but shortly afterwards, my mother was called to the hospital for a meeting with Grandma's doctor and a social worker. Their verdict: Grandma was too frail to be cared for by my mother as she had been for the previous four years and it was their recommendation that she be moved to a nursing home. My mother, who was scheduled for major surgery herself, had little choice but to agree. It was while Mom was recuperating that the hospital decided that Grandma's bed was needed. Within forty-eight hours, she was on her way to the first available nursing home.

I never went to see her. Partly it was because I had heard nursing homes called "warehouses of death" and worse, but also there was another, darker reason. My feelings toward my grandmother were ambiguous. When I thought about her, a parade of unpleasant scenes crossed my mind, most of which had taken place during the two years she had lived with my family during my adolescence. Grandma nagging and scolding, deriding my sisters and me as "overprivileged children"; Grandma urging my mother to throw hot coffee at me during an argument; Grandma reciting all of my misdeeds to my parents, looking on with self-righteous satisfaction when I was punished. Most people thought of her as an admirably stoic, high-principled, church-going woman who had raised six children on a dirt farm during the Depression, kept her house hospital-clean until she was over eighty, and survived a succession of serious illnesses that would surely have killed a lesser mortal, but to me she was a nemesis. I felt only relief when she elected to move to a seniors' lodge, and no guilt at all when I overheard my mother saying, "She won't live here because Elizabeth doesn't want her."

Gradually my resentment was replaced with a grudging admiration as I watched her cope successfully with a number of devastating incidents. She showed extraordinary courage when her husband and later her youngest daughter died, walking into both their funerals with her head held high. She was in constant, severe pain from arthritis but never complained. Several weeks before my sister Donna's wedding, she nearly died from toxaemia, but defied the doctors' dire predictions by putting up such a struggle to recover that she was able to attend the ceremony. "Grandma *die*?" I would say. "Grandma and death are polar opposites." Still, I could never bring myself to spend much time with her. Besides, the reports my family gave me on the nursing home were not encouraging. Mom, a great believer in positive thinking, managed to come up with one good thing to say about the place: it kept two cats as pets. My father said, "Well, *I* wouldn't want to live there." My youngest sister Diane said bluntly, "It's a dump."

Things seemed to go wrong from the start. Aside from Grandma's shock at leaving the hospital at such short notice, and then depression at being sent to an extended care centre, the hospital sent the wrong information about her medication dosage to the nursing home. At least that was what the nursing home officials said. The hospital board said that the nursing home officials were the culprits. Grandma also complained that the attendants treated her as if she were senile. Her physical and mental condition got rapidly worse.

"She isn't eating and she isn't sleeping," my mother said in tears. "At this rate, she won't last another month."

Finally, my grandmother was taken home until she could be moved to a more congenial nursing home. One day I helped watch her. It wasn't eventful; all I had to do was make sure Grandma was kept warm and given her lunch and medication. Although she spent most of the time sleeping, Mom handed me a ten-dollar bill at the end of the day.

"Grandma wanted you to have this for looking after her," she said. "I told her you wouldn't want it, but she insisted."

I went into the bedroom where Grandma was just waking up from her nap and tried to give the money back.

"You're welcome to anything I have," she said in a tired, faint voice. "I feel like such a burden." I assured her that nobody felt that way, but she wouldn't touch the money. She just shook her head wearily.

I felt depressed. Was this what I had to look forward to? For the first time it occurred to me that perhaps these debilitating effects of old age were the reasons behind her vindictive behaviour. It must have been difficult to be surrounded by vigorous young people and realize that their world was lost to you. But for now, I reflected, I *was* part of that world, so it was best not to think about aging. Grandma left for another nursing home, and I put the whole issue away.

That bout of temporary fear might have been the end of my confrontation with the aging process, except that my sister Donna, a student nurse, had a summer job doing homecare for elderly people. She often mentioned a ninety-one-year-old client named Mrs. Robertson who told marvelous stories.

"She's had a remarkable life," Donna said. "You should come and hear her."

So one day I found myself in the doorway of a high-rise apartment being greeted by a plump little woman with salt and pepper hair who embraced me and exclaimed, "You're beautiful! But of course no sister of Donna's could be anything else. I hope

I haven't embarrassed you, dear."

"Not at all," I said truthfully, although ordinarily I would have been ready to sink into the ground. But Mrs. Robertson had, in those few moments, completely won me over. Aside from her utterly open manner and obvious sincerity, there were her clothes. She was wearing a flannelette lounging suit in a black and white zebra design, earrings in the shape of black cats, and a large black-sequinned beret.

"This is my fun suit," she explained. "I don't usually wear it, but today a man my friends are trying to set me up with sent me the most depressing letter, so I wore this outfit to cheer myself up."

The walls of the apartment were covered with memorabilia: psychedelic hand-drawn pictures, newspaper clippings and Xeroxed poems, photographs of friends, but especially pictures of wild animals. She was particularly proud of a drawing of a tiger and her cubs which was vaguely familiar to me.

"That was the illustration on the front of the telephone directory two years ago. I had them enlarge it for me," she explained. "I never saw such love as in the eyes of that tiger." I remember thinking that anyone who associated love with a tiger had to be an unusual person, and the story she told proved me right.

II. Her Story

Mrs. Robertson: I was born at the edge of a forest. My father had some animals, a sort of farm and grew a lot of vegetables. We had to walk five miles to school and five miles home which we did in all weathers and then church on Sunday and Sunday school. We had a very happy home, love and discipline in that order, both plenty. No whippings, my parents simply said, "No," and that was enough. My mother had ten children and I was the second.

When the First World War broke out, my brothers and the farm hands went to war, so my father sold everything and we moved. I was thirteen and a half. I didn't want to start another school, so I worked as an afternoon tea waitress to avoid the principal because in those days you would be fined if you didn't go to school. I went to night school until I was seventeen because then you could choose what subjects you wanted, so I really didn't stop learning and I never have. And then, I flirted a lot with boys. I got engaged four times to four different boys, one after the other, because I thought I was in love, and then at twenty-two years of age I went to a midnight party and met my fate and then I knew that I'd never been in love because here I was totally in love. Within a month, we got married. My husband Kenneth had four degrees and spoke eight languages and couldn't get a job in 1923. Eventually, he became a writer. He worked for *National Geographic*, and then went to Africa. Two years later I joined him. Remember, we sailed on liners in those days and you were two months on the water, and I went out to the Mediterranean Sea and the Suez Canal to Mombasa, then four days by train, then by car to Kampala and there I met my husband. I promptly got pregnant with my second child, which was a great joy to me. I had a daughter five years old at that time. A firm was beginning a tourist trip for rich Americans and they wanted another hostess. They had camps, one day's run by car. And this was in a big game reserve: it had elephants, leopards, scorpions, snakes. Ten servants spoke Arabic, and I didn't. But the beautiful big black wives nursed me through a very severe attack of malaria and I could communicate with them because I had a few words of Swahili. I don't care where you are, whether it's France, Belgium, wherever — if you care, you can communicate. But then the British Governor come through on his yearly visit and saw me there and within two hours I was on my way out over the border because no white woman was allowed here. So I was taken out and came down to Uganda.

My husband was still writing, this time about a very rare animal, the okapi. He said that he would go to the Belgian Congo to photograph these animals in the company of a big-game hunter. So he set off, and he had paid for me to be in the hotel in Kampala in case I needed to go to the hospital because I was pregnant. Unfortunately, I had told him — you see, money has never been a real important thing in my life — I had said to him, "Put it all in your name" — because I'm a booklover — "so that I won't spend any on books because when you come back we're going to buy a house." He had been dead six weeks before anyone had the guts to tell me. He had blackwater fever. That's a tropical disease like malaria which attacks the kidneys. I believe they can cure it today, but I'm talking about 1930. As soon as I heard, I went straight into the hospital and within three hours I had produced my second child a little prematurely. Kathleen, a little girl. And here I had told Kenneth before he went, "Put all the money in your name," so everything was frozen! It took three years before I even got a death certificate.

Now I'm a very proud woman. So when my baby was born and I was in the hospital, somebody brought me in a daily magazine and I was reading it. It said, "Buy a ticket for the dance of such a day, for the fund for the young widow and two children who are in immediate need of money." I didn't cry over my husband's death, at first because I was in shock and, later, because spiritually I believe you go when you're called. And you should not cry when anyone dies, let them go free. You shouldn't hold them. If you cry for them, you hold them on the earth and that is the wrong thing to do. So I never cried. Some people thought I was very brave, and other people thought I didn't care. It didn't matter to me what they thought anyway. But I saw this and I had never cried but now I cried because of the pride in me. But luckily for me they raised five hundred pounds to meet expenses.

Then I left the Congo and I came back round the Cape, so I'd circumnavigated Africa. And I came back to London, England, and my mother-in-law wanted me to go and see them in Aberdeen. My husband had been an only child, very spoilt by this old, aristocratic Englishwoman married to a Scot, and she wanted to adopt my first-born, Joan, who was very, very like her father. And I refused. I said, "No" — my father-in-law was a preacher, so he would understand — I said, "No, I can't sell my daughter for a mess of pottage." I couldn't do that. To me it was wrong; she was my daughter and she would have to share what we had, even if it was nothing. But I was in a weak emotional state and so they typed out an article where they would keep her for a year and at the end of the year, if I could give her what they could give her, I could have her back. And I didn't know what to do. You know, I always prayed to God to help me and I believe completely that He certainly always has and always will. So I went to Aberdeen and I prayed all the time silently, "Dear God, please guide my footsteps to the best solicitor in Aberdeen." I walked along one street that was all lawyers and solicitors on both sides. I walked, looking at the names, and I suddenly stopped at a brass plate. And there was an open door with some steps. I had no hesitation; I went up. And the lawyer could see me right away. And I showed him this article and I explained the conditions and so he read it and said, "You must not sign this. You're signing away your daughter for the rest of your life unless you can keep her in the conditions that they can and you can't do that." So I went back to my mother and father-in-law and I said, "My lawyer says I mustn't sign it."

"Huh! Your lawyer!" my mother-in-law said. "And who would that be?"

And when I mentioned the name, she said, "That's the best lawyer in Aberdeen. How did you know?"

I had to leave Joan with them, but I wouldn't sign anything. Within six months they wrote and urged me to come and pick her up because four or five times she had wandered away with her goldfish bowl to find her way to London to her mother, and they had all the police force out looking for her. So I went and got her.

We all lived together. I cleaned people's houses, one in the morning, one in the afternoon. That's three bedrooms, bathroom, down the stairs, hall, dining room, drawing room, kitchen, scullery, step by step, three hours. Ten pennies an hour was the going rate. The baby I put in the pram and took with me until she was three years old. Then I got her into a kindergarten school and paid a little for her. I worked up quite a clientele because I was quick and thorough and honest. One woman said, "You don't even steal my tea." I said, "Madam, if I'm going to clean your house from top to bottom, I have no time to look into your tins to find tea, and I do have tea at home." And I fired her for daring to think I would steal.

And anyway, then, when the youngest was five years old I couldn't earn enough to support them. The thirties Depression was terrific, it was very, very hard, very bad. And one day I opened my purse to get money for some bread and milk. And there wasn't any money. Now, I've never been one to sit down and cry and say the world owes me a living because it doesn't, because each one of us is in the position we are in because we put ourselves there from choice. We always have the choice. And I married Kenneth, so don't let me cry about it.

So I went home and I found a cup of rice. I boiled the rice and I was able to put a bit of sugar in it and I filled our cups with water and I said to the kids, "Let's pretend this is the best cup of tea we ever had in our lives." And we drank it. And that taught me the greatest lesson of my life, that *money is not important.* To my surprise, we didn't die, we were still alive the next morning, so that put money in its proper place. Money isn't important, and most people think it's the most important thing in the world. And people *slave* till they're seventy or eighty to acquire a fortune and then drop dead. Hallelujah! It's so odd, isn't it?

Me: (with some trepidation) Are you afraid of death?

Mrs. Robertson: (laughing) Oh, no, I'm longing to go. My body is tired. No, I'm not afraid, but I also realize that it's not my choice this time; this time I have to wait. But I'm a very good example of old age, aren't I?

Me: Indeed you are.

Mrs. Robertson: You know, the reason is, because I'm *alive.* I said to the doctor, "You know, I have a lot of wonderful friends." And he said, "That doesn't surprise me. You're so sexy." I said, "Sexy? Me? I don't even look at a man." He said, "You don't have to. You're oozing sex." And I said, "Well, I have a very, very strong sexual urge." He said, "Do you go out and get a man?" I answered, "Do you think I want AIDS? No, I have a very good two-speed vibrator." Then I said to the doctor, "I want to ask you a serious question. I have this sex urge which is so terrific I don't know what to do. It's so ferocious. Shouldn't it stop? Shouldn't it be dead?" And he said, "No. Don't knock it. That's what gives you the life. That's why you're so young-looking and young-acting. Be thankful."

Me: What about the emotional aspect of aging? Has aging limited you? Do you feel isolated by it?

Mrs. Robertson: No, on the contrary. I'm busier now than I ever was when I worked. When I was working, I went home and spent the evening alone more often than not. A lot of people, they begin thinking about fifty, "*Oh*, when I retire I can sit and do nothing." That's the worst thing you can think of doing, sitting down and doing nothing. This man, for instance, that they're trying to mate me up with. He sings the blues all the time. He's lonely, he's unhappy, he wants love and companionship. Even in his first letter to me, he said, would I go out and share his home. I thought, my God, I'd have to know a person a long time before I'd think about doing that. Besides, I'm not about to give up my way of life.

Me: Then aging hasn't changed your way of life?

Mrs. Robertson: It has enhanced my life. I'm able to do what I want. I'm a great letter-writer. That's one of my chief joys, and reading. Also travelling. I told my two daughters and their husbands and my adult grandchildren about five years ago, "Please don't give me any *thing* for my birthday, Mother's Day, or Christmas. Because I have enough junk. Just give me money, from five dollars up." And it all goes into a travel fund. The last time, I went to Finland and Russia. All my sisters and brothers have lived normal lives. They bought a house and got settled in it, then they married and they had their children and they've one address for the rest of their lives. You'd need a whole book for my addresses because I'm never in one place five minutes. Movement. Freedom. Freedom is the great answer.

Me: You seem to have a great many friends.

Mrs. Robertson: Yes. A woman phoned me this morning. I've been writing to her for about twenty-five years. She wanted to meet me. Another family came the other day to take me out to lunch. And then this other woman turned up for the evening and sat till nine o'clock. I like to go to bed at eight o'clock and read. So I see that I'm going to have to start saying no to some people in order to preserve my freedom which is so very dear to me. (She paused a little, reflectively.) You see, you make your life. You have your choice.

III. In Which I Come to Terms with the Seasoning Process

I felt reflective on leaving Mrs. Robertson. Sometimes, there is no choice. Mrs. Robertson cannot dictate the time of her death; my grandmother cannot control her increasingly frail body. And I have no choice about growing older. But we can choose whether to continue to enjoy life and find it meaningful. My grandmother had chosen to keep a stiff upper lip towards the adversities in her life, but had become bitter and disapproving in the process. Mrs. Robertson had made the decision that despite bodily decay, there was still much left to enjoy, including the younger generation, to whom she left her gift of story.

I thought of something my father had told me. "Don't say 'aging.' It's negative," he said. "Say something like 'seasoning.'"

Seasoning. It was an interesting term, with connotations of ripening, maturing, the adding of a piquant flavour. I thought of Mrs. Robertson and her vigour, her resilience, her ability to savour life as long as it lasted, and of my grandmother's remarkable capacity to endure.

I agreed that it was a much better word.

~

Elizabeth Entrup was born and raised in Alberta. At various times, she has been an office worker, a bookstore sales clerk, a research assistant, an English instructor at Red Deer College, and served as an editorial assistant on *Eating Apples*. "Seasoning" is her first publication and is dedicated to the older women who have shaped us.

Letter to a dead friend who missed the high school reunion

Shirley A. Serviss

EAR SONYA,

I missed you at the twenty-year high school reunion this summer. I cried, in fact — right in the middle of the dinner and dance — when I finally realized what was missing for me that night was you. You were so much a part of my high school life, it seemed strange to be there without you. But of course you couldn't come back; you've been dead for most of those twenty years.

Norm wasn't there either; he missed the ten-year reunion too. I always wanted to tell him it wasn't his fault you died when his Volkswagen hit the bus. Do you remember the night we all sat around at your pyjama party and tried to imagine life after high school? We could picture what Elaine, Sandy, and I would be like and what we'd be doing, but when we came to you, we grew silent. We could see you in jeans, burning incense, but couldn't predict past the present.

You weren't the only one missing from the reunion. Some didn't even bother to reply to the invitation and others never received one. "I don't know where he is and I don't want to know," Eric's mother told the committee. Some, like Marjorie, live too far away; she's nursing in Hawaii now and sent photos of her family walking on the beach, but her letter didn't say anything about her fight with cancer. Others, like Susan and Mona, were finishing up degrees. Roberta had spent all her money adopting children.

Some probably didn't want to talk about the years they've lost to psychiatric wards, the relationships they've been through, their failed dreams and ambitions. Others came between jobs or between relationships because in twenty years they've learned that's not what's important. Those of us who were there weren't much changed on the surface: a few grey hairs, a few wrinkles, a few more pounds, or — in some cases — a few less pounds and a bit less hair.

Sandy phoned me to see what I was planning to wear. I haven't talked to her for at least nineteen years and she calls long distance to ask what I'm going to wear. I felt as though I was back in high school all over again. "Are you going to wear pantyhose?" she wondered. "I don't know," I said. "It depends on the weather; it depends on whether or not I've shaved my legs."

Would you have come to the reunion, Sonya, if you'd been alive? I'm not sure. Perhaps you'd have come out of curiosity, as I did. There was so much I wanted to know about people, but still didn't know how to ask. What happened to those babies our classmates had when they disappeared for a term or two and reappeared? What was it like to have a child when you were little more than a child yourself? What was it like to give your baby away?

I certainly couldn't have imagined — back in high school — that I would choose to become an unwed mother at age thirty-four. Times change and time catches up to us.

Would you have had children, Sonya? Would some of those young boys standing taller than their mothers have belonged to you? Or one of those lovely teenaged girls who danced with their fathers? Would you have been a grandmother like Linda or a late starter like Marian and me? Our daughters spilled pop down their fronts and collected caterpillars at the picnic on Sunday while our classmates talked about varicose veins.

Varicose veins! I couldn't believe that's what we'd come to in twenty years. I tried to change the subject to hemorrhoids, but it didn't catch on.

Stan contemplated not coming with me to the reunion; he wasn't sure he wanted to spend his precious holidays on another trip back to Saskatchewan, and I can't blame him. But I panicked. All of a sudden I was right back in high school, standing against the gym wall, feeling more ugly by the minute, praying someone would ask me to dance. It was so frightening to realize that all my accomplishments in the intervening years could be erased by an invitation to a high school reunion. I'm just as bad as Sandy; I'm sure she doesn't call her co-workers in the morning to find out what they're going to wear to work that day.

In the end, he agreed to come along — my trophy husband. I brought a different one to the ten-year reunion. Some of us have made a hobby of collecting wedding rings.

"Tell me how you met your husband?" Connie asked.

"Which one?" I replied. It gave me a certain amount of pleasure to go from the girl without a single date to the woman of several husbands.

You would have been proud of me at the reunion, Sonya. I actually struck up the odd conversation with boys I never dared talk to in high school who have turned into men with interesting jobs and attractive blond wives. Remember how devastated I was when I asked Dennis to a Sadie Hawkins dance and he turned me down? He wasn't at the reunion and I was disappointed. I wanted to see those frosty blue eyes of his again — eyes not unlike my current husband's, I just realized.

Do you remember us being teased about being lesbians because we walked each other to our classes and spent every moment we could together engrossed in each other's company? I didn't even know what the word meant, but you made a joke of it, and held my hand in the hallways just for spite. I spent years trying to discover if my attraction to women meant I was gay and finally did go to bed with a good friend just to put the issue at rest.

We were incredibly intimate, Sonya — sitting on your bed reading Leonard Cohen and Shakespeare to each other all those nights I stayed in town at your parents' home — but our relationship was never sexual despite what people thought.

Of course you remember Margo, my best friend until I met you. She shared seats with me all those years on the school bus, shared stories of an adolescence so unlike my own — the drinking parties at the gravel pit, the necking sessions on some back road. Margo always had some boyfriend's ring taped to her finger like a talisman and was forever taunting me for my innocence, my refusal to smoke or shoplift, swear or wear makeup, my insistence on being square.

Yet we faithfully sent each other Christmas letters all these years and I thought we were still friends — fool that I always was when it came to her. It seemed too dangerous not to be her friend; she appeared so powerful to me back then because of her popularity.

Margo looked exactly the way she had in high school, but this time I saw her differently. She wore too much eye makeup, her heels were too high and her hair was still streaked. She pretended to have mistaken me for my older sister and made a big deal about the fact that I had a beer in my hand. It turned out we really didn't have much else to say to each other, but of course I sought her out to say good-bye. (Old habits of courting favour die hard.) What she didn't know was that I meant it — no more Christmas letters.

I can't tell you how freeing it was to realize I didn't need her anymore. "You never did," my seventy-nine-year-old mother explained to me the next morning at breakfast. "She was the one who needed you." And I thought of all the adolescent poetry I wrote that she told me she's saving, waiting for me to become famous.

I still haven't become famous, you know, but I'm working on it. Maybe by the thirty-year reunion. Do you know what Dan Semchuk said to me? (Maybe you wouldn't even remember him — he was a farm boy and I think he still farms with his dad.) He came up to me on Sunday and said, "If you ever have a book published, Shirley, I'd like a copy." It made my whole weekend.

Take risks, Sonya — wherever you are.

Your friend for life (mine),
Shirley

~

Shirley A. Serviss was born in 1953 and has been writing for most of her life. She has earned a living by working in broadcasting, journalism, and public relations, but poetry is her first love. Her work has appeared in a variety of literary publications in Canada, Ireland, and Great Britain. Her first collection of poetry, *Model Families*, was published by Rowan Books in 1992. It describes her experience of living in a blended family with her husband, stepson, and daughter. Shirley lives in Edmonton and works from her home as a freelance writer/editor.

Body of Knowledge

*O*F COURSE, ALL KNOWLEDGE comes to us through the body: our mind making sense of what we touch, taste, see, hear, and smell. But these selections resonate with particular bodily knowledge, a particular self-knowledge, one traditionally conceded to women; it is a knowledge that comes not so much through as because of the body. It can involve joy; but it is often ambiguous and sometimes bitter. For too often the physical imperative includes the learning of limitations, the lesson of fear.

Usually to be a woman is to be smaller, is to be physically weaker, is to be vulnerable to attack. One *learns* one must always be careful, always curtailed. Both Desirée Freeman in "Condemned to Fly" and Lorna Millard in "Fear of Falling" recount being threatened by a strange man and the resultant fear that, in itself, becomes another kind of threat. The adrenalin rush that brings the ability to fight back later turns to anxiety and insomnia, until both learn to combat the threat and challenge the limitations.

In Roberta Morris's "A Feminist Ovary Goes Its Own Way," Laurel Wade's "Memento Mori," Shelley Banks's "The Lucky Ones," and Diana Chown's "Treatments," the threat comes from within rather than from without. It is the female body itself that is the betrayer. For Morris, a ruptured ovary becomes an occasion for celebrating female (and her own) sexuality. No self-knowledge, no mental attitude can give Wade control over her reproductive system or Banks and Chown control over cancer cells. Worse, all three are forced to submit to medical indignities that seem worse than their cause. Whimsy and an eventual distance facilitate not control, but resignation and stoicism.

Achieving an appropriate and helpful state of mind becomes even more difficult in Caterina Edwards's "Care Calling Care" and Emma Pivato's "A Song for Alexis." The limitation that needs to be accepted is twofold: a limitation of the other and a limitation of the self. What is the right thing to do? And what is possible for me to do? Edwards's and Pivato's responses are naturally different. But shining through their essays is respect for the person locked within the body (father-in-law or daughter) that is both demonstrated and created through care of the body. In exploring her complex and ambiguous emotions towards her multihandicapped daughter, Pivato has given us a reexamination of the value of service, as well as a testimony to unsung female heroism.

A Song for Alexis

Emma Pivato

Part I—Spring, 1981

T HE PAIN. IT IS HARD NOW TO even begin to recapture the pain. Loss, limitation, everything changed.

My baby. My beautiful baby. So hurt. What did this to her? What picked away at her brain? When?

Alexis was nine months old when she was finally diagnosed. I knew, of course. I knew before she was born. My training is in developmental psychology and I already had two older children. But others felt I was wrong, over-anxious. Finally, my paediatrician referred me to a specialist to satisfy me.

I don't think there is anything the matter with her but I am giving you the name of this specialist to consult just for your own peace of mind. I know how you worry about these things, Mrs. Pivato.

I went home walking on air and almost threw the card away. Alexis was all right! It *was* my imagination! But my brother, who had shared my concerns over her development, insisted that I make the appointment.

November 9, 1978

I waited with my family in the cheerful reception area outside the specialist's office. My son, age four, and daughter, three, played happily with the many toys. The sun shone through the large windows. It was a beautiful fall day outside. I had a sudden sense of euphoria. The children were on their way. My husband had recently received a full-time university appointment and I was half-way through my doctoral studies. Surely, the struggle we had been through the past few years was almost over and nothing awful would come along to mar our life now.

The resident examined Alexis carefully, questioning me closely about her history and commenting about some irregularity in the eye. Then the specialist came in, examined her briefly and conferred with the resident. After, he turned to me and said

You are very right to be concerned about your daughter, Mrs. Pivato. She is functioning at a two-month level instead of a nine-month level. She must be a great burden to you.

I felt stunned, paralysed. "Why?" I croaked, with a great effort.

The damage is central, and probably severe. From what you have told me and what our ophthalmological examination reveals, I would say it was Rubella Syndrome due to exposure to German measles during early pregnancy. In addition to the extensive central damage she appears to be blind and I would not be surprised if she was deaf as well.

When I returned to the waiting room I was surprised to see it still sunny and cheerful and Janni and Juliana still playing happily with the toys. There was my husband, interest in his face — but no fear. I could not feel the floor. The light pierced my eyes. They all looked strangely different. They *were* different. Everything was different now.

"What did he say?" I heard Joe's voice vaguely, some concern in it now. Then I told him. I waited for it to sink in, for his face to alter, to focus in on this enormous event — but it did not change. "The doctor is wrong," he said, flatly. "They don't know everything, you know. You believe in them too much." Rarely in my life have I felt so alone as I did at that moment.

When we got home I put Alexis down on the kitchen table in her snowsuit and said, "Alexis, look at me." She turned towards me and smiled. Three times I said it and three times she responded in the same way. "She hears!" I exclaimed. "I know she hears — and sees too!" Then I collapsed against the back door, overwhelmed by grief. Janni and Juliana milled around me, frightened and confused, not understanding what was happening.

Those first nights. Waking suddenly, a moment of peace — then remembering and the pain flooding over me. Alexis! — with her beautiful, sensitive face, not really there, lost somewhere in the past. Only the body left. I wished she would just die so the mockery, the obscenity of it, would end.

I thought of the life Joe and I had planned so carefully: for us — academic careers, research projects, the occasional conference together; for the children — string music lessons which I hoped would culminate in their own little chamber music trio, other languages including the French immersion program at school and Italian on Saturdays, switching easily from one to another in the home; for the family — the trips, the sabbatical years in Europe, the concerts, plays and restaurants we had hoped to share together.

Little of this plan remained viable. Alexis's remediation program, which I planned to start immediately, would be very time-consuming. I could forget about a career, at least for the next few years, and also about the children's music lessons, which consumed a lot of my energy. And, of course, there could never be a trio now. Somehow, that was the hardest dream of all to let die.

The specialist had told me that Alexis would probably never walk or talk. This would make family outings difficult or impossible. It also meant that if she were to have any chance of developing speech we could not confuse her by speaking a second language in the home. But worst of all was the fact that everything Joe and I had learned to value in life, all the skills and interests we had worked so long to develop, would be forever cut off from Alexis. There was absolutely no possibility of ever sharing any but the most basic experiences with her.

All the hopes and all the dreams I had cherished for my family were completely gone, and in their place was nothing I could see of value — nothing but endless struggle and sacrifice. My spirit revolted inside me. Hadn't I lost enough already, my first husband and both parents — all under very painful circumstances. Hadn't

I suffered and struggled enough in pursuit of education and other idols? Wasn't it time now to relax and reap the rewards of all this sacrifice? No, I could not cope with this latest twist of fate! The pain rolled over me in endless waves. I did not know how I could go on.

And that is when Eleanor came into my life. I knew her only slightly as the mother of my babysitters and the wife of a Lutheran pastor. She brought me books to read about families with a handicapped child — Christian families. I ignored that aspect of them and read them greedily. Every Friday morning she came to bring me new books and to discuss the ones from the week before. At her request, I politely allowed her to pray over Alexis. Since I was an atheist of many years' standing this embarrassed me more than a little and I kept hoping that none of my "intellectual" friends would ever visit me during these times.

With the help of Eleanor and other friends the days passed, but the nights remained very difficult. I would wake suddenly, remember, and then be unable to sleep again. I spent the better part of many nights rocking endlessly in our big living room chair and staring meaninglessly out the window. "Why this?" I asked, over and over. "Why not anything but this?" Mental handicap! My whole life had been dedicated to the development of the intellect. And now to have this — a child who could not think. It made an utter joke out of all I had struggled so hard to achieve.

One night, as I sat rocking in the chair, I thought about Eleanor and her God. He did not seem such a shocking and ridiculous idea as He once had. But no! I was simply habituating to this concept which I had now been exposed to for several months through Eleanor's weekly visits. Also, I knew I was a prime candidate for brainwashing because of my state of physical and emotional exhaustion. The additional stress of Alexis's frequent seizures night and day had then begun.

I mentally shook myself and retreated to my inner fortress of intellectual certainty. But it was no longer there! For a long moment I sat shocked, peculiarly suspended in time and space, with no frame of reference. Then, gradually, I felt cold all over —

and I realized that I was no longer alone. I recognized the God of my childhood standing waiting there for me, as if I had never been away, as if all my suffering had bridged the gap between us. I felt a strange humility and a new certainty. I drank my coffee and went to bed.

Part II — July, 1992

When I awoke the next morning there was still pain but never again the kind you could drown in, the kind that could engulf you so completely as to destroy your very identity. I had some distance now, some perspective. Alexis and I were finally two separate beings.

In the months that followed anger came, and a type of arrogance stirred by a strange logic. I knew now that this terrible thing had really happened — but I also knew that there had to be a reason. Not some ignominious, accidental twist of fate such as exposure to German measles, as the doctor had suggested, but some nobler, more purposeful reason. And if there must be a reason, then what exactly was the reason? Since I was the one who was suffering so much it clearly must be connected to me; something to do with me and my destiny.

I retreated into a narcissistic fog, mentally stroking myself, feeling out the contours of my strengths. There was a mission in this for me, something I was supposed to do. But what? Fix Alexis? Even then I knew that was impossible. No. My mission must extend beyond Alexis. It must be to right the balance, to bring more good into the world than the evil that had been visited upon Alexis and our family. During these musings the God who had so recently returned to my world remained but He gradually assumed a more peripheral position. His primary purpose now, in my world view, was teleological, to provide a paradigm into which to fit this new logic, to render plausible this new perspective.

Within a week of Alexis's diagnosis at nine months of age as severely and multihandicapped I had enroled her in an Infant Stimulation Group and begun to inform myself of every other program, technique, or device that could possibly assist children with her problems. Alexis has low and fluctuating muscle tone (athetosis). She cannot sit independently or stand. She is cortically blind and cannot talk. She communicates only by smacking her lips if she is thirsty and fussing if she is cold, hungry, bored, or uncomfortable. She has a defective swallow reflex. She can eat only puréed food and continues to have petit mal, grand mal, and apnoeic (brain stem) seizures which cannot be controlled well medically. In the midst of all my grieving and musing I was therefore aware, at a very practical level, that nothing existed which was going to help Alexis very much. This knowledge lent further legitimacy to my newfound sense of destiny and allayed any compunctions I might have about sacrificing myself and the other members of my family to this self-embraced mission.

The years that followed, from 1979 to 1984, were my peak advocacy years. I worked in a megalomaniacal fervour to fix Alexis, to change the system, to help other parents. The GRIT program (an intensive, in-home early intervention program different from anything previously tried) was launched; a collection of stories about the impact of children with mental handicaps on family life was completed; and the first breaches in the barriers to integration of children with multiple disabilities were made in Alberta. That was, and remains, the most intense and satisfying period in my life, to date.

Caught up in the endless struggles around me I finally understood Albert Camus's character in *La Peste*. An alienated man feels happy and connected to others for the first time when all around him are dying of the plague. I, too, felt more deeply connected than ever before. I was connected to other mothers struggling with seizures, operations, chronic illness, and sometimes the death of their disabled children. I belonged, belonged in a way that, as a somewhat awkward and eccentric person always marching to the tune of a different drummer, I had never belonged before. My long-term struggle to find meaning in life was over. Life now had meaning with a vengeance.

But by 1984, I was beginning to realize that this meaning was an illusion. My life was not really full, only busy. All these endless projects relating to Alexis were like pebbles skittering madly over the surface of a pond. There was no depth. To ground oneself in Alexis was to ground oneself in a negativity, somewhat akin to a black hole where everything went in and nothing ever came out. One day I looked around at all the discarded toys, devices, projects, dreams that had failed to fix Alexis. Nothing ever worked, not really. For every painful half-step forward there were two steps back because of the endless, vicious seizures and the truly overwhelming extent of her disabilities. In a moment of weakness and self-pity I focussed inward, away from "the project." With mild surprise I realized that the nagging back pain I had experienced for years was now constant and close to unbearable.

If you take complete bed rest for a month the disc material may go back in place and you may not have to have an operation. In any case you must avoid lifting completely for a year. The nerve damage you have already suffered is very close to being permanent. If you don't listen to what I am saying now you will likely end up paralysed and in a wheelchair yourself.

Tough words from a doctor disgusted by my cavalier disregard for earlier warning signs and my stubborn insistence that Alexis could not survive without my physical involvement. Somehow it became possible to organize assistance for Alexis and I had lots of time to think while lying in bed. A new crisis, a new stage. What to do now?

My husband was due for sabbatical and had an opportunity to continue his research at the University of Toronto. The older children seemed to be getting out of hand and were clearly suffering from the unorthodoxies of our family life. At that point about one hundred different people a week were coming in to help us carry out a patterning program with Alexis and that was just one part of her regimen, a grinding, demanding, soul-destroying regimen that squeezed all joy and spontaneity from our lives. Furthermore, she was now too old for the GRIT program and different arrangements would have to be made for the fall. I thought and I thought, the constant pain in my back giving a new edge of practicality to my musings. Finally, I reached a conclusion.

Alexis, we all love you and you are part of us. Surely, you must know that. We have all suffered and sacrificed because of you. If you are truly a part of this family, then part of the price of belonging is that you must take your lumps, too. We are all in bad shape at this point. Our need is overwhelming. It is your turn to take second best so the rest of us can survive.

And so it was decided. Alexis would remain in Edmonton and the rest of the family would go to Toronto for a year.

Having reasoned this far, all that remained was to determine what compromise we could offer Alexis. She could go to school in a special class setting where a good friend of mine was the teacher. It fell short of my ideal of integration but I trusted my friend to do her very best by her and felt sure Alexis would survive without too much damage. Now what about a home setting? Our GRIT assistant, who worked closely with Alexis on a daily basis, had developed an excellent relationship with her and knew exactly what it took to meet her needs. Kathy and her soon-to-be husband, Andy, were looking for a missionary-type challenge, some way to really make a difference in this world. I suggested they move into our house for a year and care for our daughter so that we could have the break we badly needed. Around-the-clock care for a completely helpless six-year-old with violent seizures would provide enough challenge for anyone, I argued. After a short deliberation they agreed. It was then March and in August, just a few weeks after their wedding, we would leave.

The night before we left for Toronto I did not go to bed. I had had no time to spend with Alexis the previous day and all night I continued my obsessive work to leave the house in meticulous order. We left at ten in the morning, before I could get the sheets out of the dryer to make the bed, the last task. I cried all the way to Winnipeg. Clouds of guilt kept wisping through my head. At times I felt I could hardly breathe. How could I be doing this? We phoned home. Alexis was fine. Slowly, I began to become human again.

Toronto. In Toronto I got my children back. In Toronto I got a job, a real job with real money where people were grateful for what contribution I made and did not criticize me and question my motives. In Toronto I got my life back. We almost moved there. That was just before the big boom. We still talk fondly of our year in Toronto.

Alexis did survive. We arranged with a friend to bring her out at Christmas. She seemed happy to see us and we spent a good ten days together. When she returned home I phoned and talked to her. She can't talk but when she heard my voice she said "eugh, eugh, eu-oow, eu-ool," with all the rising intonation of indignation. It was as close as I have ever been to her and perhaps the most bittersweet moment of my life. She was there. She felt abandoned but that meant that she knew me. I wanted desperately to reassure her, but she could not understand my words. I wanted above all else to hug her, but she was two thousand miles away. People should not have to live through such moments. They are unbearable in their poignancy. They change you forever.

After our family sabbatical we came home and picked up our life where we left it, except from that time on I have always worked for money. Alexis did have an accident in our absence and chipped her permanent front teeth. Whenever I look at them I think

That is the price you paid for our trip to Toronto, Alexis. You have your chipped teeth and I have my deteriorating disc. It is all part of the price of our survival as a family. Nothing is free in this world, Alexis. And it is particularly not free for us.

Life, in general, has been better since we returned from Toronto, although we have gone through some very bad times: the time when Alexis ended up with still more brain damage from a bout of status epilepticus; the time when a new assistant let her fall off the changing table and she broke her jaw in three places and almost died. Generally, these things happen when life has been good for a while and we have let our guard down a bit. I have learned to worry when things go too smoothly.

We have more help with Alexis now and she is generally less irritable and can go out more without incident. But this phase came too late for our family. By the time we were in a position where we could take the other two children out for some entertainment, some shared experience together, they were in the habit of managing on their own and were no longer interested in our company. They grew up without us except for scattered moments around the dinner table when Alexis wasn't fussing too much. They learned not to rely on us too much. As recently as a month ago our older daughter attended her Grade Twelve awards ceremony alone and received honours and glowing words from her teachers without us there to witness them because our care-providing arrangements for Alexis broke down at the last moment once again.

Soon we will be alone with Alexis. The older children will be gone to live more normal, peaceful lives — or so they hope. Joe and I are tired now. We both have back problems from constant lifting and we get out of bed very stiffly in the mornings. We lie awake at night listening to the monitor for the sounds of Alexis choking. Only when it is silent for a long time do we allow ourselves to go to sleep. After years of struggling we have finally worked out most of the problems in her school program and only two months ago were told that the board would no longer challenge our efforts to keep her in an integrated setting. But in another five years she will no longer be the school's problem and there is nothing at all out there at present to fill all the days of her adult life. Also, it is much harder to hire assistants now as many people can no longer lift her. Yet, as I write this, Alexis is spending three days at a wheelchair-accessible camp she enjoys very much. It is but one of many windows on the community I have found in recent years to keep her engaged and interested in life. The daunting but stimulating challenge to find activities for someone with such circumscribed possibilities as Alexis continues to take much of my time and a fair chunk of the family budget.

What about the future? What of Alexis's security? What of meaning now? If I were to die tomorrow what would my own life have mattered? I worry about Alexis but I do not care so much about more esoteric issues as I once did. Life is now. It is a series of endless little problems and challenges, both interesting and irritating, to be met. It is odd moments of recreation, just enough to give one the strength to continue. I am neither happy nor unhappy. But I am different than I once was. Alexis has truly transformed my life. I no longer have any idea of who I might have been without her.

~

In her own words: I was born and raised in a farming community in northeastern Alberta. My mother was a country school teacher and my father worked a variety of jobs from camp cook to catskinner but was most remarkable for the music he would make with his eight-string Norwegian violin. I received my Ph.D. from the University of Alberta in 1980, and I am currently employed as a clinical psychologist in a psychiatric hospital. Apart from the book I edited *Different Hopes, Different Dreams* (1984, 1990) and GRIT, the preschool program I designed and implemented with the assistance of other parents, I have devoted most of my advocacy energies towards promoting integration of people with disabilities into the school system and the community at large.

Fear of Falling

Lorna Millard

$\mathcal{J}$T WAS MY LAST DAY OF WORK AS a federal employment counsellor in Nanaimo, originally a mill town halfway up the east coast of Vancouver Island. My plan was to kick off life outside the civil service with a rock climbing trip to Squamish, the rock climbers' mecca just north of Vancouver. After a day of cards, gifts, and packing up my office life, I indulged in a farewell stroll along my favourite trail in Morrell Sanctuary, a quiet park near my home.

My usual walk wove through mossy fir and cedar trees, skirted a small beaver pond, then circled larger Morrell Lake. Dividing the lake in half was a string of logs chained end to end. I hiked as I had every day to this spot, kicked off my sandals and walked out on the first log that abutted the shore. Reaching the point where it submerged, I sat down on the sun-silvered wood. Watching dragonflies and newts, I swatted the odd mosquito and let the sun toast the air-conditioned office out of my bones. Then, fifty feet into my return hike along the lake, I was jumped.

In the second before he sprang from behind a stump, I saw him. My mind did a strange thing, spinning that eye blink of time into a ponderous eternity. "My god, it's the weirdo I saw here last week."

Then he had intruded on my dragonfly watching by skinny dipping less than fifty feet from my log, and I had made a speedy departure to the more populated end of the lake. When he didn't appear to be following, I struck out on the remote trail that led to my mountain bike and the park entranceway. But the skinny dipper put on shorts and shoes and caught up with me. He asked for directions, which I gave him, and then he ran ahead only to reappear from one trail after another, intersecting my route. Finally, I arrived at my bike and the safety of other people.

The incident spooked me enough to disrupt my daily hikes, but today I had convinced myself that there could be no repeat of that bizarre chance encounter. Not on my last day of work — a day that deserved to end with my cherished ritual walk.

Now, here he was, naked. "He looks ridiculous — squatting there like a naked gnome!" My voice was whizzing through my head, "Damn him! This isn't real. I have a whole new life to start. Don't look like a victim! This can't be happening!"

"Hi," I said, looking him square in the eye.

"Hi." He said it automatically, as if he couldn't stop the word coming out so inappropriately.

My endless second of eternity ran out. He leaped.

Screaming, I lunged sideways as he grabbed for my legs. He knocked me into a tree, then slammed me down onto the fir needles. I landed on my shins and hands, legs folded beneath me, arms braced against his weight. I heard my screams echoing through the woods and fell silent, knowing no one was there to hear. The right hand gripping on my shoulder moved to my mouth. I wrenched my head down. His palm crushed my lips to my teeth, but I broke his hold. I had to keep my mouth free. There was only the sound of the two of us panting. Feeling the weight of fat and muscle pressing down on my back, I knew I was pinned until he moved. "What if?" danced through my head and I started to panic.

Then that feeling of slow time descended again. In the space of two pounding heartbeats, a strange calmness settled over me, pushing the fear and panic out of the bottoms of my feet. Within that calm, I found determination and the words to talk him out of raping me.

When we had met before, I reminded him, I had helped him orient on the maze of trails — I deserved far better than this in return for my kindness. He said it was too late for second thoughts — I said no, so far he had only scared me, he had done nothing to hurt me. We could both walk away and forget this ever happened. I was leaving town, I had no reason to tell anyone, I wouldn't be around to pursue the matter. He could trust me.

After five minutes of desperate salesmanship, he stood me up and brushed the bark from my shoulders. "Don't turn around and don't come back, or I'll kill you," and he gave me a push down the trail. Walking quickly, but with control, I kept my head up and hoped my back radiated confidence. And I listened hard, in case his footsteps pursued me. Well away from there, I glanced back. There was no one following. I ran as far as I could, then slowed to a fast walk. For an hour I fled through the woods, until finally I reached Westwood Lake. The beach was crowded. Knowing I was safe, I felt my control ebbing away. I had to find someone fast, before I broke down.

Scanning the beach, I zeroed in on a middle-aged woman. She looked like someone's mom, steady and unflappable. Walking up to her, I said, "Excuse me, I need some help —" my voice caught and stumbled over the rest of my sentence, "Someone just attacked me."

I don't remember her name. She drove me home, where I picked up my van, then followed me to a friend's office. He heard me come in the door and was halfway across the lobby by the time I reached him. "Someone tried to rape me." Overwhelmed by safety, I began to shake and cry.

The rest of the evening was a numb dream. We called the RCMP. A constable took a statement. The three of us went to the park where I had to lead them to the site of the attack. I looked hopefully for an earring I had lost, a tiny silver dragonfly. We never found it. Then to the police station. Another taped statement. Pictures of me: my scraped and bruised legs, swollen lips, bruises and cuts on my back and shoulders. A cup of styrofoam coffee and pages and pages of mug shots. My attacker wasn't in any of them.

Later, my friend said, "The way you handled all the RCMP stuff was great. It seems like you've already dealt with the attack and moved on."

"I don't know," I said. "Right now I feel, 'Wow, I did that!' But I know I haven't begun to get in touch with the uglies. They're still down there."

Unfortunately, I was right.

For the first two weeks, I did little but sleep. I was bruised, stiff, and had no energy. My nights were shattered by nightmares and my days became plagued with panic attacks. One got me while walking in the woods with a friend in a perfectly safe place — my throat closed, my body shook and my teeth chattered uncontrollably. I groped for something to hang onto as my legs buckled. When the panic subsided, I was exhausted and frustrated. Even the woods had been taken from me, and I didn't know if I would ever get them back.

Healing had to take place. First I had to talk my fears out, then to complete the RCMP composite drawing with a police artist. Once I had done that, I had done as much as I could to protect myself and others and no longer had to hold the image of my attacker's face in my mind.

The last thing I did in Nanaimo was go for my old walk — with a friend — and sit on my log in Morrell Lake. It was a scary thing, but every time images of the attack came over me, I stopped, took a deep breath, let the memories flow, then concentrated on the peace I still found there. It was time to push ahead. I assured everyone I was feeling better, so my friend Al and I headed to Squamish.

Just getting to the base of the first climb almost did me in. Hoisting a pack over my head and onto a ledge left my legs trembling with fatigue and my chest heaving. "What are you doing here?" I asked myself.

But Al scaled Cat Crack and belayed me up behind him. As I began climbing, finger jams and hand jams sidled back into my brain. Twisting the toe of my sticky climbing shoe sideways into the fissure, I rotated onto the ball of my foot and felt the reassuring snugness of the grip. It held. I reached higher, concentrating on the climb instead of on my fear. We did a couple more climbs, then broke for lunch. I was tired, but exultant. Climbing had been strenuous but fun. Best of all, it had taken my mind off everything else.

Halfway up the next crack, I was in trouble. Stretching for a hold, my left foot slipped and I slammed both knees into the rock to stop falling. Struggling upward on precarious holds, I slipped again and was hit by a full-blown panic attack. Clinging to the tiny rock edges, I willed my mind to focus — and failed. I screamed to Al, "Get me the hell out of here!"

He hauled on the rope and I lunged upward. I couldn't see the holds or feel the rock smash against my flailing legs. All I knew was that I was drowning sixty feet up a dry cliff. On hands and knees, I dragged myself over the clifftop and onto my feet. Legs splayed and shaking, hands braced on my thighs to keep me upright, I sucked air between my chattering teeth. Slowly, the swirling waves of panic receded.

Why was I so afraid? At worst I would drop only a foot or two before the rope caught me. Falling was no big deal; it came with the territory. If I couldn't chance a fall, I'd better stick to escalators and stop dangling off mountains. A thought began to nag at me — what if I had always been afraid of falling? Maybe until the assault I had just been better able to hide my fear. But now, that trauma had pulled the lid off the truth: falling was failing and I was afraid to fail.

"Don't be silly," I told myself. Then I realized that since the assault, I had been constantly drilling for another attack. I didn't feel empowered by how I had handled that situation, I was afraid it was a fluke and that any kind of test would see me fall short next time. I knew now that I had always hidden the real, imperfect, vulnerable me beneath a whole cast of characters. I was striving to be the perfect daughter, friend, lover; the perfect counsellor, climber, hiker, traveller, writer — the list went on. I was sure that just being me wasn't good enough. For the first time, I felt the burden of putting myself on stage, madly changing costumes, trying to perfect every disguise to avoid falling flat on my face.

It had taken an attack from a stranger to make me see how viciously I had been attacking myself, for as long as I could remember. The fears I had submerged for years had all bubbled to the surface where, for the first time, I could see them. Now I had to work on them. I didn't have a choice any more, I had to learn to trust my feelings.

I started the process by climbing only as long and as hard as I really wanted to. The minute I said I "should" keep going, I quit. I even let myself fall a few times, on purpose, to get used to the feeling. On the first fall, my stomach dropped out through my feet. After that, it wasn't so bad. I began to trust myself and the panic attacks finally stopped, even when I failed a climb.

Climbing is more relaxed and a lot more fun than it used to be. Not surprisingly, as I became better at transferring this skill to other areas of my life, they too are better, failures and all.

I have even begun to take the woods back. I miss the peaceful solitude I once enjoyed on my solo hikes, but since I can't feel safe hiking alone any more, my compromise is to go with a friend. One of my best hiking partners is a massive mutt named Bear. He outweighs most people I meet on the trail and he doesn't interrupt my thoughts. I borrow him frequently for walks; he never has more pressing business, except when his owners' grandchildren require escorting home after school.

I have also found a new depth and satisfaction in my friendships and made a relieved, if rueful, discovery — my friends have been able to see through my disguises all along. They have always liked me for who I am. I have fooled no one but myself.

Even knowing that, being myself isn't always easy. I get scared, or I forget and the old habits kick in. "Falling is failing" rings in my ears. But that doesn't last very long, when I remind myself that the best things in life are worth risking a fall for.

~

Lorna Millard teaches employment preparation programs for McMillan College in Nanaimo and divides the rest of her time between writing, good friends, and hikes in the woods with a dog named Bear.

A Feminist Ovary Goes Its Own Way

(for Dr. Fay Weisberg and Dr. Caroline Bennett)

Roberta Morris

*O*UR SEXUALITY IS OUR WAY OF being in the world. I go on tour to convince women that our bodies are friendly, that we don't exist as the counterpart of male intellectual and spiritual purity. Female sexuality exists apart from men's fears and temptations. This is the lecture I deliver, the poems and stories I write: Celebrate; dance. I celebrate myself. I dance. I paint this happy face on female sexuality and then my ovary erupts, dumping half my blood into my abdomen, and I feel a little silly.

With many female diseases there is an identifiable enemy. Poor nutrition. Dangerous birth control devices. Since cervical and breast tissue absorb nasty chemicals, pollution is probably the villain in the rise of female cancers. Genetically programmed female tissue plays housewife, sweeping up nuclear dust. But this doesn't explain why my happy little ovary, from whence came Andrea and Nathaniel, turns mean.

The doctor, like a good mother separating two quarrelling children, does not lay blame but plucks up my ovary and sends me to my room. My ovary remains in O.R.

Now where did they put it? I imagine the obstetrical ward's O.R. garbage, a deconstructed image of the female reproductive system that is featured on the ward walls. A Cubist sculptor with a taste for the baroque might do it justice, a mound of uteruses, ovaries, placenta, pieces of human reproduction piled high.

An amputee continues to feel the missing limb as a ghost appendage, just as I imagine my ovary whistles at me from atop the garbage heap, "Hey cutie, but didn't we have a grand time?"

~

Born in Windsor, Ontario, and raised in the U.S., **Roberta Morris** has lived most of her adult life in Toronto. She holds an M.A. in theology from the University of Toronto. She has written and lectured on the role of women in the Christian tradition and on violence against women and children, but now writes fiction and literary criticism almost exclusively. Among her publications are the novels *Virgil; Miriam: An Autobiography* (1994); and *No Words for Love and Famine* (1994). The single mother of two children, she teaches writing and English as a second language part-time.

Treatments

Diana Chown

$\mathcal{T}$HE UNEXPECTEDLY LARGE room seems empty except for the radiation table, with its outstretched grey arms, and the white plaster moulds in human forms leaning against a corner wall.

Of course, there are cupboards and drawers and other equipment, but the room seems to exist only for the grey occupant and its visitors. With quickly moving hands, two technicians position the body and pull up the gown so that beams of light can strike the blue marks on the abdomen where radiation is to penetrate. Then the table hums its way along a track ready for the circling arms. The technicians scurry out of the room with one last reminder: "Don't move."

Once they've closed the door, the rasping sound of warning begins. "Nzzz nzzz nzzz." It signals that powerful beams from radioactive cobalt are being directed into known, or suspected, cancer cells. The total amount of "rads" to be received over the twenty-two days is four thousand. The dictionary says eight hundred is fatal; presumably that means all at once. No lead covering is used to protect the rest of the body.

I remember lying there wondering: Were the cancer cells being destroyed? Were there any to begin with? The surgery may have got them all, they had said. Then why was I there? Really, remembering all of this now seems maudlin. The sound of pheasants clucking outside and thoughts of visiting a small art gallery nearby seem much more appealing.

"Because the treatment is so refined now, only the area marked will receive radiation," they say. Then they flee from the room.

No matter. It's time for "visualization." From a great distance away, she watches as the little sweepers begin their work. Disregarding the alarm and armed with tiny brooms like thousands of sets of the seven dwarfs, they sweep all the cancer cells down to the area beside her still-remaining tuft of pubic hair, the rest having been removed before the hysterectomy. Somehow, the job gets done for the day, but the alarm is still going so a new crew of dwarfs is sent in.

"Write through it," someone said. That means writing through the memory of that horrible sound, fighting a steel grip in my chest. I must remember that the treatments were much worse than the disease, which caused hardly any symptoms at all.

Meanwhile, the huge grey metal arms are sweeping around the body — so many rays to the top of her abdomen, so many to the sides and more from underneath.

"Nzzz nzzz nzzz nzzz" then silence. Beyond, the door opens and in come the white-coated technicians. "You may get up now," one of them says — sometimes female, sometimes male — as the hospital gown is pulled back down to cover the blue marks.

The fact that it is usually the technicians who readjust the gown is due not only to a loss of modesty which usually follows the treatment and the session with the dwarfs, but also to the frequent practice of touching up the radiation marks before the gown is replaced. This experience of not only exposing her interior to the radiation, but also her exterior to the ball point pens of the white coats invariably results in a state of numbness.

I'm fighting an inclination to save this story for "some later date." What a rotten way to spend a hot afternoon — and probably bad for my immune system, too!

White feet in street shoes, she walks the distance to the hallway which leads to the waiting room door, and to the little cupboard where the patients undress. Her devil-may-care look is meant to suggest that it's all just a snap, even amusing: the huge room with its sullen grey occupant, the nausea, and the nice lady volunteers who never have plain water on their carts, only tea, coffee or juice — even though requests are made for it every day.

I remember wanting to rage that this shouldn't be happening to me — this previously inconceivable assault on my body. But who could I rage at? Not the harassed technicians, nor the well-meaning volunteers, and especially not the other patients, in varying stages of terror like me.

One solution is through art. Or, at least, decoration. Halfway through the treatments, the abdomen appears decked out with red pansies arranged delicately in each right-angled radiation mark and birds in flight poised around the navel — which, although not officially within the radiation field, had proved irresistible to the would-be artists who had done the work. The technicians seem pleased by this, although none of them has come across such a phenomenon before. One day, after the customary retracing of the blue marks, one of them chuckles softly as he produces a red pen to refurbish the fading petals.

As the treatments progress, symptoms of gastric distress appear. These are kept at bay with Chinese potions, Rice Krispies squares, and acupuncture. So when not lying on the radiation table she lies staring at the acupuncturist's ceiling, with long, golden pins sticking out of her body. At last the final treatment day arrives. "External beam radiation" is over. This is followed by a three week breathing space before the next treatment: "vaginal vault insertion."

Isn't surviving enough? "Cancer Survivors" survive, that's all, and leave out the rest. "Get on with your life," as they say. When I first heard about this next type of radiation I simply refused to go through with it.

A description of possible side effects from the treatment is laid out for her. Somehow, a "narrowed bowel"— the occasional side effect of the external radiation — seems more tolerable than the vague picture of sexual impairment which could result from the "insert." It appears that little is known about what happens to women's sex lives after they have this treatment. The assault seems unending — can the dwarfs deal with threatened libido, too?

The idea of placing radioactive pellets in my vagina was outrageous. When I told one friend about it, her response made me fear to mention it again. "It sounds like rape," she shot back.

Attempts to find a previous recipient of this type of radiation are frustrated. The radiation staff's response is to suggest a visit to the hospital room of an older woman currently undergoing this treatment. Before anyone can enter the room, the radiation pellet must be automatically withdrawn through the long tube which leads to a lead box in the adjoining room. The frightened and sedated woman speaks almost inaudibly of her illness and her resignation.

After this, matters are no longer left up to the hospital. Through a former oncological nurse, and a friend of a friend, she finds Heather. Over the telephone, this generous young woman shares details of her sexual life after having this treatment.

Could I have gone through with this without Heather? She invited me to her apartment, talked to me, reassured me, phoned me before I went to the hospital and then disappeared. Thank you, Heather, wherever you are.

In the end, she capitulates and forty-eight hours are spent as a patient in the Cancer Hospital. The first afternoon, before she is put in the lead-lined room with the little window, is shared with a slender young woman who has just been diagnosed with terminal cancer. In their room, they watch *Tootsie*, sitting very close together and laughing.

The treatment (which, in fact, causes few side effects), goes by in a blur of pain, nausea, and intermittent drug euphoria. The effect of this is a dulling of awareness of the clinking sound as the little pellets travel back and forth through the wall. The nurses are gentle and kind. While the drugs are in effect, long telephone calls help to pass the time; she says little about her present circumstances. After it is over and she is taken home, she leans against a tree and vomits in the garden before she can go in.

The next day she feels oddly well.

~

Diana Chown is a founding member of the Cross Cancer Institute's Humour Program Advisory Committee. Through her involvement in committees such as the Canadian Committee on Women's History, Women in Alberta and Saskatchewan History, and the Northern Alberta Women's Archives Association, she works to increase awareness of Canadian women's history. She is the editor of the reprint of Alice Chown's *The Stairway*, first published in 1921. A freelance writer, she lives in Edmonton.

Condemned to Fly

Desirée Freeman

$\mathcal{J}$T IS NIGHT AND SOMEONE IS following me. His stare stabs a hole into my flesh and the hollow it forms aches and expands inside my body. I lick the sweat off my lip. As long as he is in the car, I am safe. I pull my coat tight around me, stare straight ahead and try to ignore him. Peripheral vision and wind-tears have transformed his car into a blur of red steel: he hangs there like a blood blister in the corner of my left eye.

I will find a way to shake him off. Maybe, if I step very slowly, he will lose the stalker's advantage and I will become as an afterthought in the reflective eye of his rear view mirror. In the orange film skirt of a street lamp, I stop dead. He creeps ahead, and his tail-lights, lit red like the night eyes of a desert animal, retreat and disappear. He has turned onto someone else's street, and I am almost home.

As I pass the last alley, I turn my head to check for traffic. I see nothing but his red car parked tight against a fence. It is empty. I jerk my head around but cannot see him. I hear the hum of distant traffic, the buzz of the street lamp overhead, gravel carving the sidewalk under my feet. I look back over the blocks I've just won. They are dark and deserted. I cannot go back.

I make it to the corner and freeze: one side of the street is lined by dark houses set deep in their lots and fenced by tall trees. The other side is well-lit, but the sidewalk forms a treacherous tunnel between a long row of parked cars and the bulwark bluffs of adjacent walk-ups. I step onto the road itself and march up its centre. I hold my head very high, as if by acting brave, I will, somehow, feel brave.

The click of my own steps betrays me and summons him out of his hiding place. He appears, bent over like an old man, from behind a tree. He looks at me, grinning, and rises to his full height. He cuts a path across the lawn, sidewalk, and onto the pavement. I swallow hard.

His hair angles off his neck like the spikes on a dragon's back. His nostrils clench and flare. I watch his breath as it stains the air in rapid bursts. His empty fists are knotted, and there is no place for me to run. I watch him through eyes that mask fear with defiance. When he is four feet in front of me and closing in, we hear an explosion of laughter. He cranks his head around and sees the silhouette of an approaching crowd. If we can hear them, they can hear us. The dragon-man twists his face back to me and there is only a foot left between us. His eyes focus on my feet, and then slowly, deliberately, climb up my body. I stiffen in resistance. He stretches his jaws apart and in a gravelly, guttural voice letter by letter, he expels the word "sweetheart." I bolt down the street. I don't need to look back. I can feel his word still behind me, licking at the nape of my neck.

Later, inside my apartment, I tiptoe through every room and draw the blinds. The sex-crimes officer finds me shaken in the dark of my living room. "The red car was stolen some two hundred miles from here. You're very lucky."

That night I lie awake in bed. I think about milk-carton children and newspaper women. I wonder how or why he chose me. Did he know where I live? I imagine that I will wake the next morning and find a child's valentine impaled on my door with the word "sweetheart" scrawled across it in blood. My fear is interrupted by the sudden recollection of a feminist slogan: "Take back the night." Yes. Take back the night. Take it back. I repeat this phrase over and over, sitting up in punctuation and affirming each one with the nod of my head. I know what I will do. I will not be afraid. I will sleep and awake even more determined. I will not give him anything, not even a fleeting thought. Yes, starting now I will take back the night.

I settle in under the covers, and curl into an S. I am not afraid, but still I cannot sleep. I begin to think about most nights, about the generic sleeplessness that occasionally plagues us all. We lie awake, the sheets tangled like seaweed around our feet, and worry. We worry about yesterday. We worry about tomorrow. We worry over the stillness that suspends us between "what was" and "what will be," and we are afraid of hanging in midair somewhere between the past and the future. We are afraid of falling.

I arrive at this conclusion with some finality. Still, I cannot sleep. I reach over to my night table and grab my journal. I open it, letting the pencil fall onto my chest and begin reading:

Hang your wings on my bedpost
when the sky's too black to fly through
come fly with me, I'll guide you
straight into the sun.

I think of Icarus. I wonder if some stop reaching and lose their fear of falling along with their hope of height. Do these low-flying people fall easy into sleep?

It is morning, and I walk to school. I retrace yesterday's steps and take back the familiar street. The wind carries yellow leaves safely down to my feet. I squish them as I pass; they are not crunchy yet and they fold silently under my step. I look up at the sun and think of Icarus. When the Romans reenacted the mythical story they would mount wings on the back of a condemned prisoner, strap him in a catapult, and launch him off the edge of a cliff. There were only two ways for Icarus to die: launched in fear with arms flailing, he could try to stop the ground from rushing up under him, or launched in courage, his winged arms thrown back, he could fly.

~

In her own words: I'd tell you about myself but self-disclosure interferes with my delusions of grandeur.

Memento Mori

Laurel A. Wade

$\mathcal{J}$ LAY DOWN ON AN EXAMINING
table. A young Chinese doctor examined me almost immediately.
How much blood had I lost? My mind flashed to the red sheets
clinging to the mattress. How does one measure blood from a
scene like that? I checked my memory of my three previous miscarriages. About two pints. For the first time I looked directly at
the doctor. In his eyes I saw an empathy, a watery sadness. To
comfort him I told him that I had a history of miscarriages. I even
used the words "spontaneous abortion." I wondered if he thought
I was callous.

That morning I had not been so stoic. While dancing down the
stairs in our townhouse, I felt a familiar dull ache in my lower
abdomen. Wishing I had moved more slowly, wanting to deny the
sensation in my body, I checked for spotting, called the doctor,
rested. I knew the routine. This was my fourth pregnancy in the
past six years. Only the first had produced a live and healthy baby,
Warren, now four.

That night, while my husband Paul slept quietly beside me, I
writhed around in the darkness for what seemed like hours. The
contractions grew stronger. I felt very much alone, but physical
pain was not something I wished to share. When the cramps finally subsided, I welcomed the relief. A voice warned me about the
danger of haemorrhage once the cervix relaxed, told me to get out

of bed and check for bleeding. Exhausted, I drifted off to sleep. Sometime between two and three A.M. an uneasiness awakened me. The sheets were saturated with blood. I woke Paul, who dressed Warren and bundled him into the van while I washed, dressed, and grabbed two towels for the trip to the hospital.

Paul and Warren left soon after I was admitted. Now I was alone in a large private room. A nurse entered with an intravenous bottle, inserted the needle into my hand, secured it with tape, and started the drip by slightly unscrewing a dial on the long plastic tube. When I asked, she said that the bottle contained oxytocin. Since I had taken six months of nurses' training — with a particular interest in maternity nursing — I knew the drug was given to induce labour. At the time I was confused about the medication, but since I felt relatively comfortable, and the nurse offered me no further explanation, I decided to try to rest.

Fifteen minutes later I felt a contraction. Every four minutes or so brought another one. The nurse came in frequently to check for bleeding and to monitor the intravenous drip. After about half an hour, I figured out what was going on. During previous miscarriages, a doctor had been available, or made available, and a D & C (dilation and curettage) had been performed promptly, and so that's what I expected to happen this time. But when I asked the nurse when the doctor would arrive, she informed me that he usually came in around 7:30 A.M. After all my physical and emotional suffering, I was now in full labour and alone. No one had informed me exactly what was being done to me or why. I suppose they wanted the cervix dilated and the contents of the uterus expelled; I could be kept out of danger while allowing the doctor his night's sleep. I began to resent the hospital and the doctor who ordered the medication. Inducing labour for someone suffering the loss of a pregnancy — the loss of a potential child — seemed barbaric.

When I decided I couldn't tolerate any more pain, I tightened the device that regulated the intravenous drip. The labour stopped. On subsequent visits, the nurse checked the frequency of the drops, adjusted the device and left. I readjusted the device immediately, before a contraction started. I kept playing the game with the intravenous drip and the nurse. The minutes passed slowly, but without pain.

Around 7:15 the obstetrician-gynecologist finally arrived, examined me, told the nurse to prepare me for the D & C, and left. When I woke up in a four-bed ward a couple of hours later, a familiar emptiness washed over me. There was no pain, no bleeding, and no baby. I wanted to see Paul. I wanted to go home.

My longing for Paul grew. I needed comfort. I thought of my mother, who had driven out from Toronto and was now on Vancouver Island, wished she were closer. Although my sister lived only a few miles away, I felt that she could not give me what I needed right then. Perhaps no one could have helped me at that moment. Or perhaps a woman who had experienced similar trauma would have been able to comfort me. But I didn't think of that. I could only think of my husband. Somehow I thought he would be able to console me — even in his grief — because we had lost a child. I guess I was pretty naive. He was satisfied with one child. And how can a man really get inside a woman's skin to understand what it is to carry another life inside? Or to lose it. And the joy of Warren in my life revealed my loss so clearly.

I felt hollow. I watched every person who entered the room; I wanted Paul to turn the corner. Nurses moved in and out checking the other patients. Finally I walked to the telephone to call my husband. I must have sounded incensed when he answered. He told me that he and Warren were tired, that they didn't get much sleep. They had just finished breakfast. They would leave to pick me up shortly.

The next week, life went on as usual around me. Paul went to work on Monday morning. My parents decided not to stay with me because they thought they would be a burden. I dragged myself around.

Ten days after the miscarriage I saw my family doctor. I thought there might be a medical explanation for my difficulty in carrying a child, since my son's birth had been a difficult caesarean, so I asked to see a specialist. The doctor, looking at me in a rather puzzled way, said that it wasn't that serious. The intense anger that came over me gave me the courage to ask him how many times I would have to abort spontaneously before I could call it serious. I gave him the name of a doctor at Grace Hospital who had been recommended to me. He didn't know her. I didn't care. All I wanted was a referral. When he agreed, I left the office quickly, and never returned. After many tests at Grace Hospital, I still had no answers.

That fall seemed long. Indian summer prolonged the life of the flowers and leaves. Pregnant women surfaced everywhere. I wanted time to pass more quickly. I wanted birds to migrate and the cold rainy weather to begin. I thought I would feel better once the birth date of my lost child had passed.

I suppose it is the invisibility of miscarriage that disturbs me. There is no gravestone, no name, sometimes no sex. And no one talks about it. In most families there is taboo about its mention. Sometimes women with similar experiences offer condolence. But that is never enough for me. There is a very high incidence of miscarriage among healthy women, but often there are no explanations.

My Christmas baby never came. By Christmas Warren and I were in an apartment on our own.

Laurel Wade, the single parent of a teenage son, recently completed an M.F.A. in Creative Writing at U.B.C. She has lived in Manitoba, Ontario, Alberta, and British Columbia, and has worked as a waitress, nanny, factory worker, and prison guard. She currently teaches high school English and tutors. Her poems are included in an anthology of five Canadian women entitled *Light Like a Summons*. In the summers she returns to rural Manitoba to find solitude and inspiration for writing.

The Lucky Ones

Shelley Banks

$\mathcal{I}$T WAS MOTHERS' NIGHT AT THE playgroup, the annual wine and cheese. I picked up the last bottle of soda water and the flow of words washed over me as bubbles filled my glass: summer vacations, babies, and the latest kicks for kids.

I had children too, aged one and three, but instead of feeling a bond with the other women, I suddenly felt out of sync, as if I'd hurtled past them down our lifelines, and found myself at a far distant point, isolated and afraid.

At thirty-two, I had cancer. Just weeks before the party, the doctors confirmed the lump above my left breast was malignant, and with the news, friends' concerns had shifted out of focus. Beach resorts? The drugs I took made my skin so sun-sensitive I'd sizzle. Pregnancy? I had trouble coping with the two youngsters I already had. Gym classes for preschoolers? My daily treks downtown for radiation therapy were balancing act enough.

A voice cut through my thoughts.

"You're not drinking!" Lisa said, edging past me to the boxes of imported wine. She splashed a spurt of white into her glass, then studied me more closely.

"*You're* not pregnant, too?" she asked — a fair question, under the circumstances. At least six women with us were expecting their next child.

"No," I croaked. The rest snagged in my throat. I wanted to tell her I had a new growth of a different kind, the kind that calls for chemotherapy, not champagne but, by the time I'd found my voice again, she'd walked away.

I didn't keep silent for long. After the first few weeks, the words came easily. I wanted to talk about what I was going through, partly because being open diminished the fear I sometimes felt, and partly because I wanted my friends — women like myself, more concerned about the cost of diapers than the risks of getting sick — to realize the importance of breast self-examination. Within a few months, Lisa and the others knew, and their reactions became predictable:

"But you look so . . . so *normal!*" Normal. I heard that word at least a dozen times. What was I supposed to be, a freak? But my weight stayed constant, my hair as thick as ever, and if I seemed tired or forgot to mask the dark rings under my eyes, why, fatigue was only natural. With two active children, what else would anyone expect? No one seemed to notice the souvenirs of chemotherapy, the needle scars that freckled the back of my hand and the blackened veins that streaked along my arm.

Normal. I wanted to believe that, but I sometimes wondered. My moods shifted rapidly. One day, I'd be a weepy wreck, collapsing into angry tears because a child had spilled a glass of milk across the kitchen floor. The next, I'd bubble with confidence, high on the knowledge that if I could handle the big "C" and the chemical warfare waged within my body, I could handle anything.

Or could I?

I'd found the lump myself. A hard and painless growth embedded in the upper breast tissue, it would roll between my ribs and disappear when I lay down, hiding from the doctors who examined me. To my unskilled fingers, it felt slightly larger than a frozen pea, a tiny thing for all the upset it caused; I never believed until the biopsy and doctors' final verdict it could be malignant.

But it was, and close to three years later, still drawn by articles on risk factors, I still wonder which slot it was that I slipped into, for it to grow in me. I had my first child before thirty, and I nursed her for eleven months. My second baby I nursed too, though not so long. Isn't that supposed to offer some protection? I thought I watched my diet, too, though looking back, I'm not so sure. I never had a tendency to put on weight, and so, unconcerned about those extra calories, I never worried about the fats I ate, or counted those glasses of wine.

Cancer. It's been part of my medical history for years, but until recently, a very academic, minor part — an afterthought I'd offer to new doctors, if they were very thorough, right after telling them about my tonsil operation at age four.

"My grandfather died of cancer," I'd say. "Of the prostate gland." But he was in his sixties, and it happened more than fifty years ago. My father was a teenager and I was as yet unborn. I grew up with that story, though, and when I was very young, I thought cancer was a disease of aging. In time, I realized it could hit young people, too, but I never thought it would come to me. Women don't have prostates, after all, and there were no other cancers I knew of in my family.

My sister now knows differently, as will my daughter, when she's old enough. Thanks to my diagnosis, they've both moved one notch further up the scale of risks.

My surgeons confused and angered me; instead of laying out at the start what I might expect, they doled out details, bit by bit. Expectations shifted constantly, and every visit, something changed. After the biopsy, I checked back into hospital for more extensive surgery to gauge the tumour's spread. It was summer, and because of bed closures, I was on a men's surgical floor — the urology unit, in fact, where the nurses were used to dealing, not just with the other sex, but with the other end of the body as well. Three times a day, student doctors fumbled with my breasts for growths the specialists might have missed. Before the operation, a resident marked the wrong side down on the consent form, and, as a final touch, a young anesthetist dropped by to tell me the worst I could expect while I was under — "severe neurological damage or death."

"I figured I could handle that, so I signed up," I later tried to joke, affecting a bravado which I didn't really feel. And yet, I appreciated her candour; she was the only one who talked about what might be yet to come.

When it was over, I was stiff and sore, unable to lift my arm more than ten inches from my side, or use it to pin my squirming son in place to change his diaper. But walking my fingers slowly up the wall helped bring my strength back, plain acetaminophen conquered the pain, and the news was good. My cancer was Stage I, confined to the lump itself. There was no sign of spread. The ordeal was almost over.

Or so I thought, until the next week, when the doctor recommended chemotherapy. A full year of it.

When I protested that the cancer had been localized within the cyst, which he'd cut out, the doctor told me there was still a chance it might recur. Microscopic cells might have filtered out from it and lodged elsewhere. The drugs, he said, might reduce or delay the odds of that. They'd be practical insurance for my future, and my family's; I'd be part of a clinical trial, the costs would be covered by medicare, the medications mild and the side effects few.

Who could refuse? Of course, I didn't realize at the time the concept of "mild chemotherapy" would turn out to be about the same as "painless childbirth."

That first session was a waking nightmare. The tiny treatment area, with its mismatched chairs, yellowing walls, and ominous hooks along the walls for intravenous lines, made me think I'd fallen into a dream chamber of an especially sordid kind.

"Relax," the nurse said confidently, as if she thought I could. But that was impossible. When she took my hand, my heart hammered and I tried to look away. When she lodged a needle in the back of it, I closed my eyes. Chemicals dripped through the IV tube for an hour, and surged, cold as a glacial stream, up the main vein on the back of my forearm. I rocked back and forth. I gripped the edges of my chair. I closed my eyes and tried to focus on the mystery novel blaring through the headphones of my Walkman. Time ticked by until at last the needle was withdrawn, and I was free to shuffle to the hospital's front door to wait for my husband.

The rest of the day I spent at home in bed, lurching between sleep and nausea. Weeks passed before I could relax enough to talk to other patients in the clinic, sharing symptoms, complaints, and reassurances.

Five weeks of daily radiation treatments, which began at the same time, were easier to bear, despite the high-tech atmosphere and the eerie, spaceship whine of the machines. The actual treatments took only minutes; the most difficult part was to stay still. By the end, my left arm and breast were swollen, the skin brown-spotted as if sunburnt, and my nipple, cracked and sore. I also had a burning feeling, deep inside my breast, which turned into an itch too deep to scratch.

Christopher, the baby, took my absence in his stride, but Morgan found it difficult, despite the fact I'd worked full-time till she was almost two. Perhaps she couldn't understand why, drugged and dazed, I locked myself away when I came home from chemotherapy. I guess words don't all have meanings at that age. Emotions do, however, and twenty-four hours after treatments, something always happened to set off a flood of tears.

"I don't want you to go back to that hospital," she'd sob when it was over. "Mommies shouldn't be sick."

But I was. For days after those twice-monthly IV hook-ups, I felt queasy; between sessions, I fought fatigue, a deep exhaustion night-shifts and pregnancies had only hinted at, exhaustion that didn't build but would come crashing down after I'd vacuumed the carpet in one room, or pushed the stroller halfway up a shopping mall, leaving me weak and longing to crumple to the floor and cry. I knew from waiting room conversations I was not the only one; I knew from my children's faces I sometimes frightened them.

I sometimes unnerved other people, too. Many don't know what to say to cancer patients. They offer reassurances. ("Oh, you'll be fine. That lump's not serious." As if they knew.) They offer horror stories. ("My aunt was in such pain. She had a tumour in her leg. . . ." As if we should feel better knowing someone's worse. In any case, I have my own dark tales; I can remember Pam and Sue, two friends who died at my age, leaving little kids behind.)

"Are you dyeing?" asked Bruce, a family friend. It was an innocent question, but he realized what it sounded like and tried again.

"I meant . . . wool. Do you dye, wool? Not, are you. . . ." He
stumbled on, then looked at me uneasily. And then, curiosity
overcoming his confusion, he blurted out:

"You're not, are you?"

I shrugged, and tried to reassure him that I had no plans for
that just then.

Instead of saying from the start this could be a lost year, the
specialists and support staff regaled Gord and me with tales of
patients heading out to the tennis courts or golf links for quick
games after treatments. I'd like to think those stories were based
on fact, and weren't just glib reassurances springing from the
"what you don't know, won't hurt you" school of thought. But
none of the women I met felt remotely like that. Certainly, I
didn't. (Maybe if I'd been able to pay the greens fees, though,
things might have been different. I could have used the money for
a full-time nanny, and perhaps then been able to rest enough to
overcome my weariness.)

I struggled for months before I could accept the fact that I was
just too tired to cope. By spring, that mind-numbing fatigue and
the queasiness and irritability I felt for days after chemotherapy
became more than I could bear. The treatment was preventative,
and I'd said from the start if it grew too rough, I'd quit. It took
weeks to realize I had reached that point, weeks of tears and angry
questioning, weeks of weighing the future risks against my present
misery, weeks of watching my husband and children flinch and
grow silent in the face of my sudden — and increasingly frequent
— bouts of rage.

I had a new doctor by then, and she accepted my decision
calmly. Studies had shown early therapy seemed to work, she said,
but no one knew how much was needed. The latest thing at the
hospital at that point was a shorter, six-month trial, one arm of
which used the same drugs and dosages as mine. I'd been through
eight long months already, four sessions more than I'd have had
under the new regimen. Maybe I'd had enough.

It was five months before my energy picked up, before I felt once more like running in the park with Morgan and Christopher, now six and almost four, or giggling at their games; before I wanted once again to stay up late with my husband, just to sit and talk, or watch TV.

Nearly three years have passed since the diagnosis. I'm back to normal, and have been for some time, but I still bear its mark. The circulation in my left arm, disrupted by radiation and the lymph node operation, is still sluggish; those fingers swell at night when I am sleeping, and when I wake, my wedding band bites deeply into puffy flesh. My chest is branded with a half-inch-wide scar from the lumpectomy, and there's a three-inch hollow round it where skin touches bone. I pay for that muscle loss in winter; my left breast aches when I've been shovelling snow, and I wonder how women with complete mastectomies can bear it, the loss — not of their breasts, but of that precious muscle tissue underneath. My doctor says the treatments can induce menopause, so while friends worry about contraception, I think about hot flashes, osteoporosis. At thirty-six, I'm out of sync, again.

I've often wished this was someone else's story, so I could turn the page and leave it all behind. Or that it was a novel, so I could skim ahead to see: what happens next? And: was the trial worth it? The hard part is I'll never know. Most women with Stage I breast cancer will never have recurrences, with or without these drugs; a small group will have them anyway, in spite of any treatments. Early chemotherapy helps only a thin slice of women in the statistical pie, and doctors can't yet pinpoint who they'll be.

I'm not noble about illness. I don't like thinking of the years of tests and monitoring ahead. I've asked, *why me?* more times than I remember. There was even a time when I would find myself glaring at young women in shopping malls or restaurants, angered by the trivial-sounding complaints I overheard. Didn't they realize how lucky they were? To be healthy and alive?

But then I'd catch myself, and realize — once again — that I'm lucky, too.

~

In her own words: Born in a small town in the Rocky Mountains, just down the line from a whistle stop called Shelley, B.C. (which my parents deny I was named for), I grew up in Canada, Jamaica, and the Cayman Islands. I went to university in Ontario (B.A. McMaster, M.A. Western) and I've worked as a newspaper reporter in Vancouver and as a freelance writer in Pointe-Claire, Quebec. Pointe-Claire is where I now live with my husband, two children, and a golden retriever. A longer version of this essay ran in *Homemakers* under the title "Surviving" in September 1991.

Care Calling Care

Caterina Edwards

$\mathcal{D}$AY AFTER DAY, I SAT BESIDE my father-in-law and witnessed his struggle against death, against the dissolution of the flesh, against himself. For death was within him. I could smell it. It radiated from his mouth and poisoned the air. I was afraid to breathe, afraid. But I stayed. I stayed —

My father-in-law and I never did get along. From the moment I was introduced as the bride-to-be, there was tension, unease. "Why can't you live together like everyone else does?" my future mother-in-law asked. And while her husband was too much the old-fashioned Sicilian gentleman to suggest something so "improper"— marriage is forever, he told Marco, his son, my husband-to-be. Marriage lasts beyond death — his eyes, his hands, the tone of his voice added: so you must not choose her, not her. "She's a princess in a tower, a prickly, haughty girl," he later wrote.

I was not what he thought I should be: innocent, sweet, subservient. "Like Christ is to his Church," said one cousin who seemed to feel she had been deputized by the family to lead me to the light, "so must be a husband to his wife: the head, the ruler." Instead of a smile or a joke, which would have been more effective, I had argued. "Ridiculous," I'd snapped. "Outmoded. . . . Oppressive." I was too threatened to take it calmly. I had been raised to the same expectations, and they were still too close, too pressing.

Two years after the wedding, I spent two months, without my husband, in the California home of my in-laws. My mother-in-law was out all day professoring. My father-in-law had been forced into early retirement. The house was large, a sprawling bungalow, and the garden extensive, but Manuele seemed to have little to occupy him besides the odd errand or game of tennis. It was what passed for winter in northern California; there was a little rain, more fog, the slightest of chills. Manuele spent his time wandering through the many-roomed house, waiting for his wife, rocking and reading in a rocking chair, waiting for his wife, rocking and staring into space, and when I let him, talking to me of his life, never mine, his theories, his philosophy, the wisdom of a lifetime he called it, though he was only middle-aged. Some of it I didn't mind: the crassness of American culture, the richness of Italian, his student years in Genova, his war years in the Italian navy, man's basic brutality, stupidity, and venality. The inscrutability of God.

He only touched obliquely on his years of top secret work on rocket engines; when commenting, for example, on America's shortcomings, he might say — we were all foreigners: a German, a Chinese, me, all the top theorists at the company. Otherwise, he never boasted, never mentioned he'd designed first the Polaris missile and then the engine of the Apollo II, the first manned spaceship to land on the moon. (Nor did he ever complain that Marco's decision to evade the draft, because of the Vietnam war, had cost him his security clearance and his job.) Even then, when I was still sheltered by the walls of my resentment, I admired him for his discretion.

Although I did sense that it simply didn't matter to him. Work was a nasty necessity he could have avoided if he'd been born in another century. When I finally read Lampedusa's *The Leopard*, I recognized his prototype. Manuele wished to be another Prince of Salaparuta: pessimistic and wise, an amateur yet serious thinker. Most of all, respected, both listened to and catered to. If not by a fiefdom, by his family.

During those two months I stayed with my in-laws, I audited a course given by Kate Millett at Sacramento State University. If absentmindedly I happened to leave one of the texts anywhere besides my bedroom, Manuele pounced. Checking out the pictures on the backs of the feminist books, he invariably made nasty comments about the looks of the author. Flipping open a page, he would read a random sentence aloud and sneer. Or he lectured, trotting out the standard male Sicilian line. Basically, women were too powerful already (*how many times did I hear it?*); they were stronger than men, better and worse than men, and therefore had certain duties, certain responsibilities. Feminism was unnatural, a perversion. Feminism was unnecessary. Feminism was a joke. I could not listen to this in the same patient way that I had listened to the rest of his pronouncements. I grew heated; I argued back.

After those two months with my in-laws, Manuele rarely ever spoke to me of his life and his theories, but this argument continued. One Christmas at a party at my parents' home, he and I started arguing over whether a man should be expected — as I expected Marco — to divide the household chores. He shouted. I burst into tears. He grabbed my arm. "You see," he said, "You women don't play fair. You're sneaky, manipulative."

Later I realized his anger towards me and my refusal to bend, to serve, was connected to his anger at his wife and her refusal. For, eventually, she divorced him. The land, the house, and all its contents were sold. He'd already lost one son to the frozen wastes of Canada and a chilly wife. The other, having chosen acting and Los Angeles, was pushing him away. His most precious possession, his family, was no longer his.

Unfulfilled expectations. I had expected an affectionate father-in-law like the kind my sister had, my mother had had. It was part of my family's mythology: my mother would tell how horrible everyone had been to her when she arrived in England as an Italian war bride — everyone except for my grandfather. He had welcomed her, bringing her extra rations and rare delicacies like chocolate and bananas when she was pregnant.

Over the years, I grew close to my mother-in-law. But even my pregnancies, even two beautiful granddaughters could not change things between Manuele and me. We no longer argued; we were polite. Still, he made a point of favouring his other son's wife, pointedly embracing her, not me, at family gatherings. I could see why. She knew how to handle him, humouring him, teasing him about his need to control.

Was it any wonder that in 1988 when I moved down to California with my husband and daughters so that we could nurse and care for Manuele, I felt as if I were the victim of a cruel and unusual punishment?

I had just got through a bad patch. One day three years before, I walked into a classroom with a sore knee. By the end of the class, I couldn't walk out. In the space of an hour and a half, with my attention elsewhere, my body transmuted from the familiar and the taken for granted into the mysterious and the sinister. I had been struck with a rare arthritic disease that attacked various organs such as the kidneys and the eyes, as well as certain joints. I suffered from weakness, exhaustion, and pain: pain that coloured everything that I was and did; pain that isolated, that drove me inwards, farther and farther inwards, reduced, limited, alone.

The day I came home from the hospital and the radical treatment that sent the illness into remission, Manuele had a stroke. He was left unable to speak, paralysed on his right side. For close to a year he could not eat but had to be fed through a tube inserted in his chest. His ex-wife, with nursing help, cared for him for several months. Then he was sent to Marco's brother and his wife. Finally, our turn came.

Since immigration would not allow us to bring Manuele into Canada, we left our home and friends, our support system. We arrived to a new kind of servitude, being on-call twenty-four hours out of twenty-four. One of us always had to be with Manuele. And, unlike a baby, he could not be packed up and taken out. Marco did manage most of the care — the washing, feeding, and exercising. But since I found after several attempts and an anxiety attack that I could not drive on the freeways, I had to manage as well. In the first few months, we both learned patience:

we both learned to be woken at night, to follow a strict time schedule (Manuele's), to order things exactly as he wanted them, to soothe his cries of rage and frustration, to stay in, to stay close, to put ourselves third after Manuele, after the girls, third, closed in. Outside, the heat was another blow, week after week, over 100° Fahrenheit: hot, parched, merciless. Encircling the city, a ring of forest fires. We watched the acres burn on TV. We inhaled and choked on the smoke and the ash.

At a mall, I found a T-shirt that expressed how I felt. Across the front in medieval script was written the opening lines of Dante's *Inferno*. The T-shirt was half price. "They just didn't sell," the salesclerk said. They did not fit the California frame of mind. One day as I was massaging cream into the dried, broken skin of his paralysed hand, I noticed Manuele staring fixedly at my chest. I pointed and read aloud.

> *Nel Mezzo del cammin della nostra vita*
> *Mi ritrouvai per un selva oscura,*
> *Che la via diritta era smarrita.*

> In the middle of the journey of our life,
> I found myself in a dark wood
> And the straight way was lost.

He laughed and I laughed. It was the first time that we laughed together. No one else had appreciated the absurdity of my wearing those words on my chest. But he was lost in the darkest of woods and understood.

Was that the moment things changed between us? No, it was the moment that I became aware that the change had occurred. I think it happened slowly as I cared for him: care calling care. I ministered to his ruined flesh, uncurling his fingers, moving the dead weight of his arm through the range of motion exercises, lifting him off the toilet (worrying as I did so about myself; my doctor had said, no heavy weights). I had always been finicky, not at all the nursing type. Now I was surprised at what I could do and never automatically or mechanically. Still, taking him to the toilet or giving him his sponge baths or even bringing him his plastic urinal and then waiting for him to finish so I could take it away, that did embarrass me. I could not make myself wash his genitals. It felt too wrong, like the breaking of a primitive taboo.

Care calling care. Manuele could not speak, but he made himself understood. At least to me. Often, when he had trouble getting through to Marco, he turned his eyes to me, expecting that I would know. And I would. Who would have ever thought? I began to sit with him to watch "Jeopardy" and "Wheel of Fortune," programs that bored me, but that he liked. I began to cook only what he might like to eat. As month followed month, he ate less and less. His throat still worked, but he would stop after a few bites. Marco and I tried to coax him. Be firm with him, said the social worker who visited to check up on us. He seems a willful type. Don't let him run you, she said. And I felt resentful. We sensed the cancer that had been cut out a couple of years before had returned. The doctor did not believe us. No sign, he said, the flu, he said. But we felt Manuele was breaking down.

And then suddenly, there was more than a sign, there were too many signs. His bowels loosened; his stomach refused any food. We changed and washed both Manuele and the sheets. Over and over. His temperature shot up, and we were woken every hour of the night. Manuele broke apart into blood and nerves, flesh and innards, a heart, lungs gasping for air. But his will hung on. At home and then in hospital, the weeks passed. He was placed on a respirator and taken off. My husband's brother and his wife had arrived, and the four of us divided up the day and night so that Manuele was never alone. His ex-wife came every day. His skin turned dark yellow; his legs swelled; the air rattled in his throat; still he hung on, fighting that last dissolution from flesh into matter. I would lean over into the fearful stink of decay and touch his hand or face. I talked. "You can let go now. Because you got what you wanted. You and your Sicilian ideas. You won. How many have sons like yours. They gave up everything when you needed them. Everything. And look at me. I served you. I bet you liked that. Being waited on hand and foot. All of us serving you. Even your wife. Loving you. All of us. So you can let go, give in. You've won."

When Manuele called me a princess in a tower, he wasn't entirely wrong. My tower was built from books and stories and ideas. None were wrong or false. But I have still fallen out, fallen to earth — grounded by the weight of my experience.

I watched Manuele's two sons clean and dress him in preparation for burial. I helped shift and lift his stiffening body. Before the coffin lid was closed, I bent for the first time and kissed his forehead.

~

Caterina Edwards has published one novel, *The Lion's Mouth*; a play, *HomeGround*; and many short stories in literary magazines and anthologies. Her latest book, *Whiter Shade of Pale/Becoming Emma*, consisting of two novellas, came out in 1992, and a collection of stories is scheduled for appearance in 1994. She lives in Edmonton with her husband Marco and two daughters, Tatiana and Antonia. Caterina says she writes "because I have to. Otherwise, I wouldn't."

Book of Knowledge

W E GAIN KNOWLEDGE NOT JUST from our experience but from the experiences of others as configured or constructed into stories, texts: language. Science, philosophy, and critical theories may inspire and enlighten us. Literature does even more; it moves intellect and emotion. The writers in this section make texts, remaking and reflecting other texts. They write, aware that the space they inscribe is a gift, an inheritance.

For Myrna Kostash, language itself is the inheritance she must reclaim in order to reconnect her story with the stories of her Ukrainian kin. Anne Ricard Burke represents herself with stories of her Iroquois grandfather and her family's denial of his (and their) race, telling us that she can only speak what has been suppressed because Native women and their children have spoken and written their stories.

Riskin, Auerbach, and Ladha testify to the importance of female mentors in finding their voice and a place from which to speak. Riskin's mentor was an exacting nun. Auerbach writes of her cousin, a more ambiguous guide, intense and self-destructive, who nevertheless inspires because she took Auerbach seriously as a writer. For Ladha, it is Phyllis Webb, the Canadian poet, who shows her the shape of the rooftop: a metaphorical place where women can resist the patriarchal injunction to remain silent and acquiescent and where Ladha can tell tales of women of her "tribe" (Asian women in Calgary) who have been killed by male oppression.

Like Ladha, Heather Menzies is horrified by the stories she reads in the newspaper day after day. Gradually, she begins to see a connection between the atrocities in the Gulf War and the neverending violence against women and children in Canada. Here we also suffer a war which allows no sanctuary and has its massacres. In "No Words" Sheree Fitch reminds us of the limitations of language in the face of such atrocities. Unable to find words to fight the horrible vision of the Montreal Massacre, she fights back with a very different visible symbol, an image of encircling love that brings back the possibility of hope.

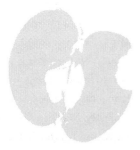

Casting Pearls

Mary Walters Riskin

HERE WERE SOFT NUNS AND hard nuns. It was in their faces — in the set of jaws, in the smoothness of cheeks and in the quickness of eyes. It was in the readiness of lips to purse, to smile, to frown. I wondered at the softness of the soft ones, and I feared the hardness of the hard. Sister Mary Isobel was one of those who could inspire fear.

I'd been sent to the Mount St. Joseph Academy, a boarding school contained within a convent, because my mother had just died. Through this pale stone building, which would be my lodging for the year, moved the nuns who taught us, and those too old to teach, and the young ones — the novitiates. I was not accustomed to nuns, and the halls seemed full of their black presences, the rustle of skirts and click of beads made audible by their quiet ways.

The Sisters of St. Joseph wore long-sleeved, full-length black gowns, crisp white wimples which framed their faces, and sheer black veils. Their rosary beads swung down against their skirts. Over time they distinguished themselves — the tall from the short, the heavy from the thin, the history teacher from the study supervisor. But learning who they were had most to do with faces. Faces framed in white. Kind faces, wrinkled faces, smooth clear innocent young ones. Hard faces and soft faces.

Sister Mary Isobel looked over the rims of her metal-framed glasses with a disdain that seemed oddly out of place in a house of piety and self-effacement. Her complexion was ruddy, as though she'd been recently working in the sun. She was not tall but she was robust and solid, and the hardness of her face was reiterated in her bearing. Her back was straight, her shoulders square and her gait measured and determined.

She seemed, more than any of the others, to be trailing bits of the outside world along with her as she strode through the hallways of the convent and the school, books closed within her arms. She'd been a newspaper reporter, before, outside. There were romantic rumours. That she'd joined the sisterhood when her fiancé was killed, in an accident or war. That she'd thrown her last cigarette away as she walked up the convent steps. Her haughty demeanour reinforced such stories, and I think the habit of a nun suited her dramatic tastes.

She was strict, and early on we learned to avoid her temper. The classes she taught were expected to be quiet and utterly attentive. If a pin did drop, she'd hear it, and she would stop, and turn, and study the fallen thing, and show it to the girls nearby, and discuss its value, until its owner was sufficiently humiliated that she would not drop the pin again. Sister Mary Isobel was there to teach us English, not to baby-sit: fifteen-year-old girls should have enough self-discipline to make that aspect of a teacher's job superfluous.

She expected all of us to be as entranced by words as she. She read aloud to us. Poetry and stories. Essays. Dickinson and cummings, Swift and Browning. She demanded our appreciation for the writers and the words. She required silence and attention. She was not popular.

By way of atonement, and to evade grief, I threw myself into my studies. So lost within myself was I, that I was surprised when my work attracted Sister Mary Isobel's attention. I hadn't done it for her; I had done it for my mother. But as she noticed me, I began to write for her. I began to read for her. I showed her things I did when I ran out of essays to write and exams to study for. She admired the phrases in my dark poetry and approved the structure and the language of my bleak stories. She showed me that writing was an activity in itself, not just a way out of — or into — despair. It had a life of its own, writing. It could be better than it was. It could be worse.

Over the course of the year, she lifted me up and out. She remarked to others on my industry and creativity, and winning the approbation of this most demanding of all the women veiled in black was like receiving a benediction.

One afternoon in March she offered us a poem, "Resurrection," appropriate to the season and the setting. But there were knots of distraction in the room, restless adolescent girls with the spring sun on us, uneasy, impatient, primed. We whispered, twisted, turned, like seeds about to burst.

Sister Mary Isobel looked up, her face reddening. Silence fell. She closed her book.

"It has been said that teaching is like casting pearls before swine," she told us. She looked over her glasses at us. We waited, breaths drawn in. The silence lengthened. She lowered her voice and raised her head. "I have cast my pearls," she said.

She swept from the classroom, head up, her veil whisked out by the suddenness of her movement. Beads swinging with her gait, she swept her skirts out of harm's way as she slammed the door closed behind her.

After a minute or two, someone began to laugh, and then others did. Laughed relief, laughed self-protection, laughed to stitch self-respect together again.

I sat and watched the door she had gone through and thought applause would have been a better response than laughter.

The following year, I went to a coed high school two thousand miles away. We didn't stay in touch. A few years later, I heard she went to Africa. Many years later, when my first book was published and I wanted to send a copy, I learned that she had died.

I, too, became a teacher. Not because of her, but because I skipped so many chemistry classes that I flunked out of Arts and into Education. However, the idea of teaching grew on me when I remembered her and one or two other real teachers I had known. I imagined I might share with eager learners my love of literature. Instead, the hours were eroded with field trips, detentions, electives, dances, counselling sessions, and film strips. How can you find literature when there are no silences?

Sister Mary Isobel wouldn't have put up with it. She'd have demanded their attention, demanded they sit still and listen, learn. If they had, they'd have been rewarded in ways they'd understand much later. If not . . . well, it wasn't her problem. She cast her pearls.

I could never have asked her why she'd become a nun. Our intimacy was on another plane. But whatever the rage, or loss — or vision — that made her want to shut herself away within those quiet confines, whatever private drama needed to be given voice by those dark gowns, she became a teacher. And inasmuch as the best kinds of teaching heal, she'd also learned to heal.

∽

Mary Walters Riskin was born in Wainright, Alberta, and raised in London, Ontario. She moved to Edmonton in 1966. She is the author of *The Woman Upstairs*, which won the Writers Guild of Alberta Award for Excellence in Writing (novel category) in 1988. She has recently completed a collection of short stories and is working on another novel. Her hour-long programme, "Reflections on Solitude," was broadcast on CBC's "Ideas" in 1993. Mary has worked as executive director of the Writers Guild of Alberta and as editor-in-chief at Lone Pine Publishing. She is currently self-employed as a freelance writer and editor.

my cousin the writer

Elaine Auerbach

*J*NO LONGER POSSESS THEM
and they no longer possess me. I threw them off the cliff at Eagle
Rock. Spilling from the edge, unravelling over dry weeds, through
clefts of stone, they unfurled and fell in soundless ripples, rushing
toward oblivion.

The hosiery — emerald green, royal blue, burnt orange, black
— had belonged to my cousin, Anne Marie. My mother had sent
it to me. A strange inheritance. Imagine. Wearing hand-me-down
panty hose. Like wearing used underwear. Can I smile now? Of
course I can. I can be cruel in sympathy. But mostly I am curious.
Death, especially the suicide of a relative, always makes a person
curious.

I could collect details about my cousin's life — she was born in
Passaic, New Jersey, she had an older brother who was an army
general, her parents owned a restaurant, she had a collie named
Lady, she was once engaged to a student who was nicknamed "The
Pirate" because he had a wooden leg. But these are simply facts
that anyone could collect. If I am to be curious, I tell myself as I
am writing this, my curiosity must be more than a simple prying
into Anne Marie's personal life; I'd rather tell, then, of two
encounters I had with Anne Marie, moments of discovery, loss,
and uncertainty, that bridge the chasm of oblivion as none of the
facts ever could.

Although Anne Marie lived in the same town where I grew up, I rarely spent any time with her or with her family. I knew where she lived and I placed her there quite easily with her dog Lady and the calico-covered sofa and the brass eagle hanging over the mantlepiece. On the night I went to the meeting of the Franklin Writer's Group at her parents' home, I was twenty-two and she was thirty-one. Gertrude Stein once said that before the age of twenty-nine, life is a great dim possibility. At thirty, it becomes a small, hard reality. I was too dim to see that Anne Marie had become intimate with hard reality.

When she telephoned me in late October, I didn't know who she was and had only clues as to who I might be. Her voice was distant, monotone. She was convinced that she knew me. She remembered a great deal of my past which I had been quick to forget, reminding me that I had once written the history column "Seems Like Only Yesterday" for the town newspaper and had a few poems in the local literary magazine *The Light Brigade*. It was peculiar talking with her. She was a stranger who was familiar to me as a character in family gossip, as someone who had gone away to university, dropped out after two years, and had a nervous breakdown. And I felt odd hearing her tell me all about myself when I had given her hardly a thought. She told me she had joined the Franklin Writer's Group and was convinced that I belonged in it. She wanted me to attend a meeting. Her request wasn't framed as a favour, even though I heard it as a favour. At that time, I was living in fragments and writing in fragments, avoiding completion of any kind. What I was writing exposed my vulnerability, my unproclaimed erotic feelings for women. I took whatever temporary jobs came along. I was comfortable. I had my own apartment. I was independent in a way many women I knew only fantasized about. But my life was a petrifying maze. I survived from day to day, inwardly terrified, trapped by my feelings. Anne Marie's life seemed so courageous, so fixed in its purpose, that I buried the terror and accepted her invitation.

We were six women seated in the colonially furnished living

room in that quaint house by the brook. Pelting rain spotted the windows. Red, white, and blue curtains framed the openings onto the black hole of night. In the middle of the floor lay a plastic yellow rain hat catching the lamplight, showering the room in reflected golden waves.

No child was present, but children were clinging to the room, to women's bodies like an extra layer of clothing. Anne Marie and I were the only ones without children. This alone could have brought us together — two women childless and mateless — but under the hovering spirit of the brood we remained far apart.

Everyone had graduated from university except Anne Marie. Though I couldn't identify with these women's lives at the time, I understood later that we were all intelligent, capable women seeking an unnameable fulfillment that family or work had failed to provide. Martha, whose husband operated the town's only pharmacy where she worked seven days a week, read two pages about her daughter's first day at school, and Clair, an elementary schoolteacher, told a tale she had written for her students about a young fish who learns the hard way not to be attracted to every shiny object floating in the sea. Sally, the vice-principal of Franklin High School, recited a poem about the war in Vietnam, while Paula, an artist who taught drawing and watercolour, offered nothing, preferring to listen with the right amount of politeness, interjecting little words of praise for each woman's efforts.

When it was Anne Marie's turn to read, the atmosphere of the room shifted. Spirited chatter gave way to solemn silence. And with rain pebbling the windows, the fireplace hissing and sparking and scenting our circle with the odour of pine, Anne Marie, swaying back and forth in the high-backed maple rocker, bathed in the honey-spreading light of a milk-can lamp, loudly announced, "I don't think I'll read anything tonight. I have to research my subject some more." Then she leaned over and said to me, "I'm glad you came. I wanted everyone to meet my cousin, the writer."

It was the first time I had noticed how crooked her eyes were. The left was a great deal lower and more heavily lidded than the right. Her speech was inordinately slow, as if she were just awakening from a long sleep that had been more tiring than restful. Her mouth was in the shape of an inverted smile. She struggled constantly, with little success, to force the downturned lines towards the opposite direction.

For the rest of the evening she was deferential to me, causing me some embarrassment in the face of women I had only just met. She smiled encouragingly as I began to read from an unfinished story. It described a woman drying the inside of a drinking glass, revolving and turning the cloth until the sides of the glass were shiny and clear.

We paid homage to our creativity on that wet evening in October, all of us who were gathered in the maple and brassy hues of the Early American living room in the quaint house by the brook. But what we excelled at best was suppressing our fear of Anne Marie and her terrible rapture of attention.

ii.

I never saw Anne Marie or talked to her again after that night.

Years after that damp autumn evening, after her descent into the basement to end her life, I had a dream.

It is the naked light before a storm, when all shadows have evaporated. Anne Marie, her body a haloed tracery of gold moving through the landscape of cinder white light, emerges from the shaded interior of her grey stone house and makes her way up the walk to a red house, cupping in her hands a bouquet of poppies in a glass filled with water. The story of the woman drying the inside of a drinking glass, the fragment I had read to the Franklin Writer's Group, has become the story of a woman leaving behind the dark room to which she has descended, to reenter the world to complete her quest.

The house Anne Marie approaches is hers and isn't hers. The roof is made of cotton, like those on the cardboard houses that I would ritually arrange under my grandmother's Christmas tree every year. The heavy brown door opens before she knocks. An old woman greets her, happy to receive her visit and her gift. As Anne Marie turns to leave the door, she still possesses the glass of flowers, even though she has given it away to the old woman. From Anne Marie I learn this paradoxical lesson: unless I give away my fragile "glass" stories, I will always wander empty-handed, feeling the loss of what could have been.

When Anne Marie told me I was a writer, I took it to heart more than when I tried to tell myself the same thing. Maybe I believed her because I was dim. But maybe it's more important that you're just being kind, as I was to Anne Marie and as she was to me. Doing a favour for a fellow human being because you feel that we're all part of a something or other that stretches far beyond oblivion, far beyond the discarded second-hand clothes of the dead and the faded first-hand memories of the living.

~

Elaine Auerbach was raised in Nutley, New Jersey. She came to Canada in 1975 and lived in Vancouver and Edmonton before moving in 1986 to Waterloo, Ontario. She works as a freelance editor, teacher, and community arts volunteer. Her writing has appeared in numerous journals and anthologies and she is currently completing a novel. "My cousin the writer" is dedicated to Anne Marie.

How I Lost My Tongue

Myrna Kostash

A T NINE O'CLOCK THE CHIL-
dren were already in school. The children prayed and sang with
the teacher. The teacher taught the children to read and write, to
paint and to sing, to draw pictures and play games. The children
loved the teacher." From *Marusia*, Ukrainian-language reader
published in Saskatoon in 1947.

The reader has fallen apart, utterly, although the pages remain
clear and clean, as though I had first read the book only months
ago. I leaf through it: the illustrations are acutely familiar to me —
the frog, or *zhaba*, the fairies floating on dewdrops like miniature
parachutists, Marusia gathering flowers from the garden, the
teacher, greeting Marusia and Roman, in a splendid green coat
and matching green hat — and even the lessons resonate like fragments of poems once memorized whole and now remembered
only for their refrains.

*Dzvony dzvoniat, bam-bam-bam. Hen vysoko u dzvinytsi, tam-
tam-tam. Dzvony dzvoniat, dzvony klychut, nas-nas-nas. Chy do
shkoly, chy do tserkvy, chas-chas-chas.* The bells are ringing, ding-
dang-dong. From afar in the bell-tower, there-there-there. The
bells are ringing, the bells are calling us-us-us. To school or to
church, it's time-time-time.

There is nothing remotely ethnic in these lessons, save for a
story about lighting candles on Christmas Eve. Marusia and
Roman live in Middle Canada, in a suburban bungalow where

Mother wears an apron and serves supper and Father appears twice — to eat, and to dandle the baby — and summer is spent at the lake, building sandcastles, and children go to sleep with teddy bears. This is upwardly-mobile, lower middle class hyphenated-Canada seduced, not by its own difference but by its adaptability.

And yet the little book reeks of that quintessential ethnic pastime — the mother, her children gathered around her, reading in the mother tongue the stories of little ones in an alien place — for this is how I learned to read *Marusia*, curled up against my mother's shoulder, my sister at her other shoulder, while the book lay open before us and we read out loud, along with her, chanting the text like a trio of cantors in church, and if not strictly *alien* (the bungalow, the teddy bear) it was nevertheless *other than* everyday life.

For these supremely banal anecdotes, about fairies and frogs, and going to school and telling the time, were told *in the Ukrainian language*, the language reserved for extraordinary occasions and places — church, concerts, speeches, the national anthem, prayers, and those mysterious but clamorous arguments that broke out between my father and grandfather, voices rising, hands slapping authoritatively at their respective newspapers — and here we were, this intimate, feminine colloquy intoning the sounds of that very same language.

And how I loved to write out the letters, all the curlicues and whorls and slanted strokes of the Cyrillic alphabet, *drawing* them, for long before the letters arranged themselves into discrete, meaningful words, the written Ukrainian language in my eyes was a picture — a design, perhaps, such as one could trace in a carpet or on an embroidered cushion. Pleasing. Like the swirl of my name written in Ukrainian in the front of the reader in my mother's hand.

Yet this sense of otherness is perhaps too self-conscious, and does not belong to the little girl at her lessons, for I don't think I then thought of these sounds and letters as strange or exotic. Private, yes; belonging to this intimate space in the pool of light in the living room or, later, in the church basement where none but

Ukrainian-Canadians would wish to gather to study. But I had seen the letters all my life — in my father's newspapers, on the envelopes that came all the way from Dzhuriv in the USSR, crabbed and cuneiform on the icons in church. And had heard the language from birth (Baba holding me gingerly, her first grandchild, as she stood in front of her root cellar) and had even, so I was told, spoken it babyishly. It was synchronous with my sensory life.

It was, in an important sense, my first language and my mothered tongue. What perverse process alienated it from my mouth?

Kiev, 1984

I stood on a street corner near a group of schoolchildren and listened to them speaking with each other in Russian. We waited together while a battered delivery truck cantered through the intersection, bearing the utilitarian inscription, KHLEB. That's Russian, for bread.

In Ukraine, legendary bread basket for eastern Europe, mythologized and memorialized as the Earth Mother cradling a sheaf of wheat in her round, stout arms, as the three-layered and crusty, coiled *kalach,* they eat bread in Russian.

All my life I had heard about this tragedy — how our kith and kin back home in Ukraine were having the Mother Tongue squeezed out of them, leaving behind a hollowed-out Ukrainian ashamed of a language which in any case he or she could no longer speak with any felicity. The Ukrainian language, as if by some scientific, philological law, was petering out. Russian, on the other hand, belonged to the ages.

I knew all this. I had heard it all my life.

I went to my baba's village. I met with her brother's descendants. They spoke Ukrainian. I didn't.

"Now," intone the elders in Canada, "do you understand why we send you to language school on Saturdays in the middle of Middle Canada?"

From 1963 to 1968, I studied the Russian language and literature as my major subject at university. The Russian language was presented to me as a World Language: millions of people in an important country —"Russia"— spoke it. It signified the language of a World Literature: major, canonical, essential. Every literate person in the world knows its writers. As I had earlier come to love the language of John Keats and then Arthur Rimbaud, I now loved the language of Alexander Pushkin. I learned whole poems by heart. I even learned how to sing one to the music scored by Glinka.

Ia vas liubil, liubov eshcho byt mozhet,
V dushe moei ugasla ne sovsem.

I loved you, and love, perhaps,
Still flickers in my soul.

I loved those words, and rolled them around in my mouth like fruity lozenges, sucking out their hard sibilants, their throaty linguals, as though wooing the poet myself with my flickering tongue.

Screened from us, however, was the official, Soviet state attitude to the Russian language. Because of the undeniable historical fact that the Bolshevik revolutionaries had spoken Russian to each other, the Russian language was deemed more "democratic" than other languages. It was not enough that this should seem to be merely "rational"; it had to be seen as irresistible. The non-Russian citizen was exhorted to learn Russian out of love and obligation to the Soviet motherland and by this means to gain access to the works of the titans, the patriarchs, the guardians of the revolution which had liberated them all, from the Black Sea to the Bering Straits.

Now in Kiev, in June 1984, a cold hard rain had been driving down all day from the steely sky and I came back to the hotel room miserable: wet, cold, and disconsolate. All day we had been trying to contact a friend of a friend by telephone in public kiosks but it had proved impossible — broken connections, wrong numbers. I was obsessed with the doleful realization that, had this been a normal country, with normal habits, we would have been able to telephone from our hotel room (here bugged), consult a telephone directory (here classified), or take a taxi to the address (here driven by a chauffeur on the KGB take). I cursed this society which was frightened even of strangers befriending each other.

I turned to the television set, a bulky console on a table by the window where thin white curtains barely screened from view the sheets of rainwater falling into the mucky, rubbishy courtyard. The set was turned on to the so-called Ukrainian channel (the other two broadcasting from Moscow). It was late in the afternoon. A children's program. Introduced in Ukrainian. A cartoon, of cuddly bears and fuzzy-wuzzy ducks and tiny, squeaky kiddies. In Russian.

And suddenly, I couldn't bear it: the Russian language vibrating in my skull in sonorous clarity, choleric, harsh, and disciplinary. I wept from chagrin, from biliousness. I turned off the television with a savage yank at the cord and turned on the radio.

A concert program. A Ukrainian baritone singing, in exquisite diction, the song by Glinka.

Ia vas liubil, liubov eshcho byt mozhet. . . .

Was I now to hate Pushkin too?

In the fall of 1984, on my return from Ukraine and still smarting from my rude encounters with russification, I decided to learn to speak Ukrainian. I began where I had left off, thirty years earlier: the Saturday School. No longer held in the church basement, the Saturday Ukrainian language classes — the Ridna Shkola — were now conducted in the church hall, a modern facility.

Together with some twenty teenagers, I enrolled in the Senior class. The teenagers radiated a self-confidence in their youthfulness and in their ethnicity that were quite absent from my generation at their age. I reminded myself that these kids were the *great*-grandchildren of Galician immigrants — their ethnic baggage carried purely Canadian content and the last immigrant in their families had died quite some time ago.

I sat at the front of the class, took notes, listened attentively, raised my hand to answer questions and did all my homework. I was a model student.

In learning to speak Ukrainian, I found myself in a stew of emotions. To be middle-aged and at the beginning of a new learning is a humbling experience but I bent my head to it and persevered, recovering as best I could from the periodic ravages of humiliation when I realized that my self-expression in Ukrainian rendered me idiotic and simple-minded in the extreme. For someone accustomed to see herself and *to be seen as* articulate, well-spoken, and opinionated, this infantilization — this forcible return to baby talk — was abusive. But I did not quit. As I became progressively more able to read complex texts I was exhilarated: I was becoming smarter.

Finally, the day came when I opened my brand-new copy of Taras Shevchenko's *Kobzar*, his collected poems, a book that is in every Ukrainian-Canadian home even if no one reads it (much like Gideon Bibles are in motel rooms). It was my very own copy, just purchased at the Ukrainian Book Store, a Soviet edition, with extensive notes.

I began with the first poem, consulting the dictionary when I had to and underlining words to remember, and so on, poem after poem, until I was a third of the way through the book and reading one of the most famous poems of them all, "The Haidamaky," when I suddenly realized I was not just reading Shevchenko: I was *inside* the language, understanding it directly, the profoundly familiar sounds of it all at once meaningful and carrying a story, a voice, a personality where before there had been only babble.

"Ah," I said to myself, with heated satisfaction, "so this is what they mean by 'Shevchenko.' "

And in picturing myself taking my place among the generations who had read these poems I had another image: that someone had just come along and wiped clean a foggy window through which I had been peering my whole life, nose pressed to the pane, steaming it up with my own breath. For just a few moments I saw through to the other side, to the company of literates who had known all along the beauty carried by the Ukrainian language and the splendid architecture of its poetry. Soon enough I was once again stumbling and tongue-tied and overwhelmed by the learning still to be done. But *I* knew that once I had been inside the words, without translation.

For at least a generation, since the catastrophic educational "reforms" of the 1960s in Ukraine which gave parents the "freedom to choose" Russian-language or Ukrainian-language schooling for their children, the Ukrainian language had been disappearing from public use — from schools and textbooks, from the mass media, even from road signs, posters, and information about trolleybus routes.

Along with this erasure was disappearing the collective remembrance of a language which had produced literature and theology and historiography, leaving many millions of Soviet Ukrainians vaguely embarrassed by this Mother Tongue which lacked status and authority.

I felt implicated in all this.

While for several years I had acquiesced in spending my Saturdays at "Ukrainian school," I had been a reluctant student, made wretched by my dim-witted understanding of what was being taught me and enlivened only by the hour devoted to singing and dancing. (In fact, I was rather good at the dancing, and this was my most successful "performance" as a Ukrainian-Canadian girl.)

Now, as a grown-up, I felt I owed a number of people apologies. To the patient if uninspired teachers, community volunteers who, like me, were spending their Saturdays in the church basement and who tried their best to illuminate for me the secret codes of the Mother Tongue. To my parents who, wishing to enrol the next generation in the Ridna Shkola, committed me to an instruction to which I was miserably unequal, failing as I did to understand not just mere words but the whole enveloping reason for being there. To my Ukrainian kin who were losing their language under the ferocious pressure of state policy while I was losing it from a supercilious disinclination.

To a Canadian-born child, the responsibility for continuing to speak a language imperilled in its own homeland was onerous but irrefutable; imagine, then, the sense of personal, intimate, and peculiar *failure* of the child — found wanting before the ancestors — who could not speak Ukrainian.

Now, as a grown-up, I would try again, almost defiantly, daring the ghosts of the martyrs, the despairing teachers, the teenaged girl, now daring them to say I couldn't do it. I *would* speak, and in speaking be granted membership, if only provisional, in that remote society of the true patriots, the sons and daughters of Ukraine, the Ukrainophiles. I had much to make up for, years and years of indifference and, worse, disrespect. I *would* be forgiven.

I would learn to speak Ukrainian so that, on going back to Ukraine and seeing the relatives again, I could speak with them. I owed this, first of all, to my baba. The relatives were the descendants of her brother, family she had never seen. She would have wanted me to visit them and to speak with them.

But I would learn this language to keep another kind of faith with her — this gentle, pink-cheeked, round-headed old woman who could speak no English but who never, with not a word, not once reproached me for speechlessness before her. Now it is I who reproach myself, that I have taken up this learning too late.

She died in a state of failed communication with me — her language and memory so much gibberish to me at the time. She was the last person in a long line of generations who spoke only Ukrainian and I broke the chain, speaking it not at all. Now I pick it up, wanting to hammer back my link in it, so that Baba might live again in my broken, stammering syllables.

I Get My Wish

In 1988 I travelled again to Ukraine, this time endowed with the power of speech.

As before, I heard the Russian language everywhere. On the so-called Ukrainian television station, an interviewer addressed his guest, a Komsomol bureaucrat, in Ukrainian and was answered in Russian. In the streets of Kiev, a television journalist chatted with a group of very young schoolchildren: he addressed them in Russian, they replied in kind. A little girl even burst forth with a poem by Pushkin.

The Russian language was pervasive, like a gas — in the airport bus, the Customs Hall, the hotel restaurant, on the rock videos, in the boutiques. But, this time, I did not stand by rainy windows and weep.

I revelled in the sounds I was making, even though I often retreated to my hotel room, my tongue swollen with exhaustion, my brain depleted of all vocabulary. Although I often failed to understand jokes, the lyrics of pop songs, and the banter of children, there was much, much I did understand — speeches, arguments, manifestoes — and although I was often too abashed to do more in conversation than to ask intelligent questions, I was exhilarated by my verve, as though I were dancing.

The Russian I once knew had been filed in some deep archive of my brain; the Ukrainian I was speaking had risen up and inscribed itself on my tongue as though I once knew how to speak it and had only now to remember.

And so I went to the provinces, to the village, met my relatives, opened my mouth, and spoke.

~

Myrna Kostash was born in Edmonton and educated at the University of Alberta and at the University of Toronto before hitchhiking in Europe for two years. After freelancing and teaching in the Women's Studies program at the University of Toronto, she returned to Alberta in 1975 to research and write her first book, *All of Baba's Children*, about the first generation of Ukrainian-Canadians. She has also published *Long Way From Home* (1980), *No Kidding: Inside the World of Teenage Girls* (1987), and *Bloodlines* (1993), based on conversations with writers and political dissidents in eastern Europe. She lives in a housing co-op in Edmonton and spends her summers on her quarter-section near Two Hills, Alberta.

No Words

Sheree Fitch

I REMEMBER WHERE I WAS; what I was wearing; what I was doing.

In the kitchen; in my terry-cloth housecoat; waiting for the toast to pop.

The radio was on.

Then I heard the words: fourteen women . . . machine gun . . . man . . . bunch of feminists.

From far off I heard the deep-bellied moan of a woman in pain: a moan that grew louder until finally it was a wail.

It wasn't until my sons came rushing into the kitchen that I realized that the woman who was crying was me.

I tried to explain to them; but I had no words.

The toaster popped.

I jumped.

~

As soon as they left for school, I phoned a friend.

I mumbled.

But she was a friend who felt and understood despite my incoherence.

I attended the vigil held in this city.

I listened to others put words to my feelings, sometimes eloquently; but still they were not my words — and I needed to have some, for words are my tools for survival, for unscrambling and ordering reality so that I might live in this world of machine guns.

~

As we left the engineering building where the vigil was held, my candle blew out. Someone immediately reached over and lit it for me. I looked up. It was a man. Someone I knew, but not well.

Somehow, this simple act of kindness gave me hope. But again I could say nothing. No words to tell him how very important it was that he care enough to light my candle . . . no words to tell him that I knew he was a kind man. Because at this moment his maleness represented my vulnerability.

~

I could not read the newspapers or watch the news. Those words laid out events, told details, gave names and faces. I, deliberately and selfishly, did not want to know. I read enough to find out that the man, the murderer, the predator, had been victim also. Of hatred, violence, abuse, as a child. Those words did not assuage the pain.

~

Several weeks later I finally figured out what I had to do.

I was in a log cabin, where the only sound I heard was snow sifting off the trees, trying to write, trying to find words for what had happened and still there was only confusion. No, it was not just an isolated act of violence by a madman. It was that and so much more. A visible symbol of something that operated in this world. It was not only male versus female; it was much larger than that. It was about conquerors and victims; love and hate; evil and goodness. It was a reminder that if we as a human race have come far, we still have a very long way to go.

Long way to go.

I wrote those words in my journal. Stared at them. Montreal was not a long way. Suddenly it seemed urgent that I should go there. I called an old friend from university days. She seemed to know immediately what I was stuttering over the phone line.

~

It was a Sunday morning in February. There was not much snow but there was a fierce wind. We walked for about an hour through the streets of old Montreal until we came to the cathedral. Neither one of us was Catholic, but it didn't matter. We sat in the stillness of the church, got up, linked arms, and stood in front of a mural of Mary. We lit our candles and left.

But it was not that act that healed me most. It was something else on that trip — something I didn't realize until after — that I had been searching for.

~

On the plane to Montreal there was a strikingly beautiful woman across the aisle from me. She was dark-skinned, young, and she held an infant on her lap. Was discreetly trying to nurse her baby in the crowded plane. When I looked at her, I thought of her beauty, of her baby daughter; of the hope that infants inspire. I thought then of those fourteen young women who would never get the chance to become engineers, or to become mothers either. Of how this tragedy was also about all that was left undone, unfulfilled, all that was in them that was stopped from shining forth.

As we left the plane, I watched the woman struggle with luggage and her baby. So I offered to help. She shook her head. She didn't understand. I tried French. She shook her head again. "*Yo hablo español,*" she said. So with a sort of sign language I asked if I could take her luggage. She nodded gratefully. We walked in silence to the baggage terminal. I set down the bags and made cooing sounds at the baby. Then, from behind us, a young man came and encircled the two of them in his arms; kissing them, hugging them, spinning them around. I disappeared quickly to the other side of the conveyor as the luggage came tumbling down.

Then the young man was there in front of me. He started speaking to me in French. I shrugged that I did not understand that well. He switched easily to English.

"My wife tells me you were kind to her, thank you."

"Your wife and daughter are beautiful," I said.

"I know," he said.

"How long since you've seen each other?" I did not even know why I asked the question.

"One month. They have been in Venezuela. Too long . . . too far away," he said.

And they left.

~

So it was, in my search for words, for healing, so that I could live with the death of these fourteen women, I discovered that it was not words I needed at all. For there were no words. But I found an image. An image of love, goodness, caring. That man and woman and child in that airport.

So when it comes rushing back to me, the images of those corridors, the images of hatred, of violence, I acknowledge the horror, but then I try to focus on the other image. Immediately I conjure up the vision of these three spinning around in an endless circle of love.

And I will hang on to that picture, in order to live with this tragedy; hang on to this picture: as a woman, a daughter, a mother, a writer, a teacher, a sister, a feminist, a human being. I can live without words, but I cannot live without a vision of hope.

~

In her own words: A mother-poet-performer-broadcaster-teacher-conference speaker-former adult learner/yearner now b.a. m.a. so what's that mean I am a ma-M.A.? In other words, a professional plate-spinner/meaning-maker with six books out now, five from the child selves inside me, and one collection of adult poetry called *In This House Are Many Women* (Gooselane Editions, 1993). I write in many voices. To roar or bellow, lament or weep, laugh or dance. I call *No Words* a Her(e)(s)say. It was first broadcast on CBC radio.

War and the Continuum of Violence
Heather Menzies

*O*NE OF MY FAVOURITE MEMO-
ries from the 1960s is of travelling to Ottawa for an anti-Vietnam
War demonstration, where I walked for a while beside the great
Tommy Douglas. What I had forgotten until recently is what happened later. Bused back to Montreal that evening, I was walking
up the street towards where I lived in a rooming house near the
university, humming "We Shall Overcome" to myself, when a man
jumped me from behind.

I'd also forgotten that in the peace movement of the day,
the men did the talking; the women kept quiet and were pleas-
ingly supportive. This is probably why I later joined the Voice of
Women, a Canadian women's peace group begun in the early
1960s. But it took me a while to define what "peace" meant for me
personally, as a woman.

The following is a meditation on my journey home: a journey
from war, of which I have no experience, into the continuum of
violence against women, in which I do.

January, 1991
Throughout the Persian Gulf War I dragged them around, the
bodies of my dead and wounded. There was no chance to speak of
them, these bruised and battered women when, there on the global news, Baghdad flared like a torch. The casualties I knew about
were local. They were reported in the local paper, though sepa-

rately as "abuse" and "family violence." I filed their stories in an old shopping bag. Week after week I carried the bag of clippings to meetings of the local chapter of the Voice of Women, trying to bring the women's experience into our discussions. The bag was in the way as we passed around press releases from the Peace Network, the Disarmament Coalition, the Coalition to Oppose the Arms Trade, and so on. One organization was spending five thousand dollars on advertising alone for a Canada-wide peace march. Would we join them, and send a donation?

The war was finished before that event got its chance. Since then, nothing, except the five hundred jobs created as Canadian law was bent permitting General Motors in Oshawa, Ontario, to manufacture armed personnel carriers. The stock market has settled back. Life has returned to "normal."

A flicker of memory interjects: my nine-year-old son Donald cutting me off midsentence in supper table conversation — something he never, ever does with his father; though I've always tried not to dwell on it.

I return to the newspapers.

On January 17, while the headline "Bombs Rain on Baghdad" occupied the front page of the *Ottawa Citizen* and a seven-by-five-inch colour picture glorified two handsome pilots riding their lethal smart-bomb planes, inside the paper, smaller unobtrusive type reported that an army colonel had been found guilty of repeated sexual assaults against his stepdaughter. The assaults began when the girl was seven. They went on until she "left home" at fifteen.

In the standard column on "police reports," that same first day of Gulf War news, three inches of type matter-of-factly reported three "incidents" of sexual assault, all coincidentally by thirty-five-year-olds: one man on his twelve-year-old stepdaughter; the second man on a twenty-four-year-old woman who'd accepted his offer of a ride home; and a third, against his eighteen-year-old ex-girlfriend.

On January 19, as the front section of the *Ottawa Citizen* continued to mythologize war — with "Small-town America" quoted as saying "Let's kick butt," the "City" section quietly reported the conviction of a man for bludgeoning his mother to death with a hammer, and another man for sexually assaulting his daughter. The incest began when she was ten years old, with forced sex up to three times a week. The experience has left her psychologically "disabled," the news brief added.

The women in our group saw the connections: Women as "refugees" in their own communities; women as "casualties" and the "walking wounded." But we never acted on them. Not because there were men in the room saying we were hitching "women's" issues onto the peace movement. We, the Voice of Women, did it to ourselves. We did it through the constraints of time and structure we embodied as career women meeting as an amateur, voluntary organization. It takes time — and courage, passion, anger — to break old moulds and old, prescribed agendas. Besides, we were busy being helpful, organizing a "media" event: a Women's Walk for Peace, for February 16.

I placed the bag of newspaper clippings in the centre of the room. Was there time to live the details of the women's experience? Time to be moved to respond no matter what the constraints? Even time to hand the stories around? But there were announcements to be made, the latest developments both in the war and in protests against it to be discussed. Just two hours, and could we please have some order here? One person speaking at a time: stay on topic, stay on target. The coffee tin is passed around: for sending press releases to the media, for advance coverage of our peace talk. Give what you can.

I too have been a target. His "smart" weapon was a credit card slipped without a sound into the crack I'd never noticed between the door and the door frame of the apartment I'd just moved into in a city far from home. I awoke to something hazy and dark obstructing my view and a prickling sharpness digging into my neck. I focussed on the darkness. It was heavy. It was on my chest. A man, here on my bed. A man I'd never seen before. Kneeling on my chest. Dark jack-shirt, dark hair, face in shadow close to mine.

Stale-cigarette breath telling me not to scream or he'll kill me. It's a knife there at my neck. And suddenly he's biting me. Biting my breasts. Breasts I'd waited for so long. When I was sixteen and they bloomed at last, I took to wearing soft fabrics so I could feel them rubbing, bouncing ever so slightly against the inside of my blouse. My breasts. Now taken, seized by this unknown man. He tore at them like they were steak. I didn't count, didn't exist as a person.

The assault did not end with his running away down the hall that night. Twenty years later, he persists in the shadows, as does the certainty that he can return. Any day. Anywhere. He's with me always, weighing me down with the knowledge of his seamless invasion. And where that memory is, I am not. Not as I was before, not fully myself within myself. Not at peace, whole and sovereign. Under the surface faith, I am always taut, poised for the next assault. Conscious of myself, as a sexual target.

The coffee can is being passed. The woman who's chairing tonight consults the agenda we'd agreed, given the time, to follow. We must plan the main elements in our "women's walk" event.

(What about the women?)

I couldn't even ask the question. The deadline drew me, chastened me. Silenced.

I drafted some participatory chants: words disembodied from the context of shared experience, though they were effective in their way — and made it to the ten o'clock news.

"They say a thousand 'sorties' a day and the 'losses' are small. We say sorties are bombs. Losses are death, grief and revenge."
"Stop the trivialization of suffering."
"All life is sacred. Nous voulons la paix."

The parallels were there: "sorties" of violence on jogging paths and back bedrooms. "Losses" calculated not just in lives, in bodies mutilated or traumatized, no longer capable of feeling. But equally in the loss of innocence, of the freedom to jog, to walk, and to breathe in peace and equilibrium. Peace is an environment, an environment conducive to communion and community.

The resonances go further. Women as D.P.s, Displaced Persons. Displaced, not just from their homes in the sense of the home as sanctuary where one can be one's own self. The violation is so deep, women are displaced from being fully at home and alive within their own bodies as well. But like the sad and seemingly inevitable refugee and D.P. of war, like the "heroic" wounded soldier as well, we are expected to be noble: to live in what's left, struggle to find ourselves in the ruins. Silently and uncomplainingly.

And "they" say, "you don't know what you're talking about!" "They" are the military experts. They hold a monopoly in the discourse on war, and by doing so, guarantee its perpetuation from one millennium to the next. Yet we know too — though our knowledge is of a different kind. Not war treated out of context as if it were a game with one side winning and making it all worthwhile. Not war discussed like it was a gun you could choose not to fire. But as context, as a lethally hostile environment which once entered, one lives in forever. That we know. We are the experts. We include the one in ten women who has been battered, the one in five women who has been raped, the one in four women who as a child has been sexually abused. We know it as the propaganda of terror in the news: another woman beaten, stabbed, shot with a crossbow, hacked with a chainsaw. We know it as we take taxis to go four blocks at night.

Violence prevails, indivisible as PCBs and global warming. And I long to live in peace.

December 6, 1991
There's a crowd looming in the shadows ahead. Men? They look big in thick coats and jackets, faceless and threatening in the dark December night. Suddenly, sparks of light. Flames catching here and there. They're candles cupped in mittened hands. Now the crowd is moving, walking forward in twos, threes, and fours with candlelight flickering up into their faces. Men and women, they're streaming down the boulevard from the front gates of Parliament

Hill to the steps in front of the Peace Tower.

The conversion process, it's happening, I think, as I fall into step with the hundreds and hundreds who've come out this cold December night for what has become an annual vigil on Parliament Hill in honour of the fourteen young women massacred in Montreal in 1989.

I stand beside a friend watching the men from the media pace impatiently on the sidelines to which they've been asked to confine themselves. I listen to the women who've helped organize the event thank the sponsors: Bouclair Fabrics which supplied the material for arm bands, sewn by the women at Harmony House, a home for battered women and their children. . . .

"No. I'll ask Dad, he's more intelligent." It comes to me that this is exactly what Donald did say. One day last week or the week before. In a flicker of a moment after supper at home, gone before I could catch it. Or rather, before I could recover from being diminished by it. It had disappeared, been disappeared. Turned to mists in my mind, like all the other lines that slip by, and the things that are not spoken as well: The fact that my time doesn't count for as much, because I make myself more available. Donald didn't want to come with me for the vigil. "Boring," he said. But would it have been if the three of us had gone as we did for the demonstration of solidarity for Native people after Oka a few months ago? To be honest and fair, I must mention that Miles would have come with me tonight — I must say too, I was surprised that he thought it worthwhile. But, he said, he saw it as a women's vigil, and didn't want to intrude. Instead, he, an engineer, wore a white ribbon to work.

The official speakers say all the right things: continuum of violence, epidemic of violence, war against women. But they do not move me to tears. The woman who does has come from the hospital after multiple stab wounds to lay a commemorative wreath. Her name is Shadikan Mohamed. She and her daughter Sharon were attacked by her ex-boyfriend. Sharon was killed.

Until her moment, she's been down at the bottom of the steps holding her candle with the rest of us. Now, leaning a little on the arm of a friend, she haltingly mounts the steps. The men from the media rush forward, getting her in their sights. Their fluorescent lights glance off her shiny black hair. Her head is down. She places the wreath against the stand. The cameras are close, microphones open to catch any sign of her emotions. Her head is still down, black hair flecked with white falling screenlike across her face. She hesitates, then she raises her head, shaking back her hair. Her gaze cuts across the beams of the camera lights, and she looks out at us. Steadily she looks. Refusing to be a target of media attention, merely another reported "incident." She connects herself instead with us — in solidarity against violence. Then there is the official minute of silence. Heads bow; there are sniffles all around me.

At home we have a late supper in front of the fire, and I try to remember the tune to a song some of us sang at the end. It's a spiralling song, with two lines endlessly folding into each other: "A river of birds in migration, a nation of women with words." Donald brings me a cartoon from the *Citizen*. The cartoon shows a man wearing a white ribbon walking through a park hand in hand with a little girl. The little girl asks if the ribbon is something like a poppy, and her Daddy replies: "Sort of. . . ."

"Is it to remember a war?"

"Sort of. . . ."

"The day the war ended?"

"Actually, it hasn't ended yet," her father replies.

"Will you tell me when it has?"

"I won't have to. . . ."

Donald doesn't get it, and asks me to explain.

"She'll know when it's ended, because then she can walk on her own in peace," I say, my voice breaking. I point to the cartoon. She'll be able to walk through that park by herself without being afraid, I say.

"I've been attacked in the street," I tell Donald, and watch his eyes pop open with surprise. I put my arm around him, tell him "everywhere I go, I am afraid to go alone. Even here. I lock the house when I'm home alone. I can't help it."

Donald has to go pee. He races away. I look across at Miles, wondering if I'm carrying this too far. The firelight catches the sheen on his lashes.

Donald is back. "Let's make lawn signs," he says. "'Let the women walk in peace.'"

"Yes," I say, my voice trembling, "let's." And I realize that I am beginning to hope. Because I've brought my experience into the open, compelling response in the here and now. I've never really hoped except in my head before, and never for myself.

But we don't get around to it. I remind Donald once; it's really his project, not mine. But he's on to other things.

Afterword:
April 1994

Donald has given a speech at school about violence, and about the socialization of boys to be GI Joes and of girls to be Barbie dolls screaming and running away. He did this, he tells me, because he wanted to: bearing witness.

There has also been more war, including in Bosnia and Somalia. Reports leaked out: women raped. Thousands of women raped. "Routinely raped," a woman originally from Sarajevo told me when I went to her home for more news.

I spoke to a network of organizations involved in violence against women, who suggested a candlelight vigil in solidarity with these women and girls for International Women's Day, 1993. And then we formed a coalition: the Women's Health Project. Its equal membership is drawn from the Ottawa chapter of the Voice of Women and women from local women's shelters and the Women's Urgent Action, plus a woman from the Canadian Council of Muslim Women, the Physicians for the Prevention of Nuclear War, and others.

We spent time getting to know each other and the women refugees (some of them rape victims) who'd been located in Ottawa. We took time to talk about our feelings, to sense the links between there and here. We wrote a mission statement:

"We have come together in grief and outrage at the mass rape and abuse of women and girls in Bosnia-Herzegovina and Somalia. . . . We seek to raise public awareness about violence against women wherever it occurs. Our vision is that all women shall be free to live in peace and safety."

Focussing first on the women of Bosnia of whom the (white) media had more immediate information, we organized a fundraising event and raised over five thousand dollars. We've since distributed this to three projects where women are helping women directly: one in Sarajevo itself, one in Zagreb, and one in a spot along Slavokski Road in the North, where many women and what families they have left have found shelter in empty garages.

Now we're working with women from Somalia. This Sunday we meet at Zeinab's home to finalize plans for a women's evening of telling each other our stories.

Listening to each other, we gather strength. Strength to hold the lights and microphones steady, to bring women's experience insistently to public attention, and to hold the men accountable.

Author's note: I wish to thank Joan Skogan and Colleen Glass for helpful comments on an earlier draft.

~

Heather Menzies is an Ottawa-based writer with a working background in journalism and film-making and a personal background in the peace movement, feminism, farming, and the outdoors. She is a full-time mother, and teaches part-time in Women's Studies and Canadian Studies at Carleton University. Her books include *The Railroad's Not Enough: Canada Now* (Clarke, Irwin, 1978); *Women and the Chip* (The Institute for Research on Public Policy, 1981); *Fastforward and Out of Control* (Macmillan of Canada, 1989); and *By the Labour of Their Hands: The Story of Ontario Cheddar* (Quarry Press, 1994).

Negotiations with the Spirit

Anne Ricard Burke

M Y GRANDMOTHER SAYS I
have her eyes but I know she is lying. My hair and eyes are Iroquois,
just like my grandfather's. I can usually pass until somebody
notices, although it's the high cheekbones some woman praises, or
it can be those eyes, dark and fathomless, like my father's father.

He sits in a corner of the store on a stool, unmoving all day,
never offering to bag the groceries, not once asking to help her: to
sell the packs of cigarettes, the tins of milk, the open packages of
fruit with the rotten ones hidden at the bottom, flies circling
them, laying their eggs for larvae in the produce. And he never
spoke then.

Earlier he used to talk plaintively of selling fruit door-to-door
that the boys stole out of somebody else's garden or off the backs
of trucks loading for market. But the women at their doors
opened them reluctantly, if at all. When they heard his accent they
scolded him, or the men drove him away with sticks. "None of his
kind" were welcomed anywhere, although it wasn't as if they had
not tried, the family moving out of one small town into another,
never finding the peace they sought.

"Don't you remember the house," his sister prompts. "The one
Papa painted, the white shutters," she prods, "the red roof," but
my father cannot. His mind is unwilling and, besides, the years
blurred, the unpaid accounts, the priests with their black robes
frightened him, especially the one who crawled into his bed at

night. He could not speak of these memories with anyone. And so his family, like so many others, were Christianized, in boarding schools, each and every one, lost the language, learned the conqueror's and have forgotten ancestral memories.

My childhood was so painful I seldom speak of it. The odyssey for the ethnic writer, moving from old culture to new, from country to country, begins with family memory and folk past. It is a golden age of childhood which shapes the whole and contributes to the ideal of country and nation. It begins again with my son, a geological tree of branches without any leaves and I wonder if it will be easier to list his father's family from Nova Scotia (Irish origins, appropriable roots) than mine, simpler but who am I fooling? Writers are, in effect, in a sociological sense, reinventing the Canadian past to multicultural ends. That the Greek root of ethnic, *ethinkos*, was used to mean "heathen," a meaning that has continued to haunt the word's scholarly uses with its negative connotations, seems relevant here. My family imposed a taboo about our origins (being French was bad enough) which my mother broke before her death, and so it is only the women's movement, in particular the telling and writing of stories by Native women and their children, which has brought to surface what I and they have suppressed. Picnics were forbidden because it involved, they said, "eating in a ditch like gypsies" or worse. "Indian" was a term of derision like "nigger" or "kike" for family members who were not acting appropriately, used among them as a reproach learned from my grandmother's "good" French family. When I braided my hair for a school portrait, my father bitterly complained to my mother that I looked like "a squaw" and he detested the photograph for years afterwards, since my mother displayed it on her dresser. I suppose he was inculcated with self-loathing from an early age, while we rejected, virulently, ethnic as "other." I cherish my mother's courage but my father, I do not know him at all, except by way of our correspondences, discovering bits of him embedded inside myself, like glass splinters. We passed years in the same house without speaking. His silences, is that how he copes with the Big Lie? I have no *place*, unable to go home because of the distances involved, between family and friend, heart and head, the past abandoning you to the world and its inscrutable ways.

Marie doesn't live here anymore. But she is my friend, on reserve or off. Off reserve, are we really Indian people anymore? Marie explains. She says Indian women who married white men were cast off reservations, but they became resource persons for Indian women. They had access, it was thought, to the white world. She says, "If you know more than the chief you're in big trouble." And I agree, "It's the same all over."

Pat is Ojibway. She recalls being chased by her father with his belt in hand and hiding behind the coat rack, never telling her mother. Mothers were not told the secrets children shared with their fathers because their "knowing" might break up the family unit. Pat was auditioning yesterday for a speaking part in a made-for-TV movie which is hiring natives for work on screen and behind the camera. "It is directed by James Rockford's buddy, you know what's his name," but I can't remember.

A newspaper reporter tells me her beat is Native issues. She confides in me, "They're such shy people, unassertive, it takes a long time to get them angry." My son's French teacher was annoyed because she claims Indian people smell. "It's the tanning process they use," she explains confidently. At Christmas the children performed as *habitants* wearing red toques.

Niçose, my Acadian friend, says, "I tried to live in Quebec but I was not understood. Too much slang." "Is it English?" "No. *That* I could understand. Too much Indian," she complains.

"You call it Métis out west," I offer. "Back home, nobody's pure."

We are filaments, some of us, wound tight and will not unravel, unless we really must. It is liberating to be able to express thoughts, feelings, and selfhood finally. Perhaps, because I have come to this slowly, somewhat tentatively, the writing deserves to be stronger. I believe my mother. I know her like the back of my hand. I have her hands. My father is a stranger to himself, a stony silence to me. I must speak volumes to contain his absence. I do know that empowerment opens the way for the spirit. I will listen a little harder and see what results.

~

Anne Ricard Burke is a Calgary writer who holds a B.A., a B.Ed., an M.A., and has done Ph.D. studies. She has many professional credits, including work in *Canadian Women and Transcendence, Atlantis, Places of the Heart, In the Language of the Enemy*, the feminist issue of *Prairie Fire*, and elsewhere across Canada and in the U.S.

To My Woman-Reader*ji*
Yasmin Ladha

Readerji, my woman-Readerji
you may say this is poetry or story or essay
the trail is yours
it is always

A ROOFTOP IS A WOMAN. There is bunchy gossip on rooftops. Back and forth, *dupatta* scarves move with the wind on rooftops (here the wind is sweeter than chinook).

Now and then Reader*ji*, wipe your hands, for my ink is sticky from warm cinnamon on saskatoon berries. Lick some off your fingers. A woman's ink is nourishing. Sometimes I squelch the berry juice on my palm. Saskatoon-henna is scarlet orange, riper than any bridal henna from Delhi or Delphi!

The distance from a woman to her rooftop (so what if her rooftop is in Delhi or Delphi) is not a journey but a lull. And never on a flying carpet. For a flying carpet is male-ridden. He holds all magic. And a woman's throat harnessed to his razor rope, "tell a story, or else. . . ."

Reader*ji*, a woman vanishes to her rooftop on a swing. Sometimes it is a lull, sometimes a thick flight, but always, always on a swing.

Hair newly washed, gossip, *dupattas* dyed dreamy, mango pickle on chapatti, twigs, berry juice, tea, and lazy, lazy sleep are landmarks of a rooftop. A male's invasion on a rooftop is unholy as entering the mosque in shoes. On a rooftop, Gaea sprouts red soil and jasmines. A mustard veil sails by. Here, two friends or three press secrets:

> *On a swing*
> *from a Jamun tree*
> *into Saturday night dream*
> *up-up-again*
> *a thick flight to*
> *beloved, beloved*

The first time I learn the shape of a rooftop/woman is in a prairie parking lot. Phyllis *bibi* (you will meet her soon, Reader*ji*) in her yellow jacket and it is shortly before the lilacs of May, we are caught in a spring rain. The frozen ground twitches and turns to rubbery waves in the warm rain. Spring in Calgary is raw or already summer. But today, we catch her in transition. We catch the wispy green reddening to summer and want to seal this startle in a thick curry. (A worthy curry must startle the tongue.) Now Phyllis *bibi* and I crave for warm chapatti to dunk in the curry. The rain melts the coarse winter skin around our nostrils. And we never make it to lectures that day.

But in Delhi, Reader*ji*, a washerwoman banishes me. No, no, let me withhold the story awhile. My Reader, have *you* been a washerwoman to the ghost woman? Of course you know her. *Stories about her:* someone said she was driving the car — she killed him, the boy you all knew. Of her motionless black eyes and how mothers covered their children's eyes (even their foreheads still soft as custard) then retreated from her. Never leaving their backs exposed to her motionless eyes. There is another story that on the second night of their marriage, the ghost woman pressed her thumb on his voice box, then lay by him until morning. So many stories. But what happened?

I have seen the ghost woman dancing in a slip in an empty gym. Such an otherness about her. Her powdery collar bone sifts light. She dances on the periphery; the dead space turns to mercury between her legs in flight.

In the Mahabharata, Arjun the archer is allowed the privacy of a single balance/application. He is allowed Tai Chi uninterrupted. Full-circle motion/concentration brings him an athlete's success, a warrior's success. But a woman is not allowed Tai Chi hush. And like the ghost woman in the gym, not even the privacy of pain. In creativity or pain, a woman is surrounded by *bazaari* hassle and *bazaari* domesticity: Phyllis *bibi* writes, "The Women writers, their heads bent under the light, / work late at their kitchen tables."[1] And Alberta poet Victoria Walker writes that there are pots and pans in a woman's piano.[2] Reader*ji* you may offer a wise-salt opinion that a woman naturally connects to the familiar when she seeks the unfamiliar. That in this is her rhythm-beat — everywhere she is simultaneously connected/womb connected. That is why she is never angular/singular. But Reader*ji*, her simultaneous connections are harnessed by male for his containment. That's why I call a male, Mr. Dam. He locks woman-water. He delivers woman-water. He turns her instinctive, curious, independent nature into a salt-rock. (But salt is a wise and keeping spice.) If a woman behaves independently/singularly/angularly, Mr. Dam calls her unnatural, unwomanly — a shame on a woman's name. He frightens her with stories of a salt-rock or an eerie ghost woman. (I heard another story that the ghost woman carried her ravenous sex organs in her sucking spine.) Terror and shame govern Mr. Dam's woman. He tells her all women have salt-rock/ghost potential, it is a matter of harnessing it. When she demurs, he asks her in his slow-slow master voice, "My dear, is this how I delivered you?" Take the example of a woman who laughs a lot, openly, widely. Fatima Mernissi in *Women in Moslem Paradise* writes:

> A modest and humble woman personifies total submission to someone else's will. Laughing is an explosive gesture in this situation: when you laugh, you raise your chin, throw your head back and plant your gaze high up in the sky which doesn't fit with the place society has decided for women.[3]

In Mr. Dam's dictionary, such a woman is loose/lay/ready. Her strong white teeth (he gave her a Paris apple once and crowned her "Miss Pearly") are "horsy." When a woman dissents, Mr. Dam brands her irrevocably ugly. In his eye, here womanhood slumps. No good.

Reader*ji*, I am an East Indian woman who likes to lick chocolate in retreat, who wants to unclasp the sweaty burden of marriage from my neck. Such a woman is said to be shameless/ *besharam*. By Mr. Dam. There are several tribes of Mr. Dam. I speak of Mr. Dam from my tribe.

Shame/*besharam* starts in a small way. As a child if I did not sit "golden," thighs pressed together, Grandmother said I was without shame. One day, she tied my breasts with a gingham cloth because my breasts jumped up and down when I skipped rope. Shame becomes big when I can't leak sons, so I throw my daughters, one by one, into the Bow. I jump in last. The final babywoman in my arms.

And I am . . . nine bullets in my body because I brought shame to my tribe. I laugh on your TV screen — have a sweetmeat in my mouth. Since the day we eloped, my husband drives me to the Indian sweet shop on Seventeenth Avenue. He buys me two *burfis* with silver under-paper. He places the box by my legs so no one can see it — a snatched secret, and one more touch. My *kurta-pyjama* is yellow with a red border. Red is auspicious but yellow is a wet colour. Yellow is Gaea in spring. My bangles are sluggish and a thicket of lips covers my arms. My brother waits for us outside the video store by Mac's. Eighteen bullets in my husband's body. My brother's hands are dry.

That's my father outside the Court House. His beard is prophet flowing. His son has restored the hymen of the tribe. The membrane on which a tribe's honour depends. (That is why I say a male delivers woman.) My father's eyes are dry like my brother's finger on the trigger of his AK-47. Male abode is always dry and territorial. In patriarchy, this is how a hymen is kept intact. My father's clan sticks close to him, reserved of western publicity. In anxiety, one of them eats roasted peanuts. How to explain that back home, my husband would have been beaten to death by a barrage of field hockey sticks? Only a father or brother hands over a women's hymen. My brother gives a thumbs-up signal to father when he is led to prison. My brother drenched my wet months.

The crow swoops low, unerringly low, even though there is a cat nearby. Crow, take a message as you do in daughter stories. Tell my mother I am happy under the Babul tree. I do not want to beget sons. Babul home is a girl's home before marriage.

There is a washerwoman who banishes me from Delhi. I still hear her noise: "quick, out of here, *fatafat* (clap, clap), *toute suite, pronto!*"

"Your foreign woman blood, a bleat of blood, husk-dry in three days." (Who told you so?)

"Ours bleed lustily, so dark, it gives of purple. Purple as a Java Plum." (I forget whether the mango or the plum is sacred.)

Frizzy hair (I have left them open) and airy breasts are worse. Worse still is an unfastened East Indian woman. Not fastened to my woman neck two gold nuggets (heavy drops of ruby nipples). An Indian-comely-Kamla has breasts full of a tigress's milk.

I rush to Phyllis *bibi* who is drinking wine on the rooftop. What is she up to? She is watching a groom's wedding party below. Oh no, Reader*ji,* she is dangling wine right above Allah's Head and He is in the groom's wedding party! With His smouldering Eye He will boot us out *toute suite!* "But where?" asks Phyllis *bibi.* It is true He can't terrorize us with hell because women have been in hell for a long, long time. Neither can He coax us with *houri*-nymphs with baskety hips. Allah promises Mr. Dam if he is religious and performs good deeds in life, He will reward him with *houris. Houris* are singularly Allah's benevolence. These nymphs remain virgins, night after passionate night. They lounge around heaven in silk underwear, digitalized into action as soon as Mr. Dam enters paradise. My Allah has forgotten to reward women. Suddenly Phyllis *bibi* spreads like a mother bear to protect our rooftop space. Woman-paradise. As Mernissi says, "Paradise is not having to live up to someone else's standards and expectations, even *God's. . . .*"[4]

Ooi, there is Nazareth-*wallah* Jesus. Oh Reader*ji*, his oval nose still *dukhi*-sad as in a Renaissance painting. He still walks with a glide. Who is Phyllis *bibi*, you ask, Reader*ji*? *Ooi* Reader*ji*, she is our Canadian-*walli* poet:

> Hieratic sounds emerge
> from the Priestess of
> Motion
> a new alphabet
> gasps for air.
> > We disappear in the musk of her coming.[5]

I am partial to Phyllis *bibi*. With her, my timidity vanishes quick, *pronto*, *fatafat*. Only in a dream of audience halls, am I the bold heroine, spitting poetry in Khomeini's face:

> When Rushdie *babu* comes home
> I will knead flour with flying colours

Yes, Reader*ji*, in a dream or on my rooftop, I am the bold heroine, in the company of Joan of Arc or the Queen or Jhansi.

Have you not got it as yet, woman-Reader*ji*? That a woman's map is romance. A woman loves herself thick. Not the glittering moonlight kind, that too, but she has the capacity to romance Allah as well as a baby. In her lies a strange other capacity. It comes out of her rooftop, her she-space, her push, like a baby pushed out of her womb, like a teacher pushes open her pupil: pupa, pupil, push.

Hair newly washed, gossip, *dupattas* hued with Saturday night dreams, and lazy, lazy sleep (these days wine too) are landmarks of a rooftop. Here, two friends or three drink tea, drink wine, press secrets.

My woman-Reader*ji*, on rooftop today, the wind is sweeter than chinook.

~

Yasmin Ladha was born in Mwanza, Tanzania. She has previously published *Bridal Hands on the Maple* (DisOrientation Chapbook, 1992), *Lion's*

Granddaughter and Other Stories (NeWest Press, 1992), and has been featured in numerous periodicals and anthologies, including *Alberta ReBound* (NeWest Press, 1990). She is presently working on a book of multiple-genre fictions, *Circum the Gesture.*

NOTES

1   Phyllis Webb, from "Sunday Water: Thirteen Anti Ghazals," *The Vision Tree: Selected Poems.* Sharon Thesen, ed. and intro. (Vancouver: Talonbooks, 1982), 146.
2   Victoria Walker, "Woman House," *The Alberta Diamond Jubilee Anthology.* John W. Chalmers, ed. (Edmonton: Hurtig, 1979), 261.
3   Fatima Mernissi, *Women in Moslem Paradise* (New Delhi: Kali for women, 1988), 5.
4   Mernissi, 12.
5   Webb, from "Naked Poems," *The Vision Tree,* 89.

Tree of Knowledge

T HE COSMIC TREE OF MANY mythologies symbolizes the relationship among the "three worlds": lower, middle, upper; underworld, earth, heaven. In some mythologies the cosmic tree, the Tree of Life, is distinct from the Tree of Knowledge, also called the Tree of Death, or the Tree of Truth. The writers we have included in this section share a vision of earthly life rooted in sometimes painful knowledge and yet bearing the fruit of wisdom. Central to this vision is a sense of connectedness that is biological, historical, mythological, symbolic.

The broadest perspective on the intimate connections between pain and joy, life and death, good and evil is Inge Israel's. She sets the tapestry of her mother's memories of wartime dislocation against the canvas of the unfolding universe. "Uncertain Signs" thus affirms the continuity of life in the face of adversity that runs like a grace note through the other selections.

Like Israel, Shaw and Landale choose women's handiwork as a symbol of their lives. The crochet hooks that kept her mother sane might have been turned, Shaw suggests, to more destructive purposes. The "Embroidered Birds" that Zoë Landale writes about testify to the strength of women's friendship. Judith Krause's motif is the "Hands" that define relationships within her family and with others.

Places, too, may symbolize the continuity of life. For Susan Drain, the sense of family — and especially her kinship with the generations of women before her — is rooted in the homestead that lies "Between the Meadow and the River." For Margaret Dyment, the "Line of Stones" in a prairie landscape not only symbolizes emotional states, family ties, and events in her life, but also connects her spiritual quest with that of the Native people who laid the stones.

In "Willow Women" Joan Crate brings many of the themes of this collection into harmony. She reaches into the mists of Greek myth, as her father reached into the Yellowknife cold, to bring us the image of "Poor Daphne, feet planted firmly in the ground, burdened with winged hearts." If the writers in this collection say much about women's burdens, they say even more about winged hearts.

Uncertain Signs

Inge Israel

1. *"We are one of many appearances of the thing called Life;*
. . . not its perfect image for it has no image except Life."

N<small>O MATTER WHERE</small> I <small>PULL OUT</small> a thread, the tiny tunnel left in the fabric is a wormhole leading into another world. I peer through as I have done all my life, in an effort to understand.

Each disjointed moment is bathed in the bright colours my mother used to depict the tapestry of all her memories.

Had she not finally said yes, he would have been put into one of the front carriages or one of those at the rear. The front carriages with their load of passengers were blown apart by a mine. Those at the rear were derailed by the impact and most of their occupants died too.

But she had said yes, so she and my father travelled in the central part of the train with all the other married couples and were safe. Their journey was an entrance into another world, new to them though both had already known several.

Had she said no, this particular egg might have been fertilized by someone else's sperm whose genes I would be carrying in me.

Of course, it was not the beginning for there is no such thing. Even the universe has none, it seems, having been around for more years than we can grasp, recreating itself, possibly in different forms. Like stars, we too are potential fossils carrying in us the remnants of former existences.

2. *"We watch the stars but the signs are uncertain."*

The stitches making up the tapestry's background were evenly spaced. As my mother spoke, I saw them in greens, some darker, the shadows balanced by splashes of yellow.

When the First World War spread into Russia, my mother's family fled from Vitbsk to Siberia. They settled in a village where her parents opened a small grocery store. She had not finished school before leaving the city. But in this new life, being able to read and write placed her above most. Soon, she became the teacher in the one-room village school. Her brothers sometimes visited the prisoners-of-war in the local internment camp and played chess with them. Through chess, they became acquainted with my father who, when he did not have to do chores at the camp, taught the other prisoners Esperanto, which he had taught himself.

The war ended two years later but my father could not go home to Germany. None of the prisoners could be repatriated. Badly damaged trains and railway lines made travel impossible. The prison camp was closed down and the men were told to find work and lodgings. Villagers were encouraged to give them jobs and a place to sleep. By the time their dream of leaving Siberia together came true, my father had spent four years there. He was now twenty-one and my mother nineteen.

Their overloaded train was the first to carry prisoners-of-war out of the country. It crawled along uncertain tracks where mines still lingered. There were frequent stops along the way, not only to clear the tracks or to get wood for the stoves. There were no facilities of any kind on board, no water and, soon, nothing to eat. At each stop everyone scrambled off. Money was worthless. In any case, no one had any. Instead of worthless currency, my grandparents had given my mother salt, a very scarce commodity at that time, which local farmers were glad to accept in exchange for food.

It took three months to cross the thirty-five hundred kilometres from the small Siberian village to Western Germany.

For my parents it was one of an endless series of journeys to new existences.

3. *"It was not the magnificent march through the breakers and up the cliffs that we fondly imagine."*

Some of the stitches were little darting orange flames. For instance, whenever she thought back to the train journey from Siberia, she still felt hot: imagine travelling with a virtual stranger! And he was her husband! Squeezed into a carriage with so many other couples. She would not let him touch her. She hardly knew him after all. And in front of all those people! Not that the others seemed to care. No shame! No modesty. But she would not. At night, she crawled on top of the stove, Russian fashion, and slept there. Up there she felt safe. The man who was now her husband was more of a stranger here than he had been among her people. She could not understand what the other men were saying to him. They laughed a lot. At him? For not asserting his rights? He looked embarrassed. Hardly spoke. Except to her. Mostly with his eyes. She felt sorry for him. But no. Not that sorry. Not here. Perhaps never. It looked . . . sounded . . . unspeakable.

What had got into her? Leave her family! Her mother had fainted. Her sisters had hurried her away. "Leave quickly. Don't linger! You'll only cause more pain," they had said. When the train began to pull out of the station, they called after her, "Fanoutchka, take care!" But she had only felt a thrill of excitement. Dressed in fine new clothes, she was leaving for foreign parts with a clever, curly-headed man who loved her madly. Hadn't he threatened to take his own life if she did not agree to marry him? She had laughed, would not believe him at first. Until he showed her the blade.

Already on the train she had begun to miss her family, wished she could tell them how it was with her. How could she have walked out on them? They would never have abandoned *her*. What would happen on this train? Would she be able to hold her own, day after day, night after night? And what monstrous thing awaited her at the end of this crazy journey?

4. *"Out of the choked Devonian waters emerged sight and sound and the music that rolls invisible through the composer's brain."*

There was always music.

My mother sang a great deal. By the time I was born, she sang as much in German as in Russian, rolling her *r*'s and *l*'s in the same delicious way for both. She sang whatever she heard on the radio, on records or on the street, anything from opera to the *Schlager* of the day. The songs sounded tragic or humorous, according to her mood. Sometimes, she seemed perfectly happy, then sang a Russian song and was at once overcome by waves of nostalgia. No singer ever matched the greatness of Chaliapin, no dancer compared with Pavlova, no poet came anywhere close to Pushkin!

The stitches spelled out ambiguous languages. Her sisters had brought her up. Her mother, my grandmother, left early in the morning for the grocery shop and only returned at night. Well, someone had to look after the customers! Earn the family's upkeep! Do what was necessary! My grandfather had no time to make a living. He spent his days in the prayer-house, studying the Talmud. When he arrived home, all six were expected to fetch and carry for him. He did not demand it. My grandmother did, on his behalf. At the prayer-house or on the way home, he usually picked up some poor man in need of a meal or a stranger with nowhere to go and brought them home to share whatever meal his daughters had prepared.

My grandfather, a deeply religious man, neither ate nor drank anything that was prepared on the Sabbath. He was distant with his children and my mother hardly knew him but was afraid of him. She called it respect. Once, a little fart escaped her just as he walked into the room. She was devastated, burst into hysterical laughter, could not stop until one of her sisters slapped her face. She never forgot that moment of shame.

Now in Germany, she desperately missed her kind mother, her bossy sisters, her stern father. She even missed the children whom she had taught in the village school. Unlike her new teenage sisters-in-law, the Siberian children had been uncomplicated, unspoilt. They had looked up to her though she was short, had black hair and brown eyes. The rest of her family were all tall, fair and grey-eyed. She was the youngest of six children and they had teased her about not really belonging with them.

In her secret moments, she wondered whether it was true. Perhaps this nagging doubt had made the decision to leave them forever easier. Of course, she had not then known that it was going to be forever.

5. *"We uncover the bones of the past and seek for our origins there but it appears to wander."*

Striking in the tapestry was the dark outlining of certain motifs.

I know my grandparents only from large photographic portraits. They travelled with us across borders, stood propped against walls wherever we lived. For a time I slept in the same room with them. My maternal grandmother had my mother's eyes. I felt at ease with her. Somehow, at her side, my grandfather seemed quite harmless in spite of his long beard, black skull cap and severe expression.

But my paternal grandparents looked sinister to me. I could not come to terms with them, could not escape their piercing eyes even when I pulled the cover over my head. Sometimes I got out of bed to turn the heavy, black-framed pictures to face the wall, but still felt their stare. I had recurrent nightmares: they were being placed in their coffins. They pushed against the lids while nails were being hammered in, and called out in choked voices, "We're not dead!"

Perhaps my mother had passed on to me some of her feelings about her parents-in-law. With what apprehension she must have arrived in Germany to meet them, clinging to her few precious belongings, fingering them nervously as I've so often seen her do! My father had tried to reassure her: they were simple folk, like her own. They had arrived in Germany from Poland without a cent, sold men's ties and suspenders from door to door. Gradually, from that hand-to-mouth existence, they had built up a small business. Only much later did they become wholesalers.

Still my mother must have wondered how they would greet her. She did not know their language, would not be able to speak to them! What would they think of her? True, she was from an orthodox family. But would that weigh in the balance? They were bound to be resentful: though they were not German but Polish, to them she would nevertheless be an enemy alien. Married to their son who had run away. The one they had forced to become an apprentice at the bank, when he wanted to be a mathematician. He joined up and was promptly sent to the Russian front.

My father did not know that his parents had died while he was in Siberia. No trains had meant no mail either. The blank post-cards, given to the prisoners-of-war for them "to write home," could not be sent. My father used his to draw on. He drew scenes from the internment camp: men turning the water-wheel, lying in their bunks, standing in line for their soup, even using the latrines. I still have the drawings. My mother gave them to me shortly before her death. She had always kept them in a photo album. But I had them framed and hung them up. Though they were mounted on acid-free paper, exposure to daylight made them fade rapidly. No museum or art gallery could help. It is not considered ethical to retouch someone else's work. But I could not bear this second death and retouched them myself. Now his lines and mine are intertwined.

Though spared the ordeal of meeting her parents-in-law, my mother often studied their stern faces in the photographs. Their spirit still reigned in the house and, as the wife of the eldest son, she was expected to carry on where they had left off. She was almost the same age as my father's brothers and sisters, but it was she who now had to take over the mother's responsibilities. She was expected to know what each of them liked, what their food preferences were. The youngest brother, the joker in the family, accused her of trying to economize by scrambling only one egg for him instead of his usual two. "Let her economize in other ways, on herself!" he said. To her it was no joke. She took it to heart and never forgot.

6. *"In a universe whose size is beyond human imaginings, where our world floats like a dust mote in the void of night, men have grown inconceivably lonely."*

When she became pregnant for the first time, my mother tried to run away. She was still very much the foreigner in Germany. With new life forming in her womb, the longing to be among her own flesh and blood became vital, desperate. She made it as far as the border but was stopped there. Her papers were no longer valid and she was turned back. Oh, the humiliation, the despair of that surrender! Whenever she spoke of these events, she trembled, reliving the moment, and I see the tapestry trembling.

True, my father had promised her a modern house with undreamed-of comforts. She even had a maid, Gikka, in the kitchen. They were good friends, she and Gikka — a country girl whose train journey to the city was the first in her life; a girl who had never seen bananas before, and wrote home to her family about the sweet yellow sausages from Africa. My mother understood her, could sympathize and identify with her.

Only in the kitchen with Gikka, where there was no pretence, did she feel completely at ease. Especially if guests came to the house, she found "urgent" things to do in the kitchen. To the end of her life, she was only comfortable in the company of those who related to the earth, or to one another on a compassionate level, "genuine" people. She went out of her way to avoid the pompous, the self-serving, the greedy.

My father, thoughtful, quiet, infinitely patient, and deeply in love with this small, dynamic woman, never tired of pointing out the truth as he saw it. Endlessly, he repeated how much better everything was in a modern country among reliable, honest people. In Russia he had been robbed several times of the little he possessed, even from under his pillow while he slept! In Russia nothing functioned because no one worked properly. In Russia the New Order claimed to equalize society but instead took away all freedom.

No! No! my mother cried passionately. Everyone she knew there was honest. His experiences had been unlucky accidents. Besides, people in Germany couldn't be that honest, or why was she expected to keep even the linen closets locked? Why did his brothers, who lived in the same house, insist that she, as wife of the eldest, wear a heavy, jangling bunch of keys on her belt like a jailer? Her own family had never locked anything. Not even the front door.

As for changing society, it would take time. The process had only just begun. People had to be educated first. Yes! She firmly believed it would work. She had stood on boxes, perched on walls at street corners where new, idealistic leaders explained how there would never be any more poor or disadvantaged. Everything would be shared equally among everyone. She was all for it! Anything else was pure selfishness. The accumulation of wealth — who needed it? It made people fight. Led to war. He didn't know how tragic war could be! She had helped to nurse in a hospital. He hadn't really experienced it! Wasn't he taken prisoner on his very first day on the battlefield, a mere boy of seventeen? And hadn't he chosen to fight, pretending to be one year older in order to be accepted as a recruit?

Now, now. My father shook his head in a familiar gesture. It was true he had joined up voluntarily. But only as a way to escape from home, from the apprenticeship at the bank which he hated. He had seen plenty at the front. She knew perfectly well that he was strongly opposed to war. Esperanto was the only solution. If everyone spoke the same language, all differences would soon disappear. People would trust one another.

Trust? my mother asked with derision. Where there's trust, there's honesty.

No, no. Honesty must be there first. Or how could you trust?

Sometimes my father made the mistake of recalling how unclean Russia was, how he and the other prisoners had squatted on the ground for hours at a time, delousing themselves.

That was Siberia! my mother cried. Russia was different. But even in Siberia her family had no trouble keeping clean! . . . .

At this point her temper would flower to the full, and her eyes flash. Never, never, as long as she lived would she forgive his brothers for burning all the clothes she had brought with her! Treating her as if she were dirt! Her entire trousseau! So carefully put together by her family. And at what sacrifice! Perfectly clean everything was!

These same words, feelings, and reactions were repeated every so often throughout their long married life. Small, inadvertent things could trigger the cycle — in every house in which they lived, in every subsequent country to which they moved, through endlessly changing world orders. And just as the argument never varied, neither did the stalemate at its end. When it was reached my father retired to another room with his books, or took his hat and went for a walk, while my mother went to the kitchen and rattled pots and pans.

7. *"A world in which living creatures flow with little more consistency than clouds. . . ."*

Without putting his ear to the ground, my father could sense the approach of trouble, long before it materialized. He sensed it when my mother was pregnant for the second time and he wanted her to board a ship, so that I might be born on the open sea. He hoped such a birth would make me, if not internationally acceptable, at least able to go through some doors which would otherwise remain locked. Ours has always been a many-worlds interpretation.

But the first birth had been a very difficult one. My mother was advised not to travel and I was born on land, in a country from which we soon fled. We were among the lucky ones, those who got out in time. Some of my aunts, uncles, and cousins were not so fortunate. They perished in concentration camps.

Soon thousands of refugees like us were streaming across borders into countries where they were unwanted. Permits to remain in those countries were given arbitrarily. Most people could not get any. Some managed to move on elsewhere, others became "illegal." For those who stayed, work permits were impossible to obtain. Therein lies another story.

At one point, my mother, my sister, and I were allowed to stay on in France but my father was not. My mother, who hated charity with all her heart and soul, could neither feed nor clothe us. She lived through the nightmare of having to let us go to a distant children's home, while she stayed in Paris alone, living on the pittance she managed to earn by making hats, her earnings too small to allow her the luxury of taking the metro to her few customers. She had to walk wherever she went. Paris became a dirty word for her and remained so for the rest of her life. We were separated for years. When my father finally managed to send for us, we were very excited. A stranger met us at the station in Ireland. It was my father. We no longer knew him, did not even speak the same language any more.

Often, in new places, we dared not speak for fear of being called "dirty Germans" or "dangerous Reds" because of my mother. Yet no matter where we were, if she was there it felt like home.

8. *"There are still small scuttlings and splashings in the dark,*
   and out of it come the first croaking, illiterate voices
   of the things to be."

While we lived in Germany, before we fled, my mother must have had some happy moments there. When she became a mother. When her sisters-in-law did sometimes look up to her. When the business prospered and a new house was bought and fitted with furniture of her choice. When she picked up the merry songs from operettas and kinky hits of the day. When she was on holiday with her children. But later these moments were difficult for her to recapture, the threads knotted.

I do my best. Somewhere, there were cherry orchards, Herr Kirchner's ladder propped against the trees. Pipe in mouth, he helped me climb up and reach for shiny red fruit. Somewhere there were forests. Picnics in a clearing. Out of pieces of his newspaper, my father made hats as shields against the sun. Also little boats. They floated in a stream and, when they met with some danger, my father was there at once, freeing them with a deft flick of a stick. My mother was quickest at finding wild strawberries. Or sorrel leaves, their acid puckering our mouths as we chewed them.

I still hear my mother singing Schubert's *Serenade*, "*Lasse Dir die Brust bewegen*," the literal meaning of the words going round and round my head, making me see breasts able to move like arms, beckoning, all-important. Breasts were special.

My sister's friend Blümi, who lived across the street, coming to play, sitting at our open window and saying to my sister, "You should have bitten your mother hard when she breast fed you. I bit mine so hard it made her cry. Serves her right!" The vindictive remark upset me deeply, making me feel I had overhead a terrible secret, one I could never tell my mother. And the look on my sister's face, as though she had been initiated.

I still see the cat suckling her kittens. The smallest one, my favourite, always pushed out of reach by the others who monopolized the teats, tiny paws with needle-sharp claws extended, greedily kneading and pricking the cat's belly. Klaus, the boy next door, killing my kitten with a metal grill. My mother helping me to bury it at the end of the garden.

Soon after that, Klaus telling me on the street that he wasn't going to play with me any more because I was a Jew. My hating him because of the kitten, but running home crying, crashing headlong into a lamp-post. My mother applying the cold blade of a large knife against my swelling forehead. My asking her between sobs: what is a Jew? I don't remember her answer. Perhaps she simply said, "Wanderers." To prepare me.

Author's note: The section headings are quotations from Loren Eiseley's *Immense Journey*.

~

Born in Germany of Russian/Polish parents, **Inge Israel** spent her childhood during the turbulent 1930s mostly separated from her family — in Belgium, France, and Switzerland, often in children's homes. In France, she attended school for six years, then was finally reunited with her family in Ireland. The postwar years included long stays in Brussels and Copenhagen where her first adult literary contributions were published in Danish when she was twenty. Since 1958 her home base has been Edmonton but she still spends extended periods abroad. Her work includes two books of English poetry, three books of French poetry, short stories, radio dramas, and two song cycles set to music by Canadian composer Violet Archer. Her last book of French poems, *Aux Quatre Terres*, was awarded the 1993 Prix Champlain.

Rows and Rounds

Janis Shaw

$\mathcal{E}$VELYN VIOLET ORDERED HER
life, in rows and rounds, with a crochet hook. Cane-wielding
school mistresses taught her to stand erect, in silent lines; to sit in
her place, stone-still, eyes lowered; and to crochet, in neatly-boxed
filet stitches, a tray cloth picture of a parrot telling "Polly" to "put
the kettle on."

Evelyn Violet brought those lessons with her to Canada where,
at sixteen, she fell in love — with an endless blue-black prairie sky
and its crackling northern lights and with Jim, the red-haired,
broad-shouldered fourth cousin who sat on a grassy hill in
Meadowbrook, watching her watch the dancing colours.

She married Jim and his Canadian wilderness, but she'd
known better. She'd known shops and street cars, days off in
London. She'd known soft rains in the gentle Welsh hills which
she had thought were mountains. She had known mild men with
music on their lips and in their fingers. She'd known better, but
she married Jim and settled on the emptiness of a turned-back
Alberta homestead.

In the first months of their marriage, she thought she'd lose
her mind. Instead she found her crochet hook and secured her
sanity in a circle of stitches. For want of crochet cotton, her first
doily was a delicate web of fifty-weight sewing thread. Hundreds
more lacy mandalas, in white and ecru, followed. Evelyn Violet
crocheted skeins of rippled edgings for tablecloths and pillowcases.

She worked pineapples and swans on antimacassars to protect the backs and arms of worn chesterfields. She interlaced tiny shells to make booties and sweaters to warm her infant daughters. She even crocheted stiff baskets which she stuffed with ugly crepe paper roses.

Sometimes, as she followed her patterns, she wished she could take back her mistakes as easily as she could undo her crocheted errors. When she suspected her last, unwanted pregnancy, she considered a crochet hook abortion. Then, remembering her rows and rounds, she picked up her crochet hook and started my layette.

~

Janis Shaw is a radical housewife who lives in Spruce Grove, Alberta, with her husband, son and daughter. Her respect for personal writing continues to deepen with the surprising discoveries she makes in her recording of family history and in her journal-keeping.

Line of Stones

Margaret Dyment

Journey Dream Story
Story Journey Dream
eggstone

*O*N MY SISTER'S VERANDAH IS a large pink granite stone, perfectly rounded. Enclosed in it, showing at one side and rounded and smoothed into the lines of its container, is a smaller white stone. Quartz, someone said. The effect is of a two-coloured egg, or perhaps the human eye. She and her husband found it on one of their "Easter rambles." They liked it and so they lugged it home. It's not an Easter egg. It's not a symbol of anything. They just like it.

Inside their house are many other objects they like. A feather mask from New Orleans lights up one place on the living room wall. A green mask made by their son hangs in the hall. In the children's bedrooms are large wooden structures made for them by my sister's husband, who took over the fathering of these kids at the usual point in second marriages of change and pain.

My niece was six when she received her dolls' house. She is fifteen now and still it dominates her room. Inside it she cares for babies. Every room has its tiny cradle, crib, playpen, or high chair, complete with babe. My sister says that her daughter has become a collector of miniatures. When they go for trips together, they look for stores that carry tiny furniture and exceedingly small books, rattles, toys, cups and saucers, even a minuscule roll of toilet paper. All to scale, more or less, except in the living room a gigantic seated mother brushes the ceiling with her head. In her arms, a gargantuan baby, dressed in long white clothes.

My nephew's room has the castle. Superheroes guard turret and balustrade. When we go on our trip to the medicine wheel, chosen heroes accompany us in the back seat. Behind and under the larger journey, my nephew and his heroes go about their whispered business, their death-defying leaps.

On the night before we were to visit the medicine wheel, we stayed in a cheap motel at Lake Kenosee. I was the reason for this trip. I slept in a room by myself and I dreamed I was clinging to the side of a dangerous castle moat.

I intended to dream: it was written into the schema I had outlined already on three different blackboards: *Journey*, I wrote. (The original trip to the Gatineaus near Ottawa with a group of friends, slogging around in the March bush, breaking through ice, stopping to listen to wind in the trees. We were: two married couples, each with tensions; a recently-divorced and very beautiful young woman; a twelve-year-old girlchild; an older woman who, when I broke through the ice over my boots, looked back and, before she turned to lend her hand, hesitated.)

Journey. Then: *Dream.* I had dreamed of sacred land. A woman in green leads a group of affluent yuppie tourists over contoured terrain. She unfolds an aerial-photo map and shows us that the land has been deliberately altered to resemble a temple and amphitheatre from ancient Greece. I wake and think: it's true: we were on sacred land. Each of us involved in an inner trip, scarcely able to make one another out through the fog of internal myth. Only the child danced through the day in the real Gatineaus, in real snow, under the shadow of a real hill. ("Don't be so sure," say friends I tell this to, remembering being twelve.)

So in *Story* (next in my schema) I eliminated the child, amalgamated the two quarreling married couples, and paid attention mainly to the two other women. The younger one seemed outside all their tensions, observing, treading her own path, yet surely not easily: so much going on in her own life. In the story I made her the recorder, and had my group travel to the only truly ancient sacred place I knew of in Canada: a prairie medicine wheel.

There was no money to travel there myself, and so I researched it second hand. I interviewed a Cree friend and local poet, looked up maps and the meaning of Saskatchewan names in the library, discovered a very useful article had been saved in a scrapbook by a New Age friend (synchronicity, we both believed), made phone calls and accepted Xeroxed articles and photos and personal accounts from my sister in Saskatoon who has an eggstone at her door and masks on her wall, but rarely remembers her dreams.

Perhaps, I offered, you don't need to remember them because you bring so much of this stuff into your everyday life.

We both felt shy. Well, I know that I felt shy. The fires in my sister that I had felt flare soon after my arrival tamped down. I remembered that we always go through this rough bit, feeling close, then jarring against difference.

I pulled out the gift I had brought: a grey stone. I had picked it up on Galiano Island when I visited there with my husband two years before, and had kept it ever since on my dresser, a reminder of my sister and a reminder to bring it to her whenever I could find my way to Saskatoon. In some ways it was an ambivalent gift. I felt quite bad about it, yet determined, when I plucked the stone out of salt water. A lady limpet was sweeping along its smooth surface, trailing her long fanned skirts. I was enchanted, wanted to keep her. Would have preferred to keep her alive. But as the rock dried and the limpet became still, I had to accept — I was a long time letting myself know this and would even now rather not be told for sure — that, if restored to salt water, the creature cannot revive. The limpet died, slowly or quickly, tight to her rock, conserving to the end whatever moisture she had inside her skirt. I wrapped her and her death stone gently in tissues in my suitcase, but I needn't have worried: the limpet adhered to her stone. She and it became one.

It's a limpet.

Oh — what is a limpet.

Don't you remember? I used to call you that name. When you used to ride on my back! I liked the sound of "limpet" — with the "pet" in it, too.

It sounds better than barnacle!

But really she is pleased, and places the stone in front of the photograph, the gift from last time, a fuzzy old photo taken with my very first camera, a picture of my little sister in a white nightie, come outside in her bare feet so I could take her picture on our cold front porch.

Limpet stone in front of the photograph seems to have been always there. To this house of living plants and beautiful dead weeds and paintings of prairie landscape and sky, with the egg-stone out front, I have brought the right gift.

Story, I write on the blackboards. I wrote the story. The child danced back in, changed into a Cree lad who holds more keys to the mystery than does any guru in green.

Next I got a grant, and asked for extra money to visit the wheel. *(Grant)* I write on the blackboards, parentheses because I feel apologetic about this component of the internal/external flow of the writer's life. But now because of the grant I have come to Saskatchewan to visit the medicine wheel and also some family places. *But really to visit my sister. It's a kind of scam so I can visit my sister.* Truth in its own peculiar way turns out to be both true and not true. My sister has fallen in love with our family roots, the history and prehistory of Saskatchewan. She and her prairie husband are delighted to take me on this trip. They want me to come back another time and visit the petroglyphs, the badlands, Big Muddy and. . . . My sister shows the paintings she has made, trying to capture earth colours of the prairie. I gaze at her paintings and later, as we travel, at the fields and, surprising me, the hills and wooded valleys of the prairies, flowing by. I try hard to pay attention.

Paying Attention, my Cree friend back home has informed me, is the essence of Native religion. It is what the Amerindian would have been doing up on that windy hill three thousand years ago.

The same friend told tales from her girlhood in a Catholic residential school where you were in serious trouble if you spoke your own language to anyone after you came there at the age of six. At the solstice, she said, we'd skip school and we'd go up into the hills. The nuns thought we were practising secret rituals up there, but we were paying attention. Now it is spring, we would say. We spoke to one another in Cree. We looked about us. It's not a symbol of anything, that limpet on its rock, the water receding from under its skirts.

Journey Dream Story (Grant)
eggstone limpetstone blackstone whitestone two-coloured stone for throwing away.

When does your love become a pointed grey pimple clinging to a stone that is older than the hills. If restored to salt water will your love spread her skirts and skim once more across the surface of this hard, hard earth.

On the lee side of the medicine wheel, sunwarmed, we sisters traced an old line of stones. We wanted to see how far it would go.

"You start imagining things," she smiled at me. "But I love this." We pointed out stones to one another, stone stone stone another stone. When at last we could not persuade even ourselves that the line continued up the hill, we agreed that perhaps it didn't matter any more: we were in a sight line now for one of the great wheel's spokes. Its small end cairn lay directly ahead. We looked back and marvelled at how far we had come: the line held all the way from the teepee rings laid out below the hill.

I, too, am following a line of stones, as I did with my sister that October morning, and as the ancients did, painstakingly placing the stones they gathered one by one by one. They made two concentric circles and then five lines, across the summit of their highest hill. Their intention, it is believed, was to discover the moment of equinox, spring and fall. Mine, too, is to discover a point of transition, a coming or fading of light.

When I applied for a grant to complete a manuscript of stories, I included a request for money to visit my sister, although I said it was to research a story. I intended to climb a hill among the Moose Mountains, sit with the wind in my hair looking out over land that is much the same as it was two thousand, three thousand years ago, when small dark people, perhaps joking among themselves, laid out these lines of stone. I believe that if on Moose Mountain medicine wheel I had reached out my hand and overturned a stone, I would have been the first to commit this sacrilege, the first two-legged creature in three thousand years not to hold sacred the earth and the bright eyes of the human beings who spring from her and return to her and who have held this place sacred, have honoured the line of stones.

When you have said that, you have said everything there is to know about this place. It is here, it is fragile, human beings washed over it for three thousand years and for all that time it has not been destroyed. A man with a pick-up truck could remove this wheel in less than a day. In some parts of the province, this has happened: wheels identified in the seventies have disappeared. But this one is on grazing land and it is on Native land.

A fieldstone warm under my hand, I thought I saw that in forcing our attempt to understand ourselves, we devalue and destroy the parts we cannot understand. Some of the few farmers who remain on this prairie land, riding high-removed from it in agribusiness machines (each one costing more than a house), have uprooted stones like these, cast them from their fragile moorings, sent them adrift again across the prairie sea, in fence rows, foundations, crushed in gravel or cut in facing for city bungalows, patterns new and possibly not even wrong. Each in our own way we search to find our place, our grid pattern of streets, roads, fences, backyards: privacies from which we take our bearings and to which sometimes we can return.

The thing is that we run into gaps in what we know, hiatus in the lines we trace on our experimental trails. Someone removes the clues. Hard-won tenuous insights shift and we have to win them again. If only someone had stopped and laid a mandala of stones, to hold in place the little we know. If only the bulldozer or the giant combine had not come by. But then, in three thousand years stars themselves shift. Only the smell of prairie grass must be the same. Perhaps this small yellow flower.

My sister was in charge of our journey, and she led me first to several family spots: the site of the hospital where I was born fifty years ago; a pink granite gravestone, Selena and Thomas, Indian Head; the house in nearby Kendal where Selena, without much help from Thomas, cared for our father. I was taken to visit that house when I was three, and carry faint memories from that time.

I am slow to add the pink granite headstone to my line of stones. It was a stone of my journey, but one shaped, smoothed, shined, engraved. On it Selena, my namesake (I am Margaret Selena, after two prairie grandmothers) — Selena has no surname of her own, her history dissolved into what remains of Thomas. In life it was not like this. Selena was broad, big-armed: she ran a boarding-house. Besides her own daughters, she raised as her own a neighbour's son. Four trees were planted in memory of her beside this stone, by this son, our father, as a very young man. I pick up a pinecone. From the beach where we picnic I take a black feather. No stones.

In the motel room in the night I dream of clinging, of fear I will fall, and of climbing with care from the castle moat. Enjoying being alone, I arrange paper and lamp on the round table provided and write down my dream. Then I dress and walk to the lake. Its borders have receded twenty feet. Docks have extensions built onto extensions, and still they end up high and dry. I decide to go to the water's edge and retrieve stones new-birthed from this retreating water.

Five stones I gather, put them in my pocket, smile good morning at a man walking three dogs, and meet my young nephew, the superhero, coming down to find me, and then his mother my sister with a camera, who takes a photograph of my nephew and me walking along companionably. I am a little lopsided in the picture, one jacket pocket filled with stones.

Before we leave, I wash the stones in the motel room sink. There is a crumpled black stone, grey granite, pink granite, and one that is two colours, yellow and white. My nephew and I admire how pretty they are when they are shiny with water. I tell him how, with my husband, his uncle, when we were first married, I picked up little stones all the way to Newfoundland. Our first possession as a couple was a green tent. Our second was a Volkswagen van. We sat in the tent in the evenings with the van outside loaded with our books and clothes and wedding gifts, and we polished stones. We made love, too. This part I do not say out loud. We had bought the finest grain of sandpaper and before we made love we talked and paid attention and polished stones. We had been one summer together and seven months apart and one month of family preparations for getting married. There was an enormous amount still to say.

Soon we will be thirty years married and sometimes he says, over breakfast or perhaps over a muffin and coffee in the afternoon, That's it, then, is it? After all these years? We've run out of things to say?

On the medicine wheel, I choose the black stone. It is folded in on itself and at first I think it might be coal. I hold the black stone in my hand and look out over the land of my mother and my father and my two grandmothers my namesakes, and my grandfather who ran the post office in Kendal, my grandfather who turned virgin prairie sod and built himself and his brothers their first home.

From the end of each of five great spokes I gaze across brown hills. The wind lifts my hair. I feel nothing and everything. Other women have stood here, other men and young children. My nephew and niece have gone off by themselves and are sitting down and being still. No one told them to do that. The folded black stone warms my hand as if with its own heat. There are no flashing neon signs, no strange rites. One has only to pay attention.

I find that so difficult to do.

eggstone limpetstone (gravestone) blackstone whitestone
White stone is manna stone, the vanishing, the Other. Once I

had a stone that looked like the white fudge called "divinity." It was squarish and sugared-looking; one longed to sink in one's teeth. The hollows in its square sides were made not by human hands for human needs but by water in a prehistoric lake. I felt drawn to it, yet alien; it could not be bitten or hollowed to my needs. It stayed as much as a year or two in my jacket pocket. Finger it, look at it, feel frustrated by it. Then it disappears. I find a reference in the front of Joy Kogawa's novel *Obasan* to Revelation 2:17 and the white stone with one's name on it, a white stone that like manna brings nourishment only for a time, and on its own terms.

The white stone was my own symbol, and I lost it years ago, but just near the parked van, as we return from our visit to the wheel, my sister stoops and picks up a stone.

It's a hide scraper, with a curved edge for the scraping, and a smooth edge to fit into a palm. A hollow chip has been chipped out, suitable for the placement of human thumb. Women scraped hides, so this was made for a female hand. But it is small. It has been made for a little girl, hardly big enough to sit by her mother and learn woman's work. It is almost a toy.

My sister hands me this white stone.

It had not been on the hill: it lay by the public road, in earth churned by beef cattle who had been run into a corral.

What are the ethics of moving a stone? Stone set down by a tired small girl, or lost out of her pocket as I lost that divinity stone so long ago. It was right for the ancients to place stones in a line, sighting from earth to stars in the sky, catching and marking the first rays of summer sun. It was right all those years for humans to hold those lines sacred and to sit quietly there, or to pitch teepees and sing loudly, pounding on their drums. To dance.

"Here."

We could hurt each other very easily. She in her anger and tension over emotion, over rituals. I in my arrogance, acting as if there is only one path up the hill. Psychoanalyzing a dolls' house and a castle, failing to notice the colours of the prairie or the fire behind the sociological jargon words with which my sister reports on the reality of children who are hurting.

Toward the end of the visit, we exchange a few words about the state of our hearts, fierce inner journeys we guard jealously yet want, when we are together, to share.

From my remaining collection of prairie stones I select the one with two colours, a fragment broken from some larger structure that also had a stone encircled by a stone. I turn it in my hand. Worrystone. I plunge into the enigma of my foolishness.

Stone of two colours, yellow and white, fragment broken from some larger dream.

Shit, I cry to my sister as we near the airport. I intended to throw this away when we were behind the art gallery. I forgot.

What is it you want to do?

Awkwardly. I just wanted to throw this away. A small personal ritual.

No problem, she says. She who was so tense about rituals on the hill.

She pulls the van to the side of the road and smiles. Self-conscious but determined, I climb out of the van. The two-coloured stone flies from my hand, returned to a prairie field. Worrystone, good-bye.

I get back in.

"You never know," I say.

She starts the van again. "You never know."

We take three more pictures with airplanes in the background. Then she rewinds the film in her camera and hands it over.

The journey is done, and one dream. Now there is a story to write.

Journey Dream Story
Story Journey Dream
eggstone limpetstone blackstone whitestone worrystone for throw-ing away

I've brought stones, I'd said casually as we climbed the hill to the wheel. In case we want to do some ritual up there.

Fire leapt: I felt scorched.

What's wrong with what we are doing? Why can't we just go up there, just poke around? Why do you have to add to it?

All right, I said. It's fine. I can just do something for myself.

I love this, she says later, wind lifting her fine fair hair, face alight in the sun: you start imagining things, don't you. I love to follow a line of stones. Let's see how far we can go.

~

In her own words: I'm a writer and teacher of creative writing who moved from Ottawa to Victoria in 1991: another journey, dream, and story. Three stories have been published in the anthology *Best Canadian Stories* (Oberon, 1983, 1989, 1991) and another in McClelland and Stewart's *Journey Prize Anthology* in 1990. Other stories and poems have appeared in literary magazines and in Victoria's *Focus on Women*, and I have completed a collection of short fiction. There have been three chapbooks, two of poetry and most recently a story, "The Personals," published by Reference West in 1992. I write book reviews and also have a regular column on the book page of the *Times Colonist*. "A Line of Stones" appeared in a collection of short fiction, *Drawing the Spaces* from Orca Book Publishers. On the personal side, I have been married for over thirty years and we have two adult children, a son and a daughter.

Hands

Judith Krause

MINE ARE BIG FOR A WOMAN, with stumpy fingers prone to puffiness. They are not graceful or long-nailed but rather hands built for work, hard work; yet even short stints on a shovel clearing snow or using a pitchfork to turn over soil in the spring will cause large waterfilled blisters to form.

~

My mother's hands are volcanoes, redhot eruptions of internal steam, peeling off layers of skin and forming pustules that surface like small boulders, leaving holes when they drain. She wore gloves, white cotton gloves, through most of my childhood. I do not recall the feel of her hands on my skin, but I bear in mind her sharp cries of pain if, by accident, one of us touched her.

~

Itchy bubbles sometimes burst open in the palms of my hands. The nuns told the boys about hair growing on their palms. I never knew whether to fear thick, bristly hair or the open, weeping wounds of stigmata, the holy marks of love.

~

My sister buried her hands in the ashes. Her thin, four-year-old wrists burrowed deeply into the soft, grey feathers, still hot from a fire the night before. Her screams drew us from all corners of the yard. The family doctor said she might never regain full use of her hands. All summer she rocked herself, holding her white bandages in front of her like little claws.

~

On New Year's Day, my grandmother reads aloud the cards she received from her only surviving brother and sister. Their shaky hands trace the calligraphy of age over the pages. Her brother, eleven years younger at nearly eighty, cuts his greetings into two because she may not receive the first card he sent — addressed, in error, to her phone number, area code and all. Her sister, much closer in age, though never in spirit, sends her wishes in a verse: "As I prepare for the Great Beyond, oh that I was eighteen and blonde."

~

I have the hands of a peasant.

~

My new boss says he can smell fear. He knows I am phobic about hands, especially shaking or holding hands with strangers. The very thought makes me sweat.

~

In old family photos, my mother's mother, Florence, and my mother's aunt, Kitty, perch at the end of the dock. They share a small oriental parasol that provides no shade. Sunbathing beauties in the twenties must squint. Neither sister will raise a hand to shield her gaze, neither admits to weakness.

~

Winter evenings my father and I walk, hand in hand, to his mother's house, a long way from ours. The smells of fresh coffee and baking greet us at the door. Before we set out for home, we warm our hands and feet on hot water bottles my grandmother brings wrapped in towels. Under the bridge, my father shows me the place where a man's body was found, frozen or murdered, I no longer remember. We take off our mitts to feel the cold ground. At home we must blow on our hands to warm them.

~

Whenever my father fixes something for me, we work together as smoothly as a medical team — he, the surgeon, me, the operating room assistant, handing him tools and anticipating his next move. We do not need to speak. Our hands do, in the cool semaphore of fathers and daughters.

My mother sends me to pick saskatoons for the pies she wants to make for company. All afternoon I stand in the bushes in our coulee, swat flies, and drop berries by the handful into my pail, stopping only to sample the plumpest ones. Their juice stains my hands and mouth. Later, when I turn under the pastry for the crust on my own little pie, I use my purple thumb, instead of a fork. It leaves a mark on the pale dough just like a bruise.

~

When my daughter is born, we have a party in the hospital. The four grandparents, the obstetrician, and the delivery room nurses join us for champagne an hour after her birth. Everyone claps when the cork pops and there is a round of *well done, well done*, handshakes and backslaps. My mother pats me on the arm, tells me she's so glad it's over. My father touches my daughter's small hand. She grabs his finger, holds it tight. Years later, this is the image he will hold in his mind as the anaesthetist puts him under. After the operation, my daughter quietly strokes his swollen hand, smoothing away the puffiness.

~

Driving in the car, I sometimes take one hand from the wheel and place it in my daughter's lap. Her small warm hands encircle my large cold one. If I squeeze her hand, she says I'm just like a baby, tightening and releasing, tightening and releasing in the game of mother's tug of war.

~

Judith Krause, a Regina writer, editor, and educator, comes from a long line of strong-willed women. She presently juggles parenting with a full-time teaching job and her own writing. Her first collection of poems, *What We Bring Home*, was published by Coteau Books in 1986. Her second collection, *Half the Sky*, appeared with Coteau in 1994. She is the current poetry editor for *Grain* magazine. She coedited the anthology of stories and poems *Out of Place* in 1991. "Hands" was aired on the Saskatchewan CBC program *Ambience* in the fall of 1992.

Embroidered Birds

Zoë Landale

BARB, I WISH I KNEW WHO gave you those embroidered birds. I thought they were from the time you spent at the mission in Mexico, but I was wrong. When I see them it's as though my eyes come up short in their ravelling. Why do I have to know these things, wind all the meanings back into nice tidy balls of yarn? Is it the domesticity of colours I want to be soothed by, or texture?

It's dangerous to recognize with my gut: I am driving along a strange highway yet I know that house set beside the lake, I could live there. The car rushes me by, but for miles I go up to that front door and knock.

Barb, I would have come to see you at the end if I'd known. Forgive me, but you were dying all the years I knew you. You were so weak I didn't think you'd live to see our wedding. I remember you standing outside the church, a friend holding you up. Your friend's long hair was the same shininess and colour as the braces of copper candlesticks John had fastened to the back of the pews, and in my memory, her hair and your face blaze together on the porch. I knew what it cost you to come.

I would never have started visiting you once a week if I'd known you were going to live so long. Two months at the most, I thought. All around it seemed as if women I knew were withering like California poppies in the frost, silky petals shattered on hospital beds.

~

On my wall, your embroidered birds are brave and bright against a black ground.

~

Your sister was there when I arrived for our last visit. She'd brought over cold chicken and a green salad for your supper. She was glad to see me. *How's your husband, where's the baby?* We caught up on our news in the awkward half-shouting manner people use to be heard above running water and around a corner. Then she went out to feed your remaining puppies and clean out their run, chores the homemaker was forbidden to do for you, as livestock is not considered a necessity by the government.

When your sister came back in, she sat with one leg over the wooden arm of her chair and chatted about her new bed-and-breakfast place. The chair squeaked as it rocked and the sound picked at me in five-second intervals like a toothpick snapping.

I'm sorry, your eyes kept saying, *but what can we do?* Your sister cared for you with the bewilderment of a child. She shared the congeries of memory which come from growing up in the same walls but you could not talk to her about certain things. Wound-bounded, they became invisible or else turned and twisted so their meaning became unrecognizable. We loved your sister and did not say, *Please* or *This is the last time.*

I got up and made orange spice tea; for you, unsweetened lemon juice in hot water. I stayed two minutes longer than I'd promised the friend who was babysitting, then five, then ten, fifteen minutes, feeling my breasts swell and harden and knowing my girl would be wanting to nurse. It was our second try at a last visit. Yesterday the man who was to take your original wire-haired dachshund came just as we were settled in. The dogs barked and woke up the baby and an altogether distracted time was had by all.

Your great green eyes grew sheeny with tears, long-lashed eyes with veins now a startling Christmas red. We never commented on your physical deterioration, you and I, not directly. You hadn't been able to wear anything but maternity clothes for the last couple of years: the tumour was too big. You liked a tent dress of mine and bought a brown corduroy one in the same style, I remember. That was when you could still get out.

My tea tasted too strongly of cloves.

At last your sister got up and stretched. *Well, bye. Drop in and see us. Here's a brochure, it has a map right on it.* It was a hot June day but you wanted the door closed and you had a crocheted blanket tucked around you on the couch. I remembered your house as always having a faint, delightful fragrance of wood smoke, an invisible thread above floor level. I missed it.

I asked you then, for the embroidered birds. They were thumbtacked to the wall in your spare room and until I put the baby down for a nap the day before, I'd forgotten them. I am amazed now at my own boldness, but I knew you would see the gesture not as acquisitiveness, but as I meant it: give me something to remember you by. We speak in symbols; you say to me, *I wish all this stuff were gone* for at last you have a place in Intermediate Care, and I say, *May I have. . . .* What we mean is, we won't see one another again, the smaller loss, our leisurely teas together prefiguring the greater one, your leaving entirely. And this we have spoken around, but not today. You're too frightened and it's been six months since I moved away and the pattern has shifted. For us there is a close.

They're from an island off South America, you said, breath rasping, waving away the gift. *Some friends gave them to me. But that's not important now.* Your hand was impatient with me.

The sun makes green aquarium shadows in your living room, across your face. We will not see one another again. I know this. You know this. I am here to call blessings upon you, as many and swift as the dust-moted air will hold, to smooth and place you in a house built without hands.

The doctors puzzle over how you could last so long but we know. No one can keep coming to that fountain without being changed. Drenching brightness amid the pain, the small courtesies and kindnesses you display, you are being transformed into someone whose stature your bodily limitations would like to deny but cannot. It is true you are irritable at times but behind this, there is a rush and flutter of new form. I know when you wake at night in pain, you tug at your boundaries, releasing, being soothed. The ancient dances of hurt must move into new patterns, peacock-brightness, shimmer of air. It is as though the bird-bones I hug are a disguise for the other person I keep glimpsing, large and laughing and healed.

Next year in Jerusalem.

~

I had your South American birds framed. At first I was disappointed they were not from your six years in Mexico, but I have almost grown used to the idea they were a gift and I will never know the story behind them. In fact they are not embroidered but are reverse applique, stitchery with layers of fabric cut away to reveal different colours beneath. No matter, I feel a rush of tenderness for you whenever I glance at the wall. Often when I am driving, the toss of sunlight on green branches will remind me of the familiar route to your house, the sudden glint of water as the car eased down the steep hill into the bay.

To be honest, Barb, what I found hardest about your death was that you never got the Christmas presents I made. Foolish, yet the sight of those glistening red ribbon-tied rolls of cranberry apple leather on my kitchen counter made me cry until I had to put them away. I'd made rose hip jam, too. It smelled wonderful when it was cooking, sugar, tart fruit and lemon. I made frilly cloth tops for the jars so they looked like something from *Gourmet*. And you would never eat any.

~

After you died, your sister phoned. I was awake most of the night, alternately holding you up in love and reproaching myself for not being there at the end. About four o'clock I got up to go to the bathroom and as I passed the daybed in the dining room, it was as though the world cracked open like a dark velvet egg. I could remember my whole last letter to you with its funny story about the baby and the cats and I knew you had often reread it. In between lifting a foot and bringing it down on the creaky wooden floor, there it was, news from a month before, the spiritual insights and the continuing battles and it had come at the right time. You had read it and laughed. The sudden knowing made the unlit house ring and shiver with comfort, a great soundless bell.

~

Caveat lector. There will always be something left out, something I hold back. Why don't I name your animals, or say how much they meant to you, the chickens which kept getting picked off by raccoons, or your dogs, one large, white, and dignified, the other tiny and all twirly tongue? Menageries. There is overlap and shimmer; quiddity not of a single unit of meaning but of experience, this is how it was. Is, because it goes on reverberating. I come in and find our girl asleep in her crib with two empty bottles. She smells of milk. The night light glints orange on the polished wooden floor. Stanley the Fox is there with his crumb-smeary nose. You sent him to Jocelyn; he was her first toy.

A year later, you sent another present, one for Christmas. I remember taking off the brown wrapping paper in the hall and placing it into a box to take over to Mum's with the others, standing there reading the label over and over. Your writing on the package was our last exchange; you'd been dead for three weeks. How had you been able to buy it at all when you were so weak? Commission your sister?

With love, you had written on the shoe box which contained the truck with Winnie the Pooh and all his friends. It was exactly right, just the sort of thing a nurse who worked with babies and children would know to get. It's been in use for years now.

We exist in recognized links, squeak of a rocking chair, the fragrance of the orange spice tea I keep in my cupboard, the soups I brought over for you (I'm still finding notes in my cookbooks from that time), the way your wretched dog would slurp its tongue over my hands while I yearned to thump it. Echoes of order, a woman pushing a baby in a blue stroller with fat white tires. *What's zat? Whazzat? A power pole. A bush with prickly leaves, no they're too sharp, don't touch. Here, feel the leaves on this bush.* How our conversations walked and struggled with meanings, the ideas behind a leaf, the forces we tread upon.

Word-eggs. Let's hatch some and protect them as best we can from the coons.

On my wall, your bright birds, outlined in red, gaze in opposite directions. Two are bold and broad-shouldered with the dangling arms and legs akimbo posture of humans. Their beaks, held at a ten degree angle skyward from the horizontal, convey an impression of eager curiosity. Only when you look closely do you realize there are four small birds worked into the design as well. Like the others, they gaze alertly away from the centre toward the boundaries of two dimensions, ready to move out. Against the black ground, their bright colours are glad as a shout of recognition.

They're from an island off South America. That much of the story I know.

~

Zoë Landale lives in the old fishing village of Ladner, B.C., with her husband, small daughter, and two cats. Her third book, *Burning Stone*, is forthcoming from Cacanadadada Press. Her work has appeared in numerous literary journals and anthologies. A longer version of "Embroidered Birds" was published in *Grail*, an ecumenical journal, and won an award for best narrative published in 1992 by The Canadian Church Press. Zoë has worked as a freelance writer for years. Recently she returned to the University of British Columbia to work on her M.F.A. in Creative Writing.

Between the Meadow and the River

Susan Drain

OWN BY THE RIVER, IT IS
easy to understand how they might have been misled. The river
winds through meadows as promising as any pastorale: tall elms, a
screen of poplar, the grass waist-high and green even in the driest
weather. Those meadows must have looked sweet from the river;
they made a green space between the water and the black spruce
woods.

Meadows are not sweet spaces, though: that waist-high grass
cuts like any other sharp blade; it is thickest and greenest over the
boggy patches, left from the spring floods. Mosquitoes rise whining when the long grass is disturbed.

They brought their belongings on rafts, upstream to this new
settlement. However did they manage, I wonder, swatting mosquitoes as I cross the meadow and slide over the riverbank into the
river. I am half distracted, yet I am only moments away from
immersion and relief. How could they have worked all day with
black flies and sweat in their hair and under their clothes, and the
whine of mosquitoes and the crash of axes and hammers in their
ears? Need, I suppose. With nowhere to retreat to, and the realities of winter both remembered and feared, what else to do but
endure the heat and the hurt. I am in the water now. The mosquitoes have been left behind, and the deerflies have not yet realized
that I am here.

Need, and smoke, I suppose. They might not even have

needed smudge fires, there would have been so much burning of brush and stumps, and a fire smoking under the cookpots, with perhaps a Dutch oven buried in its ashes. Flies and sweat, the mosquitoes' whine and the crash of axes; smoke in the eyes and throat.

I take a deep breath now, and dive under the water.

~

The men must have come here to the water, and washed — at least sometimes. At evening, when I was a child, when the haying was done, there was no better way to end the tickle and itch of grass than the river water. At twilight, no light catches the ripples, and the river flows dark and smooth between its banks. Occasionally a trout jumps for a fly, or, with a swish of grass and only a little splash, a muskrat slides into the water. The water feels warm as the air cools, and it resists the diver as if a thin skin had formed over its darkening surface. Sometimes when the summer was very dry, and the well low, we took soap and shampoo with us, and watched a slick of bubbles slide away in the darkness. Soap isn't slippery when it is crusted with sand, and even a perfunctory washing left us almost raw.

I can imagine the men here, but the women? They must have come down, too. Did they tent themselves in petticoats? or was the riverbank private enough in the twilight, the men smoking their pipes in the clearings, perhaps, and the children subdued by vigorous scrubbing.

Winter came, of course, and snow followed the wind through the chinks of those first houses. From my desk in the upstairs window, I look towards the river over the roof of the summer kitchen. That drafty space, little more than shed now, was the original house. You can see where the old stovepipe hole was boarded in. There they waited out many a storm, blanketed against the wind, the wood stove steadily devouring the woodpile. Did morning bring joy, or just relief? The snow white and trackless down to the river, drifted over the frozen meadow, leaving only the dark curve where the water runs swiftest and deepest under the ice-carved bank. If, storm-bowed and sundazzled, you can spare a thought for anything but replenishing the wood box, then you have probably inherited a house made snug by generations of improvements.

~

Hasten the spring. How welcome the slow melting of the meadow ice, the widening curve of open water. Less welcome, the mud in the pathways and roads, equally impassable to wheel or sled-runners. Daily we tramp down to the meadow's edge, to chart the rotting of the ice and the receding of the flood. Gradually the drowned meadow growth appears, and eventually we can squelch right to the river's edge. Swift and lightless, the water scours the river bottom, tumbling gravel into sand. It snatches at the crumbling bank, spins flotsam into eddies, and leaves it snagged on a deadhead. In a week or two, fresh green will start through the meadow debris: we will have to mow the path, if we want to get to the riverbank in summer. No one cuts hay here now, so the violets creep thick where last year's path went, and purple flags mark the wettest patches.

There is no need for hay now, for there are no cows in the cedar-railed fields. Poplars and little spruces grow up among blueberry bushes, and the deer feed in abandoned dooryards. The meadow promised richness, but the fields those settlers dug out of the tangled woods are only sand. One or two crops exhausted them.

Blueberries from these overgrown fields are bitter-tinged with the scent of bracken and fir. I will not eat them on my way to the river, lying sunk to its summer depth between its banks. The sandbar is scorching in the sun; I slide down the bank and plunge again into the simplicity of water.

~

That water fascinates me still — dark brown and clear, like transparent mahogany. With the sun behind you at the right angle, you can see right to the bottom, to the weed patches and mussels and your own feet walking. Then the other way, and you see nothing but the glint of the sun on the surface ripples — vision denied, sealed off from the watery world. Swimming underwater is unlike any other experience; without salt or stinging chlorine, it becomes natural to observe the bottom, watching for shy trout, but seeing only minnows. So natural, that it seems an easy next step to breathe underwater, gliding and turning in the current without ever coming up.

But time swells the lungs to bursting with staling air, and I bluster through the surface and find myself farther downstream than I thought.

Time *is* a current, at least as much as it is any metaphor. It sweeps inexorably in one direction, and to go with it gives confidence at the same time as it removes responsibility. It is possible, however, to face strenuously into the flow, and with strong exertion remain poised in the flood. The reward is vision — the clarity of the river bottom, the waving of the weeds, the rush of the water itself. The act of writing is to face into the current and slow time into vision.

Once or twice, when the light is right and the water low, I have seen the glint of something alien on the river bottom and fetched up an old square bottle. Its soft green is pitted and clouded from the washing of the sand, but raised letters proclaim its once-upon-a-time contents to have been "Sarsparilla," and its provenance, "Lowell, Mass." I carry it back to the house; perhaps it came from here.

My great-grandmother loved to fish, they tell me. A photograph of her, paddling her own canoe, wearing her husband's old pants, hangs in the dining room. I wash the sand out of the bottle and put it on my desk.

The evening mist is beginning to rise in the meadow, and the children come in from their chores, sniffing the kitchen air. Make some biscuits, Janie, she says; the door slams behind her and she is off, down to the river bank with rod and basket. The trout rise greedily to the cast fly; she can be back at the house with enough for supper before the biscuits are finished baking. But she lingers a little on the riverbank. This is her time. Out of time. Woodsmoke is rising from the summer kitchen; no breeze sweeps it away. The poplars are hardly moving. It is so quiet a doe's hoof crunches audibly on the coarse sand. The river smell rises — a scent of earthiness, darkness, and silt, a smell of decay and rot, but washed thin and almost clean, a shadow of a smell.

A voice rings across the still meadow. The doe raises her head, and steps precisely through the screen of poplar and scrub. The women gather up their towels and children, flurrying back to the clearings and the cookfires. My great-grandmother watches them leave, shadows in the river's memory, then shoulders her rod and her responsibilities again. I am the laggard on the riverbank now, but not alone, while the river dissolves time and floods the memoried meadow.

~

In her own words: My grandmother Janie Libbey brought her children home to Brockway from Quebec City every summer; my mother did the same thing, whether from Britain (where I was born), Vancouver, or Montreal (where I grew up). Wherever I have lived, studying in Ontario and later in Britain, and then teaching, first on the prairies, then in Halifax, Toronto, and now in Halifax again, Brockway has been a constant. I hope that my own daughter's Brockway summers are giving her a similar strong sense of place and of family.

Willow Women

Joan Crate

$\mathcal{T}$HESE DAYS I WEAR IT ALWAYS, a silver medallion on a silver chain, sometimes tucked discreetly under T-shirts and blouses, but usually worn overtop where it settles between my breasts. People notice it, stop and look at the engraving — the profile of a woman's perfectly sculpted head, her hair wind-wild, and around her branches ripe with birds. There's something in the hair at her crown, and I've gone cross-eyed trying to figure out what it is. Blossoms perhaps. Budding fruit. It could even be a young bird.

"Beautiful," people say when they look at this medallion. "Never saw anything like it." A friend once suggested that the woman is Daphne, transformed by sympathetic gods into a willow tree so that Apollo, in hot pursuit, was unable to rape her. One has to wonder if there were no other alternative. Out of the frying pan and into the fire, as my mother would put it. Poor Daphne, feet planted firmly in the ground, burdened with winged hearts.

This medallion and a bigger one just like it were found near the town of Yellowknife October 14, 1957. It was night but a white powdering of stars dazzled the snow. How clean it always looked at night — the grimy road, the humped cars, even the skeleton of the dump in the distance — all cleansed by shadow. My father walked and his boots squeaked. Perhaps that's all he heard. Or maybe sounds from across the lake mingled with those close by, the way they seem to on cold clear nights, so he couldn't tell if the groaning car engine, the intermingling howls of huskies and wolves, the frosty air surging in and out and in and out were part of him or not. He never mentions this when he tells the story, but I know those nights, how you don't know what's near and what's far away, how all the sounds stalk you, and shadows too, darting behind telephone poles, lurking under the stiff skirts of trees, and you can't run because you'll breathe too deeply and your lungs will pinch, your nose and eyes will water and freeze. You can freeze if you forget yourself. Like Old Michael Bichon. Like the Warner boy, drunk as a skunk, and only sixteen.

At home my mother sang as she baked the last of the flour and sugar into a cake. *"There'll be bluebirds over / The white cliffs of Dover."* She sang for her daughters giggling under blankets on the bed they shared, peering through red flannel at the light bulb in the ceiling that was suddenly a hot Hawaiian sun. She worried about them, about the eldest whose birthday was the next day, about the paper sacks in the pantry and their empty rustling sound. At least there was wood for the fire. October should never be this cold, and her husband outside, walking in the snow, a fool always making trouble, fired for trying to organize a union, black-listed, and the bags in the pantry rustling, the girls giggling with anticipation, and she singing the songs she heard in the London underground when the bombs fell.

Carrie would be seven years old the next day and there were no gifts except the slippers she had knit from an unravelled sweater, and the boots Leigh next door gave her, miles too big, because Carrie's were worn through. You couldn't call those gifts. *"There'll be love and laughter."*

He saw them on the road as he walked, head bowed against cold and despair. Two discs. He was on the way to Old Town and the lights from dilapidated trappers' shacks flared coldly from the bottom of the hill. Snow was everywhere, permeated with grey flakes of arsenic ash. It made a rash around the mouths of children who ate the snow, red spots on their skin; it made them sick and it poisoned dogs and cats who drank from puddles in the spring, yet it was something you got used to. Not that there was a choice.

He picked up the discs. One was about an inch in diameter, the other smaller, three-quarters of an inch, but the imprint on each was the same — woman, hair blowing, branches filled with leaves and birds. They sang suddenly in the night sky — I believed they did. At least I could always hear them when Father told the story, a bright chorus of birds that were smaller and more colourful than ravens, beacons from somewhere else where October was warm and light, the breeze playful. Then they were gone, wing tips caressing skull, eyes, fading into daydream. Only the discs remained in his big miner's hand.

My sister Carrie opened a crude bark box and her eyes danced. She "oohed" with pleasure as Mother slipped a length of string through the ring at the top of the medallion and tied it around her thin, red-spotted neck. The smaller medallion was mine and as I gobbled my cake in the hot yellow kitchen, I gazed at it, wanting to know all about the beautiful woman surrounded by branches, but neither Father nor Mother knew anything about her. Her silver eyes watched two birds perched, but with wings reaching skyward, and her mouth was slightly open, is slightly open now as I look at her, as if she's ready to say something, to cry out, as if she has been seized and she begins to gasp, surprised but not yet relieved, not yet horrified, the action perpetually incomplete.

Implicit in her expression is the genesis of something I recognized even then, as familiar as my mother's face: acceptance. Like a tough skin, it protects against the bite of envy, of promise and hope — those glittering teeth. Acceptance allows the perception of fate. We tell ourselves this is the way things are; it's for the best; this is the way things have to be. And so we accept the sparse birthday celebrations, the too-big boots and too-small coats, the skin rashes and illness. "Life goes on," we learn to announce cheerfully, trudging through seasons — spring, summer, autumn, and winter — that cold star we bend our hopes around, its sinking of ice into the heart. We accept the nagging worry of our mothers, a litany that plays over and over in our ears and then years later when we have our own children, on our lips.

My father got back on at the mine once the union was instated, and the pantry filled again. There was an accident at the mine and Father was hurt. Rock fell from the darkness and crushed his vertebrae, but it wasn't as bad as it first seemed and after a month or so in bed he was able to return to work. Winters were long and cold, but there was always enough wood to keep the kitchen steaming hot. While Carrie was at school and Father was at work, Mother baked and I played at her feet mixing imaginary cake and cookie batter and feeding it to dolls who were endlessly ill. Mother sang and I muttered a lullaby of words, wrapped my dolls warmly and told them, as Mother told me, as I tell my children today, "Everything will be all right."

At some point in my childhood, I, like Carrie, became a hoarder. I kept buttons of various colours and shapes, marbles, feathers, the braids of hair Mother clipped neatly away one summer day, and that silver medallion — in a purple draw-string bag with "Crown Royal" embroidered in gold on the front. Sometimes now when I touch a baby's skin, or when I'm gesturing in the air, describing something magnificent with my hands, I stop. I feel it again in my fingers, the rich felt of that Crown Royal bag before it became thin with age and wear. Or maybe it never really felt that sumptuous.

Years later I threw out my treasures — the buttons, marbles, hair, and feathers — when I quit high school to marry a boy three years my senior. I was an adult, I told myself, sixteen and about to become a wife and mother, someone interested in cookware and budgets, practical things; I no longer needed the keepsakes of childhood. But I kept the medallion.

After our hodgepodge wedding, Ned and I moved to Victoria where asphalt streets throbbed with wet colour and car engines, a real city — I was so happy to escape Yellowknife at last — so busy. But so lonely. Ned's uncle got him a job through a friend, and though it didn't pay well and I was pregnant, we were lucky. Very lucky, Mother reminded me. She had sobbed at the airport when we left, but her letters were cheery and matter-of-fact. Everything would be all right. We were young and we tried so hard to be in love. While Ned was at work I read recipe books from the library, and I learned how to bake bread. I sang as I kneaded dough in the kitchen, *"Here comes the sun / Here comes the sun,"* and sometimes, *"There'll be bluebirds over / The white cliffs of Dover."*

Ned's and my son was born the week before Christmas. We named him Paul after Ned's uncle, and Ned and I held him close as we huddled around our small Christmas tree.

One day when Paul was about a year old, he yanked at the silver chain that anchored the medallion around my neck and it fell to the floor, broken. I threw the chain away, but wrapped the medallion in a torn bit of cloth diaper and tucked it at the bottom of my jewelry box. There it remained for years.

Ned was promoted to salesman and his salary increased. He was good at his job and some days he even liked it. Paul grew bigger and smarter, and although there were no other kids in our building for him to play with, he loved to splash in the puddles when I took him to the park. One winter it snowed and I'll never forget his excitement over what was so dreary to me. He's a teenager now, sombre; he seldom smiles, but I still remember the way he laughed at the silver flakes that fell into his open mouth and disappeared. Like magic — here and gone. Like everything.

Ned was transferred to Regina. It was there we met Marina and her husband Richard.

Marina and I looked alike, Ned said, with our dark hair and hazel eyes. Neighbours asked if we were sisters, and often we told them, "Yes." We giggled together on her front steps or mine while our children played in the yard. She was such a good friend, and I hadn't felt close to anyone since I left my parents' house. Carrie was living in Vancouver working as a nurse's aide and seeing a man named Roy. "He's a fabulous storyteller," she wrote in a letter. "He wants to marry me." I was happy for her; I missed her, but how Marina and I laughed the hot prairie summer away.

Winter came and Regina was almost as cold as Yellowknife, for almost as long. I pulled Paul on a toboggan over to Marina's house and against the moan of wind, we exchanged concerns. Richard had lost his job. He didn't know how to get along with people; he was acting crazy again. And Ned was drinking. More. At first on

Friday and Saturday nights after work with the other salesmen, but soon it was every night, and with anyone. Paul called for him at bedtime and I tried to comfort him. Daddy was out. Daddy was gone. He would be back.

I thought Paul would stop asking for Ned, accept his absence as I had, but he kept calling from his small bed. Finally I let Paul sit in bed with me munching popcorn and watching TV until we both fell asleep. Now when he and I reminisce, we don't recall that we were waiting, always waiting. In fact, we remember those nights fondly.

I never noticed how thin and distracted Richard had become until Marina mentioned it. When he spoke, it was nonsensical. He would become a monk, the prime minister, a Mormon patriarch; he could not be confined to just one wife, a handful of mortals. And he started making passes at me and other women, even as Marina stood near. Money was tight for both our families. Marina and I talked about that — neither of us wanted to leave our children — but we started looking for jobs. One night Carrie called me from the hospital in Vancouver to say she had just delivered a beautiful baby girl, and together we shrieked our delight. Soon afterwards Marina discovered she was pregnant. "Everything will be all right," I told her.

It was a week after the birth of Vincent and two months after Richard's suicide that I slipped into Marina's bedroom to lay her tiny baby in his bassinet. Downstairs she was sitting at the kitchen window sipping coffee and staring out past the children flying about in the yard like bright leaves, past the far hedge and the autumn sky, a sky too bright for eyes like bruises. Except for the distant squeals of the children, everything was quiet.

I was about to leave the room and shut the door on the sleeping baby when I decided to look more closely at the wedding photograph on the dresser with Richard standing over Marina, his smile nervous, his hand clasping hers. He was wearing shiny black shoes, but all that was visible was the shine against the black floor. He was standing in liquid, sinking in liquid, holding on to Marina with slippery fingers.

Beside the photograph was an old brush and mirror set backed with heavy silver. I turned the pieces over. Engraved on the back was the head of a woman, lips ajar, hair blowing free, and branches of trees filled with birds. The pattern was identical to the one imprinted on the medallion I had buried in my jewelry box at home.

I wanted to ask Marina about this coincidence. Where did her dresser set come from? But no, the time wasn't right. There were the children to think of, what to do with the house, the tangled finances. It hadn't been a model marriage, but it had been — something where now there was nothing. Richard was gone. In a sense Marina was free of his pain and illusions, but the children — what about the children?— and such sorrow, her terrible sorrow!

Ned and I moved away when Vincent was just a few months old. I didn't want to leave Marina like that. How I would miss her and her kids; yet Calgary was closer to Carrie who was pregnant again, and my parents whom I hadn't seen for so long; and perhaps it would be a new beginning for Ned and me. I started wearing the medallion again — as a symbol of my connection with Marina perhaps, a tribute to Mom and Dad, Carrie and our past together — but this time anchored by a stronger silver chain.

In Calgary I signed up for two courses at the university, and I began to get up early to study. I left for classes when Paul banged out the back door to school.

Ned came home later and later at night, and sometimes not at all. I wanted to think that it was work, all work that kept him away. I wanted him to sleep on the couch when he stumbled in the house so I wouldn't smell liquor on his breath, and I wanted to believe it when I told our son that Daddy was busy, very busy, but everything would be all right.

Ned and I divorced not long before Carrie left Roy. She found out that his past was very different than the one he had invented so colourfully for her, and the present was not what she had believed. There was another woman and other children. "A life of lies," she told me bitterly over the phone, "And I became one more." She escaped to the Okanagan where she and her two daughters rent a small house with a wood stove. She stokes that stove the same way Mother stoked our old stove in Yellowknife. And she sings and tells her girls everything will be all right.

Ned moved back to Victoria, and I applied for a student loan. Paul spent hours in his room. In the evening when I returned home from university I'd knock on his door. "I'm home," I'd call into the shadows on the other side. "Are you okay?"

Marina and I wrote, though erratically, as we still do, and despite the infrequent letters, the fewer visits, the miles between us, we are close. She took a lover a year after Richard's death, and she has him still though he and the kids just don't get along. I know how she feels. I now have a new husband and two new children whom I love as much as is humanly possible, but there's friction between my husband and Paul. And he's not really my husband, not legally. When friends ask me why we don't marry I say, "What difference does it make?" Though perhaps it makes a difference to me.

Several years after that day when Richard had died and I lay Vincent in his bassinet, Marina and her boyfriend dropped in on their way back from a conference in Banff, and I asked her where her silver-backed dresser set had come from. "It was from my mother-in-law," she said. "Passed down from her mother, I think." But Elsa had died since then and she didn't know anything more about it. I showed her my medallion with the identical engraving and told her the story of how my father found it and Carrie's larger one in the snow. We smiled at each other, and although I, and I think Marina too, felt seductive words like "portent" and "destiny" tease the tongue, we would not say them. In our daily routines of bills, quarrels, bag lunches, and worn running shoes, they have little meaning. And she left. For home.

In and out of our seasons we plod, Marina, Carrie, and I, with our children. We hoard our dreams, our memories. We have a lot to be thankful for; we all know it. And we laugh. We laugh whenever we get the chance.

But there are days.

Sometimes my babies sob big salty tears, or Carrie's voice over the telephone cracks like pond ice, or I glance at the picture I have of Marina with Vincent, wrinkled and brand-new, nestled in the crook of her arm. I see her face, the shock imprinted there but beginning to fade, to become familiar, and I acknowledge the acceptance we all live with, that we cannot live without. Like Daphne, like all women, we accept the shortfalls, the inevitable consequences of actions we frequently have little control over, the bonds that root us in home, in schedules that chase the sun daily, daily across the sky, in worry. And in the thoughts of each other. We reach for the glitter of dreams, yet often find our arms filling — oh, we would not have it any other way — with young lives that nest and then plan escape.

~

Joan Crate was born in Yellowknife, Northwest Territories. Hers was the first creative writing M.A. thesis at the University of Calgary. She has published two books, *Pale as Real Ladies: Poems for Pauline Johnson* (Brick, 1989), and *Breathing Water*, NeWest's first Nunatak new fiction novel, in 1989. She has published poems and short stories in *Grain, Secrets from the Orange Couch, Red Dress Anthology, Canadian Author and Bookman, blue buffalo, Quarry Magazine, Canadian Forum, Fiddlehead, Ariel, Dinosaur Review, NeWest Review,* and the Calgary *Herald.* Presently she resides with her family in Red Deer where she teaches at Red Deer College. Joan has four children, each one born in a different decade.